The Essential
Theodore Roosevelt

———— ★ ————

LIBRARY OF FREEDOM

The Essential Theodore Roosevelt

★

EDITED, WITH AN INTRODUCTION, BY

John Gabriel Hunt

GRAMERCY BOOKS
NEW YORK • AVENEL

A NOTE ON THE TEXT

The original sources for the selections in *The Essential Theodore Roosevelt* have been indicated after the title of the entry. For the speeches, the identification is usually by place and date, with, if appropriate, a secondary heading that refers to the content or is the title given the address when published. Many of the magazine articles also appeared in Theodore Roosevelt's own books; in these cases both periodical and book appearances are noted beneath the main heading or in a footnote. All selections are complete and unabridged except for: the gubernatorial and presidential messages; the article on civil service reform; the chapters from *The Rough Riders* and *African Game Trails;* and the speech at the Progressive party's national convention. The text has been edited to modernize punctuation and spelling, but Roosevelt's language remains unaltered.

This 1994 edition is published by Gramercy Books,
distributed by Random House Value Publishing, Inc.,
40 Engelhard Avenue, Avenel, New Jersey 07001.

Random House
New York • Toronto • London • Sydney • Auckland

Printed and bound in the United States of America

Library of Congress Cataloging-in-Publication Data
Roosevelt, Theodore, 1858–1919.
The essential Theodore Roosevelt.
p. cm.—(Library of freedom)
ISBN 0-517-11848-3
1. United States—Politics and government—1865–1933.
2. Outdoor life. 3. Conservation of natural resources—United States.
I. Title. II. Series.
E660.R72   1994b
320.973—dc20   94-14793
                                                      CIP

8 7 6 5 4 3 2 1

CONTENTS

INTRODUCTION

THERE HAS BEEN no American president quite like Theodore Roosevelt. His status as a folk hero is due not merely to the circumstances of war or to service in the presidency, but is based upon the whole of a remarkable life. Roosevelt was a man of bold ideas and enormous energy. Alternatingly conservative and liberal, he epitomized patriotism and was committed to American military strength, yet he advocated progressive programs that could turn the nation upside down. Roosevelt pursued with equal enthusiasm his passions for politics, social reform, the outdoor life, and the printed word. He knew exactly what he believed, conducted his own life in accordance with a strict ethical code, and never stopped telling the American people how they, too, could be decent and extraordinary.

The Roosevelt legend has its roots in his childhood, in the transformation of a sickly boy into a vigorous young man. Born on October 27, 1858, Theodore was the second child of Theodore Roosevelt, Sr., a member of one of New York City's oldest and wealthiest families, and Martha Bulloch Roosevelt, a cultured and elegant woman from a prominent Georgia family. Physically weak and suffering from severe asthma since the age of three, young Theodore rarely played with other children and turned to solitary pursuits. He became a voracious reader, kept a detailed diary, and began a lifelong interest in natural history by collecting live and dead animals and practicing taxidermy. Theodore's early years were spent in the family's fashionable homes in New York City and Oyster Bay, Long Island, and on tours of Europe. The elder Theodore Roosevelt—who died at the age of forty-six, during his namesake's sophomore year at Harvard—was a partner in the family import business. He worked hard, was affectionate to his wife and four children, reveled in outdoor activities, was highly ethical, and considered it his duty to help those less fortunate. He devoted much of his time and wealth to cultural and humanitarian causes, helping to found the Museum of Natural History, the Metropolitan Museum of Art, the New York Orthopedic Hospital, the Children's Aid Society, and the Newsboy's Lodging House. Much of the elder Roosevelt's character and beliefs were eventually reflected in his son, who wrote in his 1913 autobiography: "My father . . . was the best man I ever knew. He combined strength and courage with gentleness, tenderness, and great unselfishness." With his father's encouragement, young Theodore balanced his intellectual interests with a rigorous regimen of bodybuilding and athletics that eventually turned a weak youngster into one of the most robust men ever to live in the White House.

Theodore attended Harvard, where he excelled in natural history and boxing and was an editor of the literary magazine. In 1880, just a few months after his graduation, he married Alice Hathaway Lee. During the next year, he attended Columbia Law School, took a belated European honeymoon, worked on a book about the War of 1812, and became involved in local politics at New York's Twenty-first District Republican Association. Although his desire to become a lawyer quickly waned, Roosevelt's potential was recognized by some of the district politicians, who nominated him for the New York State Assembly. He easily won his first election in November 1881. Within six months he was the published author of his first book, *The Naval War of 1812*—which was well received and quickly became a classic military history textbook. As an assemblyman, he soon drew attention—and praise from the press—as an independent and courageous lawmaker, as a crusader for honest government and the sponsor of numerous reform bills. During his years in the legislature—from 1882 to 1884—he also pursued the physical challenge of life in the great outdoors with a buffalo-hunting trip to the North Dakota Bad Lands, and suffered an incredible double-tragedy with the deaths, in the same house and on the same day—February 14, 1884—of his mother and his wife. Alice died of a previously undiagnosed kidney ailment, Bright's disease, just two days after giving birth to a baby girl, who was soon christened with her mother's name. "The light has gone out of my life," wrote Roosevelt in his dairy on February 14. He rarely spoke or wrote of his wife Alice again.

Over the next two years Roosevelt adopted the lifestyle of a western ranchman in the Bad Lands: he became part-owner of the Maltese Cross ranch on the Little Missouri River, and built a second cattle ranch, the Elkhorn, nearby. One result of the adventure was the publication in 1885 of his *Hunting Trips of a Ranchman,* which attacted fine reviews in both the United States and England. When he returned permanently to the East, stronger and more energetic than ever, he reentered politics as the Republican candidate for mayor of New York City, lost that election, and on December 2, 1886, married a childhood sweetheart, Edith Kermit Carow. The couple spent the next few months traveling in Europe, and then settled in a newly built house, Sagamore Hill, in Oyster Bay, where Roosevelt began work on an ambitious series of books, *The Winning of the West.*

During the 1888 presidential election, Roosevelt visited a number of states to speak on behalf of the Republican candidate, Benjamin Harrison, who ultimately won. Because of his efforts, and through the intercession of his good friend Congressman Henry Cabot Lodge—an important figure in the Republican party—Roosevelt was appointed to the U.S. Civil Service Commission; the fairly lackluster post soon took on excitement and importance in the hands of the dynamic young commissioner. His enthusiasm for merit appointments and other reforms, and his accomplishments during his service in the position from 1889 to 1895, kept Roosevelt in the public limelight and are detailed in his article "Six Years of Civil Service

Reform," written for *Scribner's Magazine* at the end of his tenure.

Eager for a new challenge, in April 1895 Roosevelt accepted an appointment as New York City's police commissioner. He embarked on a systematic cleanup of the department, using publicity as a weapon and nightly prowling the streets incognito to surprise any officers who might be shirking their duties; but his efforts to enforce the Sunday closing of saloons met with shrill opposition. As he began his duties, he wrote another significant article, defending his reformist approach, "The Enforcement of Law," for the September 1895 issue of the *Forum*. Roosevelt was establishing a pattern of writing opinion pieces, many expressing the need for political honesty and reforms, for publication in popular magazines. By the end of his career he had written hundreds of articles—on such varied subjects as ancient Irish sagas, Christmas dinner on a ranch, factory laws for women and children, the birds of Louisiana, and even the origin and evolution of life—as well as more than twenty books.

With Republican William McKinley elected president in 1896, Roosevelt was once again appointed to a position in the federal government. As assistant secretary of the navy, Roosevelt's basic belief in national military perparedness was translated into the forceful promotion of a large and up-to-date navy. But he created chaos in the administration—and the usual publicity—with his strident advocacy of U.S. military intervention in the ongoing Cuban insurrection against Spain's rule. Roosevelt's position was finally strengthened by the sinking of the U.S. battleship *Maine* in Havana Harbor, and within two months President McKinley declared war on Spain.

So in 1898, Teddy Roosevelt responded to a calling deep within him: to fight the dutiful fight, to fearlessly defend his country in a righteous war. The effort to banish Spain from Cuba and the Philippines was, for Roosevelt, such a war. He resigned his government post, and organized a volunteer regiment. Within a month of landing in Cuba, Colonel Theodore

Roosevelt was famous as the leader of the Rough Riders and hero of the Battle of San Juan Hill. Of course, he wrote a book about it all, *The Rough Riders,* and his fame and popularity propelled him into the New York governorship and, ultimately, into the vice presidency of the United States.

As governor of New York, Roosevelt's independence and idealism caused so much trouble for the state's Republican political machine that Senator Thomas Platt, the party's influential boss, saw an opportunity, in the election of 1900, to push Roosevelt out of New York. Platt and others sponsored him as a candidate for vice president at the Republican National Convention—where the charismatic hero of the Spanish-American War was loudly acclaimed. Ohio Senator Mark Hanna, the powerful Republican national chairman, opposed him—"that damned cowboy"—and with incredible irony asked Roosevelt's supporters, "Don't you realize that there's only one life between that madman and the White House?" Nevertheless, Theodore Roosevelt became William McKinley's running mate in his bid for reelection to the presidency.

Roosevelt stole the show. He campaigned so vigorously—giving hundreds of speeches and covering more than twenty-one thousand miles—that it seemed *he* was the presidential candidate. Teddy was, of course, famous as a Rough Rider, but now the country came to know him as a person—whose flashing white teeth, energetic gestures, good humor, infectious enthusiasm, and strong ideas made him a forceful and unforgettable personality. The Republicans easily defeated the Democrats and their candidate, William Jennings Bryan.

As vice president, Roosevelt continued to give powerful and attention-getting speeches. His address at the Minnesota State Fair of September 2, 1901, resounded with the rhetoric of duty, responsibility, and national strength and included one of Roosevelt's many memorable phrases, "Speak softly and carry a big stick."

From the moment of his nomination, there appeared a multitude of editorial cartoons of Teddy grinning from ear to ear and taking charge, with the apparently insignificant president unable to control him. From then on, whether as a political official or as a private citizen, Roosevelt was always in the public eye, masterfully attracting editorials, headlines, caricatures, and attention and using the era's mass-circulation periodicals as his soapbox.

When McKinley was assassinated just seven months into his second term, Theodore Roosevelt became the twenty-sixth president of the United States. It was the role he was born to play. He served nearly two full terms in the office, giving but one inaugural address in March 1905, after his resounding election victory the previous November.

From the beginning, the press realized that the public was eager for news about this charismatic president and his youthful family, who were clearly different from most of their predecessors. Edith Roosevelt literally brought a breath of fresh air to the musty White House, throwing open windows, clearing out old furniture, filling the residence with flowers and cheerful decorations, and supervising the addition of a new West Wing in 1902. Edith's husband created an atmosphere of openness and informality, daily welcoming all visitors, from reporters and dignitaries to politicians and reformers, who were invariably impressed by the president's warmth, exuberance, hearty laugh, and willingness to discuss any subject. Although he was the first president to set aside a specific room for a White House press corps, Roosevelt was quick to criticize the excesses of journalists; his famous speech and article "The Man with the Muck-Rake" almost immediately gave rise to the term *muckrakers* to describe journalists who concentrate only on the worst aspects of society.

While sons Ted and Kermit were away at school, the antics of the young Roosevelt children—Ethel, Archie, and Quentin —and their friends, as well as the president's fatherly devotion and own recreational escapades, were a source of constant fascination for the public. Alice, the eldest daughter, was particularly newsworthy: pretty, fun-loving, and fashionable, she seemed to enjoy attracting attention through outrageous public behavior. Dubbed "Princess Alice" by the press, her favorite fashion color inspired a popular song, "Alice Blue Gown," and her White House wedding to Ohio Congressman Nicholas Longworth on February 17, 1907, was a spectacular social event.

President Roosevelt also captured the nation's imagination with his powerful ideas. In his First Annual Message to Congress on December 3, 1901, Roosevelt presented his goals and beliefs with convincing, reasoned clarity. From praise of McKinley he dove immediately into the larger problem of unchecked immigration and the danger from anarchists. He spoke of the need to preserve the nation's forests; the importance of using a merit system in making government appointments; the necessity of regulating the corporate trusts; the righteousness of U.S. policy in the recently acquired possessions of Hawaii, Puerto Rico, and the Philippines; and the ambitious goal of building a canal across the isthmus connecting North and South America.

Roosevelt's dedication to rooting out the abuses of the big corporations increased with the passage of time. But he never failed to warn Americans about the good and bad on both sides, and linked his signature slogan of "a square deal" with respect for all people, regardless of class, religion, or race. In his address on September 7, 1903, at the New York State Fair in Syracuse, he stated:

> There must be ever present in our minds the fundamental truth that in a republic such as ours the only safety is to stand neither for nor against any man because he is rich or because he is poor, because he is engaged in one occupation or another, because he works with his brains or because he works with his hands. We must treat each man on his worth and merits as a man. We must see that each is given a square deal, because he is entitled to no more and should receive no less.

Throughout his presidency, Roosevelt strengthened his commitment to political reform, progressive social legislation and programs, the conservation of natural resources, and the military preparedness of America, with visible results in many areas. He gave a major speech on conservation at the laying of the gateway cornerstone at Yellowstone National Park in April 1903, and held an important White House conference on conservation, which he addressed passionately on May 13, 1908. He negotiated an end to the Russo-Japanese War of 1904–1905, and for his efforts won the Nobel Peace Prize. He pushed for child-labor laws, pure-food laws, an eight-hour workday, and the continuing buildup of the navy. He railed against race and class hatred and prejudice of every kind, poverty in the cities, and political extremists. He successfully began the massive American project to build a canal across the Isthmus of Panama —and reported, in a special Message to Congress on December 17, 1906, on his personal inspection of working, housing, and sanitary conditions at the site. In addition, he consistently injected into his writings and speeches an emphasis on what he felt was the measure of good citizenship and effective goverment— personal ethics. Responsibility, duty, goodwill, "fellow-feeling," respect—these formed the basis for good government, civic justice, and even foreign policy.

When Roosevelt did not run for reelection in 1908, he chose to support his secretary of war, William Howard Taft, as the Republican candidate for the presidency. Taft overwhelmingly won the election, largely due to the public's continuing regard for Roosevelt. Immediately following the inauguration, Roosevelt left for Africa with his son Kermit on an eleven-month exploration and hunting expedition—the details of which were recorded, naturally, in a book, *African Game Trails*, published in 1910. The former president's exploits, both in Africa and on a contiguous European tour filled with important speaking engagements, attracted extensive press coverage in America and abroad. In England, when he was awarded an honorary degree at Cambridge University, Roosevelt received a playful tribute— similar to that previously accorded Charles Darwin—when a large teddy bear was dropped from the ceiling. (Eight years before, Roosevelt's refusal to shoot a bear under what he considered to be unsportsmanlike conditions inspired an editorial cartoon based on the incident, which in turn inspired a Brooklyn toy-shop owner to create a stuffed "Teddy" bear for children. The toy—which had the real Teddy's approval—quickly became a phenomenal international success.) On his return to the United States, Roosevelt received a rousing welcome, including a parade, in New York.

In the year and a half following his departure from the presidency, Roosevelt had developed a deep disappointment in the policies and performance of Taft. Teddy Roosevelt, the battling reformer, eagerly returned to political life. In a startlingly progressive speech in Osawatomie, Kansas, on August 31, 1910, during the midterm election campaign, Roosevelt broke with Taft and the conservative wing of the Republican party and declared a New Nationalism built upon social justice.

> The national government belongs to the whole American people, and where the whole American people are interested, that interest can be guarded effectively only by the national government. The betterment which we seek must be accomplished, I believe, mainly through the national government.
>
> The American people are right in demanding that New Nationalism, without which we cannot hope to deal with new problems. The New Nationalism puts the national need before sectional or personal advantage. . . .
>
> The object of government is the welfare of the people. The material progress and prosperity of a nation are desirable chiefly so far as they lead to the moral and material welfare of all good citizens.

Despite Roosevelt's speeches of that year, the voters' dissatisfaction with Taft and the Republicans was obvious, and the Democrats won many races. Roosevelt retired to his Sagamore Hill home and once again concentrated on writing, this time as a contributing editor to the *Outlook* magazine. In 1912, however, Roosevelt returned to the political battlefield, directly challenging his old friend Taft. He entered the presidential campaign in the hope of gaining the Republican nomination, but Taft's delegates outnumbered Roosevelt's at the Republican National Convention. Taft became the party's candidate for reelection, alienating hundreds of progressive-leaning Roosevelt supporters.

Within a few weeks Theodore Roosevelt became the presidential candidate of a new Progressive party. His address on August 6, 1912, at the party's national convention, based upon his lifelong beliefs and unequivocally directed toward achieving "social and economic justice," outlined a specific agenda for progressive reforms and legislation.

On October 14, 1912, just before delivering a campaign speech in Milwaukee, an attempt was made on Roosevelt's life. Far more, perhaps, than his accomplishments as a Rough Rider, a big-game hunter, a former president, or the builder of the Panama Canal, this incident illuminated the Roosevelt legend. With a bullet lodged in his chest, the indomitable candidate began his speech:

> Friends, I shall ask you to be as quiet as possible. I don't know whether you fully understand that I have just been shot; but it takes more than that to kill a bull moose. . . . The bullet is in me now, so that I cannot make a very long speech, but I will try my best. . . .
>
> I have altogether too important things to think of to feel any concern over my own death. . . . I am telling you the literal truth when I say that my concern is for many other things. It is not in the least for my own life. I want you to understand that I am ahead of the game, anyway. No man has had a happier life than I have led; a happier life in every way. I have been able to do certain things that I greatly wished to do, and I am interested in doing other things.

Roosevelt continued the address until he had finished most of what he had come to say. It seemed that he was, indeed, unstoppable. His wounds were not serious: newspapers printed pictures of the tattered manuscript of his speech, which had slowed down the bullet, and his doctors marveled at his massive chest and superb physical condition, which also helped mitigate the damage. But Roosevelt's status as a living legend was not enough for his party—so identified with him that it was also known as the Bull Moose party—to wrest power from the dominant Democrats and Republicans. Although the Progressives, in the 1912 election, garnered an amazing 28 percent of the popular vote and finished second—ahead of Taft and the Republicans—Democrat Woodrow Wilson became president.

True to form, the intrepid Roosevelt once again sought adventure in the wilderness. From October 1913 until May 1914 he explored a tributary of the Amazon in Brazil and collected animal and plant specimens for New York's Museum of Natural History, all the while sending back articles to *Scribner's Magazine*. As a private citizen, Roosevelt continued to give speeches and write essays and books during President Wilson's administration. After the First World War began in 1914, he became increasingly strident about the dangers of America being unprepared militarily, criticizing the pacifists and reiterating an old theme with the catchphrase "the peace of righteousness." In a syndicated newspaper article of November 8, 1914, he wrote:

> We must insist on righteousness first and foremost. We must strive for peace always; but we must never hesitate to put righteousness above peace. In order to do this, we must put force back of righteousness, for, as the world now is, national righteousness without force back of it speedily becomes a matter of derision.

The United States entered the Great War in 1917, and Roosevelt's four sons served in the American Expeditionary Force in Europe; Quentin, an aviator, was shot down behind enemy lines on July 14, 1918. Roosevelt was devasted by the death of his youngest son. Nevertheless, he continued to be faithful to his beliefs, and just before the end of the war he wrote an article for the *Metropolitan* magazine that unhesitatingly renewed his call for American patriotism, bravery, and duty, while at the same time espousing his philosophy of living life to the fullest. It was a testament to Quentin's sacrifice, as well as to his own life.

> Only those are fit to live who do not fear to die; and none are fit to die who have shrunk from the joy of life and the duty of life. Both life and death are parts of the same Great Adventure. . . . Never was a country worth living in unless its sons and daughters were of that stern stuff which bade them die for it at need; and never yet was a country worth dying for unless its sons and daughters thought of life not as something concerned only with the selfish evanescence of the individual, but as a link in the great chain of creation and causation, so that each person is seen in his true relations as an essential part of the whole, whose life must be made to serve the larger and continuing life of the whole.

When he died on January 6, 1919, Theodore Roosevelt was mourned the world over. America and other nations knew that they had lost a man of enormous stature. In the colossal stone portraits of Mount Rushmore, completed in 1941, Roosevelt is one of four U.S. presidents immortalized, in company with Washington, Lincoln, and Jefferson. He would have been pleased to be overlooking the Black Hills of South Dakota, in the rugged wilderness just south of his cherished Bad Lands. At the majestic Mount Rushmore National Memorial, Theodore Roosevelt remains, as he always was, larger than life.

JOHN GABRIEL HUNT

New York
1994

TRUE AMERICANISM

From the Forum, *April 1894, and* American Ideals, *1897*

Patriotism was once defined as "the last refuge of a scoundrel"; and somebody has recently remarked that when Dr. Johnson gave this definition he was ignorant of the infinite possibilities contained in the word "reform." Of course both gibes were quite justifiable, insofar as they were aimed at people who use noble names to cloak base purposes. Equally of course the man shows little wisdom and a low sense of duty who fails to see that love of country is one of the elemental virtues, even though scoundrels play upon it for their own selfish ends; and, inasmuch as abuses continually grow up in civic life as in all other kinds of life, the statesman is indeed a weakling who hesitates to reform these abuses because the word *reform* is often on the lips of men who are silly or dishonest.

What is true of patriotism and reform is true also of Americanism. There are plenty of scoundrels always ready to try to belittle reform movements or to bolster up existing iniquities in the name of Americanism; but this does not alter the fact that the man who can do most in this country is and must be the man whose Americanism is most sincere and intense. Outrageous though it is to use a noble idea as the cloak for evil, it is still worse to assail the noble idea itself because it can thus be used. The men who do iniquity in the name of patriotism, of reform, of Americanism, are merely one small division of the class that has always existed and will always exist—the class of hypocrites and demagogues, the class that is always prompt to steal the watchwords of righteousness and use them in the interests of evildoing.

The stoutest and truest Americans are the very men who have the least sympathy with the people who invoke the spirit of Americanism to aid what is vicious in our government or to throw obstacles in the way of those who strive to reform it. It is contemptible to oppose a movement for good because that movement has already succeeded somewhere else, or to champion an existing abuse because our people have always been wedded to it. To appeal to national prejudice against a given reform movement is in every way unworthy and silly. It is as childish to denounce free trade because England has adopted it as to advocate it for the same reason. It is eminently proper, in dealing with the tariff, to consider the effect of tariff legislation in time past upon other nations as well as the effect upon our own; but in drawing conclusions it is in the last degree foolish to try to excite prejudice against one system because it is in vogue in some given country, or to try to excite prejudice in its favor because the economists of that country have found that it was suited to their own peculiar needs. In attempting to solve our difficult problem of municipal government it is mere folly to refuse to profit by whatever is good in the examples of Manchester and Berlin because these cities are foreign, exactly as it is mere folly blindly to copy their examples without reference to our own totally different conditions. As for the absurdity of declaiming against civil service reform, for instance, as "Chinese," because written examinations have been used in China, it would be quite as wise to declaim against gunpowder because it was first utilized by the same people. In short, the man who, whether from mere dull fatuity or from an active interest in misgovernment, tries to appeal to American prejudice against things foreign, so as to induce Americans to oppose any measure for good, should be looked on by his fellow countrymen with the heartiest contempt. So much for the men who appeal to the spirit of Americanism to sustain us in wrongdoing. But we must never let our contempt for these men blind us to the nobility of the idea which they strive to degrade.

We Americans have many grave problems to solve, many threatening evils to fight, and many deeds to do, if, as we hope and believe, we have the wisdom, the strength, the courage, and the virtue to do them. But we must face facts as they are. We must neither surrender ourselves to a foolish optimism, nor succumb to a timid and ignoble pessimism. Our nation is that one among all the nations of the earth which holds in its hands the fate of the coming years. We enjoy exceptional advantages, and are menaced by exceptional dangers; and all signs indicate that we shall either fail greatly or succeed greatly. I firmly believe that we shall succeed; but we must not foolishly blink the dangers by which we are threatened, for that is the way to fail. On the contrary, we must soberly set to work to find out all we can about the existence and extent of every evil, must acknowledge it to be such, and must then attack it with unyielding resolution. There are many such evils, and each must be fought after a fashion; yet there is one quality which we must bring to the solution of every problem—that is, an intense and fervid Americanism. We shall never be successful over the dangers that confront us; we shall never achieve true greatness, nor reach the lofty ideal which the founders and preservers of our mighty federal Republic have set before us, unless we are Americans in heart and soul, in spirit and purpose, keenly alive to the responsibility implied in the very name of American, and proud beyond measure of the glorious privilege of bearing it.

There are two or three sides to the question of Americanism, and two or three senses in which the word *Americanism* can be used to express the antithesis of what is unwholesome and undesirable. In the first place we wish to be broadly American and national, as opposed to being local or sectional. We do not wish, in politics, in literature, or in art, to develop that unwholesome parochial spirit, that overexaltation of the little community at the expense of the great nation, which produces what has been described as the patriotism of the village, the patriotism of the belfry. Politically, the indulgence of this spirit was the chief cause of the calamities which befell the ancient republics of Greece, the medieval republics of Italy, and the petty states of Germany as it was in the last century. It is this spirit of provincial patriotism, this inability to take a view of broad adhesion to the whole nation that has been the chief among the causes that have produced such anarchy in the South American states, and which have resulted in presenting to us not one great Spanish-American federal nation stretching from the Rio Grande to Cape Horn, but a squabbling multitude of revolution-ridden states, not one of which stands even in the second rank as a power. However, politically this question of American nationality has been settled once for all. We are no longer in danger of repeating in our history the shameful and contemptible disasters that have befallen the Spanish possessions on this continent since they threw off the yoke of Spain. Indeed, there is, all through our life, very much less of this parochial spirit than there was formerly. Still there is an occasional outcropping here and there; and it is just as well that we should keep steadily in mind the futility of talking of a northern literature or a southern literature, an eastern or a western school of art or science. Joel Chandler Harris is emphatically a national writer; so is Mark Twain. They do not write merely for Georgia or Missouri or California any more than for Illinois or Connecticut; they write as Americans and for all people who can read English. St. Gaudens lives in New York; but his work is just as distinctive of Boston or Chicago. It is of very great consequence that we should have a full and ripe literary development in the United States, but it is not of the least consequence whether New York, or Boston, or Chicago, or San Francisco becomes the literary or artistic center of the United States.

There is a second side to this question of a broad Americanism, however. The patriotism of the village or the belfry is bad, but the lack of all patriotism is even worse. There are philosophers who assure us that, in the future, patriotism will be regarded not as a virtue at all, but merely as a mental stage in the journey toward a state of feeling when our patriotism will include the whole human race and all the world. This may be so; but the age of which these philosophers speak is still several eons distant. In fact, philosophers of this type are so very advanced that they are of no practical service to the present generation. It may be, that in ages so remote that we cannot now understand any of the feelings of those who will dwell in them, patriotism will no longer be regarded as a virtue, exactly as it may be that in those remote ages people will look down upon and disregard monogamic marriage; but as things now are and have been for two or three thousand years past, and are likely to be for two or three thousand years to come, the words *home* and *country* mean a great deal. Nor do they show any tendency to lose their significance. At present, treason, like adultery, ranks as one of the worst of all possible crimes.

One may fall very far short of treason and yet be an undesirable citizen in the community. The man who becomes Europeanized, who loses his power of doing good work on this side of the water, and who loses his love for his native land, is not a traitor; but he is a silly and undesirable citizen. He is as emphatically a noxious element in our body politic as is the man who comes here from abroad and remains a foreigner. Nothing will more quickly or more surely disqualify a man from doing good work in the world than the acquirement of that flaccid habit of mind which its possessors style cosmopolitanism.

It is not only necessary to Americanize the immigrants of foreign birth who settle among us, but it is even more necessary for those among us who are by birth and descent already Americans not to throw away our birthright, and, with incredible and contemptible folly, wander back to bow down before the alien gods whom our forefathers forsook. It is hard to believe that there is any necessity to warn Americans that, when they seek to model themselves on the lines of other civilizations, they make themselves the butts of all right-thinking men; and yet the necessity certainly exists to give this warning to many of our citizens who pride themselves on their standing in the world of art and letters, or, perchance, on what they would style their social leadership in the community. It is always better to be an original than an imitation, even when the imitation is of something better than the original; but what shall we say of the fool who is content to be an imitation of something worse? Even if the weaklings who seek to be other than Americans were right in deeming other nations to be better than their own, the fact yet remains that to be a first-class American is fiftyfold better than to be a second-class imitation of a Frenchman or Englishman. As a matter of fact, however, those of our countrymen who do believe in American inferiority are always individuals who, however cultivated, have some organic weakness in their moral or mental makeup; and the great mass of our pepole, who are robustly patriotic, and who have sound, healthy minds, are justified in regarding these feeble renegades with a half-impatient and half-amused scorn.

We believe in waging relentless war on rank-growing evils of all kinds, and it makes no difference to us if they happen to be of purely native growth. We grasp at any good, no matter whence it comes. We do not accept the evil attendant upon another system of government as an adequate excuse for that attendant upon our own; the fact that the courtier is a scamp does not render the demagogue any the less a scoundrel. But it remains true that, in spite of all our faults and shortcomings, no other land offers such glorious possibilities to the man able to take advantage of them, as does ours; it remains true that no one of our people can do any work really worth doing unless he does it primarily as an American. It is because certain classes of our people still retain their spirit of colonial dependence on, and exaggerated deference to, European opinion, that they fail to accomplish what they ought to. It is precisely along the lines where we have worked most independently that we have accomplished the greatest results; and it is in those professions where there has been no servility to, but merely a wise profiting by foreign experience, that we have produced our greatest men. Our soldiers and statesmen and orators; our explorers, our wilderness-winners, and commonwealth-builders; the men who have made our laws and seen that they were executed; and the other men whose energy and ingenuity have created our marvellous material prosperity—all these have been men who have drawn wisdom from the experience of every age and nation, but who have nevertheless thought, and worked, and conquered, and lived, and died, purely as Americans; and on the whole they have done better work than has been done in any other country during the short period of our national life.

On the other hand, it is in those professions where our people have striven hardest to mold themselves in conventional European forms that they have succeeded least; and this holds true to the present day, the failure being of course most conspicuous where the man takes up his abode in Europe; where he becomes a second-rate European, because he is overcivilized, oversensitive, overrefined, and has lost the hardihood and manly courage by which alone he can conquer in the keen struggle of our national life. Be it remembered, too, that this same being does not really become a European; he only ceases being an American, and becomes nothing. He throws away a great prize for the sake of a lesser one, and does not even get the lesser one. The painter who goes to Paris, not merely to get two or three years' thorough training in his art, but with the deliberate purpose of taking up his abode there, and with the intention of following in the ruts worn deep by ten thousand earlier travelers, instead of striking off to rise or fall on a new line, thereby forfeits all chance of doing the best work. He must content himself with aiming at that kind of mediocrity which consists in doing fairly well what has already been done better; and he usually never even sees the grandeur and picturesqueness lying open before the eyes of every man who can read the book of America's past and the book of America's present. Thus it is with the undersized man of letters, who flees his country because he, with his delicate, effeminate sensitiveness, finds the conditions of life on this side of the water crude and raw; in other words, because he finds that he cannot play a man's part among men, and so goes where he will be sheltered from the winds that harden stouter souls. This emigré may write graceful and pretty verses, essays, novels; but he will never do work to compare with that of his brother, who is strong enough to stand on his own feet, and do his work as an American. Thus it is with the scientist who spends his youth in a German university, and can thenceforth work only in the fields already fifty times furrowed by the German ploughs. Thus it is with that most foolish of parents who sends his children to be educated abroad, not knowing—what every clear-sighted man from Washington and Jay down has known—that the American who is to make his way in America should be brought up among his fellow Americans. It is among the people who like to consider themselves, and, indeed, to a large extent are, the leaders of the so-called social world, especially in some of the northeastern cities, that this colonial habit of thought, this thoroughly provincial spirit of admiration for things foreign, and inability to stand on one's own feet, becomes most evident and most despicable. We believe in every kind of honest and lawful pleasure, so long as the getting is not made man's chief business; and we believe heartily in the good that can be done by men of leisure who work hard in their leisure, whether at politics or philanthropy, literature or art. But a leisure class whose leisure simply means idleness is a curse to the community, and insofar as its members distinguish themselves chiefly by aping the worst—not the best—traits of similar people across the water, they become both comic and noxious elements of the body politic.

The third sense in which the word *Americanism* may be employed is with reference to the Americanizing of the newcomers to our shores. We must Americanize them in every way, in speech, in political ideas and principles, and in their way of looking at the relations between church and state. We welcome the German or the Irishman who becomes an American. We have no use for the German or Irishman who remains such. We do not wish German-Americans and Irish-Americans who figure as such in our social and political life; we want only Americans, and, provided they are such, we do not care whether they are of native or of Irish or of German ancestry. We have no room in any healthy American community for a German-American vote or an Irish-American vote, and it is contemptible demagogy to put planks into any party platform with the purpose of catching such a vote. We have no room for any people who do not act and vote simply as Americans, and as nothing else. Moreover, we have as little use for people who carry religious prejudices into our politics as for those who carry prejudices of caste or nationality. We stand unalterably in favor of the public-school system in its entirety. We believe that English, and no other language, is that in which all the school exercises should be conducted. We are against any division of the school fund, and against any appropriation of public money for sectarian purposes. We are against any recognition whatever by the state in any shape or form of state-aided parochial schools. But we are equally opposed to any discrimination against or for a man because of his creed. We demand that all citizens, Protestant and Catholic, Jew and Gentile, shall have fair treatment in every way; that all alike shall have their rights guaranteed them. The very reasons that make us unqualified in our opposition to state-aided sectarian schools make us equally bent that, in the management of our public schools, the adherents of each creed shall be given exact and equal justice, wholly without regard to their religious affiliations; that trustees, superintendents, teachers, scholars, all alike shall be treated without any reference whatsoever to the creed they profess. We maintain that it is an outrage, in voting for a man for any position, whether state or national, to take into account his religious faith, provided only he is a good American. When a secret society does what in some places the American Protective Association seems to have done, and tries to proscribe Catholics both politically and socially, the members of such society show that they themselves are as utterly un-American, as alien to our school of political thought, as the worst immigrants who land on our shores. Their conduct is equally base and contemptible; they are the worst foes of our public-school system, because they strengthen the hands of its ultramontane enemies; they should receive the hearty condemnation of all Americans who are truly patriotic.

The mighty tide of immigration to our shores has brought in its train much of good and much of evil; and whether the good or the evil shall predominate depends mainly on whether these newcomers do or do not throw themselves heartily into our national life, cease to be Europeans, and become Americans like the rest of us. More than a third of the people of the northern states are of foreign birth or parentage. An immense number of them have become completely Americanized, and these stand on exactly the same plane as the descendants of any Puritan, Cavalier, or Knickerbocker among us, and do their full and honorable share of the nation's work. But where immigrants, or the sons of immigrants, do not heartily and in good faith throw in their lot with us, but cling to the speech, the customs, the ways of life, and the habits of thought of the Old World which they have left, they thereby harm both themselves and us. If they remain alien elements, unassimilated, and with interests separate from ours, they are mere obstructions to the current of our national life, and, moreover, can get no good from it themselves. In fact, though we ourselves also suffer from their perversity, it is they who really suffer most. It is an immense benefit to the European immigrant to change him into an American citizen. To bear the name of American is to bear the most honorable titles; and whoever does not so believe has no business to bear the name at all, and, if he comes from Europe, the sooner he goes back there the better. Besides, the man who does not become Americanized nevertheless fails to remain a European, and becomes nothing at all. The immigrant cannot possibly remain what he was, or continue to be a member of the old-world society. If he tries to retain his old language, in a few generations it becomes a barbarous jargon; if he tries to retain his old customs and ways of life, in a few generations he becomes an uncouth boor. He has cut himself off from the Old World, and cannot retain his connection with it; and if he wishes ever to amount to anything he must throw himself heart and soul, and without reservation, into the new life to which he has come. It is urgently necessary to check and regulate our immigration, by much more drastic laws than now exist; and this should be done both to keep out laborers who tend to depress the labor market, and to keep out races which do not assimilate readily with our own, and unworthy individuals of all races—not only criminals, idiots, and paupers, but anarchists of the Most and O'Donovan Rossa type.

From his own standpoint, it is beyond all question the wise thing for the immigrant to become thoroughly Americanized. Moreover, from our standpoint, we have a right to demand it. We freely extend the hand of welcome and of good-fellowship to every man, no matter what his creed or birthplace, who comes here honestly intent on becoming a good United States citizen like the rest of us; but we have a right, and it is our duty, to demand that he shall indeed become so and shall not confuse the issues with which we are struggling by introducing among us old-world quarrels and prejudices. There are certain ideas which he must give up. For instance, he must learn that American life is incompatible with the existence of any form of anarchy, or of any secret society having murder for its aim, whether at home or abroad; and he must learn that we exact full religious toleration and the complete separation of church and state. Moreover, he must not bring in his old-world religious race and national antipathies, but must merge them into love for our common country, and must take pride in the things which we can all take pride in. He must revere only our flag; not only must it come first, but no other flag should even come second. He must learn to celebrate Washington's birthday rather than that of the queen or kaiser, and the Fourth of July instead of St. Patrick's Day. Our political and social questions must be settled on their own merits, and not complicated by quarrels between England and Ireland, or France and Germany, with which we have nothing to do: it is an outrage to fight an American political campaign with reference to questions of European politics. Above all, the immigrant must learn to talk and think and *be* United States.

The immigrant of today can learn much from the experience of the immigrants of the past, who came to America prior to the Revolutionary War. We were then already, what we are now, a people of mixed blood. Many of our most illustrious Revolutionary names were borne by men of Huguenot blood—Jay, Sevier, Marion, Laurens. But the Huguenots were, on the whole, the best immigrants we have ever received; sooner than any other, and more completely, they became American in speech, conviction, and thought. The Hollanders took longer than the Huguenots to become completely assimilated; nevertheless they in the end became so, immensely to their own advantage. One of the leading Revolutionary generals, Schuyler, and one of the presidents of the United States, Van Buren, were of Dutch blood; but they rose to their positions, the highest in the land, because they had become Americans and had ceased being Hollanders. If they had remained members of an alien body, cut off by their speech and customs and belief from the rest of the American community, Schuyler would have lived his life as a boorish, provincial squire, and Van Buren would have ended his days a small tavern-keeper. So it is with the Germans of Pennsylvania. Those of them who became Americanized have furnished to our history a multitude of honorable names from the days of the Mühlenbergs onward; but those who did not become Americanized form to the present day an unimportant body, of no significance in American existence. So it is with the Irish, who gave to Revolutionary annals such names as Carroll and Sullivan, and to the Civil War men like Sheridan—men who were Americans and nothing else: while the Irish who remain such, and busy themselves solely with alien politics, can have only an unhealthy influence upon American life, and can never rise as do their compatriots who become straightout Americans. Thus it has ever been with all people who have come hither, of whatever stock or blood. The same thing is true of the churches. A church which remains foreign, in language or spirit, is doomed.

But I wish to be distinctly understood on one point. Americanism is a question of spirit, conviction, and purpose, not of creed or birthplace. The politician who bids for the Irish or German vote, or the Irishman or German who votes as an

Irishman or German, is despicable, for all citizens of this commonwealth should vote solely as Americans; but he is not a whit less despicable than the voter who votes against a good American, merely because that American happens to have been born in Ireland or Germany. Know-nothingism, in any form, is as utterly un-American as foreignism. It is a base outrage to oppose a man because of his religion or birthplace, and all good citizens will hold any such effort in abhorrence. A Scandinavian, a German, or an Irishman who has really become an American has the right to stand on exactly the same footing as any native-born citizen in the land, and is just as much entitled to the friendship and support, social and political, of his neighbors. Among the men with whom I have been thrown in close personal contact socially, and who have been among my staunchest friends and allies politically, are not a few Americans who happen to have been born on the other side of the water, in Germany, Ireland, Scandinavia; and there could be no better men in the ranks of our native-born citizens.

In closing, I cannot better express the ideal attitude that should be taken by our fellow citizens of foreign birth than by quoting the words of a representative American, born in Germany, the Honorable Richard Guenther, of Wisconsin. In a speech spoken at the time of the Samoan trouble he said:

> We know as well as any other class of American citizens where our duties belong. We will work for our country in time of peace and fight for it in time of war, if a time of war should ever come. When I say our country, I mean, of course, our adopted country. I mean the United States of America. After passing through the crucible of naturalization, we are no longer Germans; we are Americans. Our attachment to America cannot be measured by the length of our residence here. We are Americans from the moment we touch the American shore until we are laid in American graves. We will fight for America whenever necessary. America, first, last, and all the time. America against Germany, America against the world; America, right or wrong; always America. We are Americans.

All honor to the man who spoke such words as those; and I believe they express the feelings of the great majority of those among our fellow American citizens who were born abroad. We Americans can only do our allotted task well if we face it steadily and bravely, seeing but not fearing the dangers. Above all we must stand shoulder to shoulder, not asking as to the ancestry or creed of our comrades, but only demanding that they be in very truth Americans, and that we all work together, heart, hand, and head, for the honor and the greatness of our common country.

SIX YEARS OF CIVIL SERVICE REFORM

From Scribner's Magazine, *August 1895, and*
American Ideals, *1897*

No question of internal administration is so important to the
United States as the question of civil service reform, because the
spoils system, which can only be supplanted through the agencies which have found expression in the act creating the Civil
Service Commission, has been for seventy years the most potent
of all the forces tending to bring about the degradation of our
politics. No republic can permanently endure when its politics
is corrupt and base; and the spoils system, the application in
political life of the degrading doctrine that to the victor belong
the spoils, produces corruption and degradation. The man who
is in politics for the offices might just as well be in politics for
the money he can get for his vote, so far as the general good is
concerned. When the then vice president of the United States,
Mr. Hendricks, said that he "wished to take the boys in out of
the cold to warm their toes," thereby meaning that he wished to
distribute offices among the more active heelers, to the raptur-
ous enthusiasm of the latter, he uttered a sentiment which was
morally on the same plane with a wish to give "the boys" five
dollars apiece all around for their votes, and fifty dollars apiece
when they showed themselves sufficiently active in bullying,
bribing, and cajoling other voters. Such a sentiment should bar
any man from public life, and will bar him whenever the people
grow to realize that the worst enemies of the Republic are the
demagogue and the corruptionist. The spoils-monger and
spoils-seeker invariably breed the bribe-taker and bribe-giver,
the embezzler of public funds and the corrupter of voters. Civil
service reform is not merely a movement to better the public

service. It achieves this end too; but its main purpose is to raise the tone of public life, and it is in this direction that its effects have been of incalculable good to the whole community.

For six years, from May 1889 to May 1895, I was a member of the National Civil Service Commission, and it seems to me to be of interest to show exactly what has been done to advance the law and what to hinder its advancement during these six years, and who have been the more prominent among its friends and foes. I wish to tell "the adventures of Philip on his way through the world," and show who robbed him, who helped him, and who passed him by. It would take too long to give the names of all our friends, and it is not worthwhile to more than allude to most of our foes and to most of those who were indifferent to us; but a few of the names should be preserved and some record made of the fights that have been fought and won and of the way in which, by fits and starts, and with more than one setback, the general advance has been made.

Of the commission itself little need be said. When I took office the only commissioner was Mr. Charles Lyman, of Connecticut, who resigned when I did. Honorable Hugh S. Thompson, ex-governor of South Carolina, was made commissioner at the same time that I was, and after serving for three years resigned. He was succeeded by Mr. George D. Johnston, of Louisiana, who was removed by the president in November 1893, being replaced by Mr. John R. Procter, the former state geologist of Kentucky, who is still serving. The commission has never varied a hand's-breadth from its course throughout this time; and Messrs. Thompson, Procter, Lyman, and myself were always a unit in all important questions of policy and principle. Our aim was always to procure the extension of the classified service as rapidly as possible, and to see that the law was administered thoroughly and fairly. The commission does not have the power that it should, and in many instances there have been violations or evasions of the law in particular bureaus or departments which the commission was not able to prevent. In every case, however, we made a resolute fight, and gave the widest publicity to the wrongdoing. Often, even where we have been unable to win the actual fight in which we were engaged, the fact of our having made it, and the further fact that we were ready to repeat it on provocation, has put a complete stop to the repetition of the offense. As a consequence, while there have been plenty of violations and evasions of the law, yet their proportion was really very small, taking into account the extent of the service. In the aggregate it is doubtful if 1 percent of all the employees have been dismissed for political reasons. In other words, where under the spoils system a hundred men would have been turned out, under the Civil Service Law, as administered under our supervision, ninety-nine men were kept in.

In the administration of the law very much depends upon the commission. Good heads of departments and bureaus will administer it well anyhow; but not only the bad men, but also the large class of men who are weak rather than bad, are sure to administer the law poorly unless kept well up to the mark. The public should exercise a most careful scrutiny over the appointment and over the acts of Civil Service commissioners, for there is no office the effectiveness of which depends so much upon the way in which the man himself chooses to construe his duties. A commissioner can keep within the letter of the law and do his routine work and yet accomplish absolutely nothing in the way of securing the observance of the law. The commission, to do useful work, must be fearless and vigilant. It must actively interfere whenever wrong is done, and must take all the steps that can be taken to secure the punishment of the wrongdoer and to protect the employee threatened with molestation.

This course was consistently followed by the commission throughout my connection with it. I was myself a Republican from the North. Messrs. Thompson and Procter were from the South, and were both Democrats who had served in the Confederate armies; and it would be impossible for anyone to desire as associates two public men with higher ideals of duty, or more resolute in their adherence to those ideals. It is unnecessary to say that in all our dealings there was no single instance wherein the politics of any person or the political significance of any action was so much as taken into account in any case that arose. The force to the commission itself was all chosen through the competitive examinations, and included men of every party and from every section of the country; and I do not believe that in any public or private office of the size it would be possible to find a more honest, efficient, and coherent body of workers.

From the beginning of the present system each president of the United States has been its friend, but no president has been a radical civil service reformer. Presidents Arthur, Harrison, and Cleveland have all desired to see the service extended, and to see the law well administered. No one of them has felt willing or able to do all that the reformers asked, or to pay much heed to their wishes save as regards that portion of the service to which the law actually applied. Each has been a sincere party man, who has felt strongly on such questions as those of the tariff, of finance, and of our foreign policy, and each has been obliged to conform more or less closely to the wishes of his party associates and fellow party leaders; and, of course, these party leaders, and the party politicians generally, wished the offices to be distrubuted as they had been ever since Andrew Jackson became president. In consequence the offices outside the protection of the law have still been treated, under every administration, as patronage, to be disposed of in the interest of the dominant party. . . .

The Cabinet officers, though often not civil service reformers to start with, usually become such before their terms of office expire. This was true, without exception, of all the Cabinet officers with whom I was personally brought into contact while on the commission. Moreover, from their position and their sense of responsibility they are certain to refrain from violating the law themselves and to try to secure at least a formal compliance with its demands on the part of their subordinates. In most cases it is necessary, however, to goad them continually to see that they do not allow their subordinates to evade the law; and it is very difficult to get either the president or the head of a department to punish these subordinates when they have evaded it. There is not much open violation of the law, because such violation can be reached through the courts; but in the small offices and small bureaus there is often a chance for an unscrupulous head of the office or bureau to persecute his subordinates who are politically opposed to him into resigning, or to trump up charges against them on which they can be dismissed. If this is done in a sufficient number of cases, men of the opposite political party think that it is useless to enter the examinations; and by staying out they leave the way clear for the offender to get precisely the men he wishes for the eligible registers. Cases like this continually occur, and the commission has to be vigilant in detecting and exposing them and in demanding their punishment by the head of the office. . . .

Congress has control of the appropriations for the commission, and as it cannot do its work without an ample appropriation the action of Congress is vital to its welfare. Many, even of the friends of the system in the country at large, are astonishingly ignorant of who the men are who have battled most effectively for the law and for good government in either the Senate or the lower house. It is not only necessary that a man shall be good and possess the desire to do decent things, but it is also necessary that he shall be courageous, practical, and efficient, if his work is to amount to anything. There is a good deal of rough-and-tumble fighting in Congress, as there is in all our political life, and a man is entirely out of place in it if he does not possess the virile qualities, and if he fails to show himself ready and able to hit back when assailed. Moreover, he must be alert, vigorous, and intelligent if he is going to make his work count. The friends of the Civil Service Law, like the friends of all other laws, would be in a bad way if they had to rely solely upon the backing of the timid good. During the last six years there have been, as there always are, a number of men in the House who believe in the Civil Service Law, and who vote for it if they understand the question and are present when it comes up, but who practically count for very little one way or the other, because they are timid or flighty, or are lacking in capacity for leadership or ability to see a point and to put it strongly before their associates.

There is need of further legislation to perfect and extend the law and the system; but Congress has never been willing seriously to consider a proposition looking to this extension. Bills to provide for the appointment of fourth-class postmasters have been introduced by Senator Lodge and others, but have never come to anything. Indeed, but once has a measure of this kind been reported from committee and fought for in either house. . . .

On the other hand, efforts to repeal the law, or to destroy it by new legislation, have uniformly been failures, and have rarely gone beyond committee. Occasionally, in an appropriation bill or some other measure, an amendment will be slipped through, adding forty or fifty employees to the classified service, or providing that the law shall not apply to them; but nothing important has ever been done in this way. . . .

The classification of the railway mail service was ordered by President Cleveland less than two months before the expiration of his first term of office as president. It was impossible for the commission to prepare and hold the necessary examinations and establish eligible registers prior to May 1, 1889. President Harrison had been inaugurated on March 4, and Postmaster General Wanamaker permitted the spoilsmen to take advantage of the necessary delay and turn out half of the employees who were Democrats, and replace them by Republicans. This was an outrageous act, deserving the severe condemnation it received; but it was perfectly legal. During the four years of Mr. Cleveland's first term a clean sweep was made of the railway mail service; the employees, who were almost all Republicans, were turned out, and Democrats were put in their places. The result was utterly to demoralize the efficiency of the service. It had begun to recover from this when the change of administration took place in 1889. The time was too short to allow of a clean sweep, but the Republicans did all they could in two months, and turned out half of the Democrats. The law then went into effect, and since that time there have been no more removals for partisan purposes in that service. It has now recovered from the demoralization into which it was thrown by the two political revolutions, and has reached a higher standard of efficiency than ever before. What was done by the Republicans in this service was repeated, on a less scale, by the Democrats four years later in reference to the classification of the small free-delivery post offices. This classification was ordered by President Harrison two months before his term of office expired; but in many of the offices it was impossible to hold examinations and prepare eligible registers until after the inauguration of President Cleveland, and in a number of cases the incoming postmasters, who were appointed prior to the time when the law went into effect, took advantage of the delay to make clean sweeps of their offices. . . .

Whether bad legislation shall be choked and good legislation forwarded depends largely upon the composition of the committees on civil service reform of the Senate and the lower house. The makeup of these committees is consequently of great importance. They are charged with the duty of investigating complaints against the commission, and it is of course very important that if ever the commission becomes corrupt or inefficient its shortcomings should be unsparingly exposed in Congress. On the other hand, it is equally important that the falsity of untruthful charges advanced against it should be made public. . . . In both the Fifty-first and the Fifty-second Congresses charges were made against the commission, and investigations were held into its actions and into the workings of the law by the House committee. In each case, in its report the committee not only heartily applauded the conduct of the Commission, but no less heartily approved the workings of the law, and submitted bills to increase the power of the commission and to render the law still more wide-reaching and drastic. These bills, unfortunatly, were never acted on in the House.

The main fight in each session comes on the appropriation bill. There is not the slightest danger that the law will be repealed, and there is not much danger that any president will suffer it to be so laxly administered as to deprive it of all value; though there is always need to keep a vigilant lookout for fear of such lax administration. The danger-point is in the appropriations. . . . Every man interested in decent government should keep an eye on his Congressman and see how he votes on the question of appropriations for the commission.

The opposition to the reform is generally well led by skilled parliamentarians, and they fight with the vindictiveness natural to men who see a chance of striking at the institution which has baffled their ferocious greed. As a rule, the rank and file are composed of politicians who could not rise in public life because of their attitude on any public question, and who derive most of their power from the skill with which they manipulate the patronage of their districts. These men have a gift at office-mongering, just as other men have a peculiar knack in picking pockets; and they are joined by all the honest dull men, who vote wrong out of pure ignorance, and by a few sincere and intelligent, but wholly misguided, people. Many of the spoils leaders are both efficient and fearless, and able to strike hard blows. In consequence, the leaders on the side of decency must themselves be men of ability and force, or the cause will suffer. For our good fortune, we have never yet lacked such leaders.

The Appropriation committees, both in the House and Senate, almost invariably show a friendly disposition toward the law. They are composed of men of prominence, who have a sense of the responsibilities of their positions and an earnest desire to do well for the country and to make an honorable record for their party in matters of legislation. They are usually above resorting to the arts of low cunning or of sheer demagogy to which the foes of the reform system are inevitably driven, and in consequence they can be relied upon to give, if not what is needed, at least enough to prevent any retrogression. It is in the open House and in Committee of the Whole that the fight is waged. The most dangerous fight occurs in Committee of the Whole, for there the members do not vote by aye and no, and in consequence a mean politician who wishes ill to the law, but is afraid of his constituents, votes against it in committee, but does not dare to do so when the ayes and noes are called in the House. One result of this has been that more than once the whole appropriation has been stricken out in Committee of the Whole, and then voted back again by substantial majorities by the same men sitting in open House.

In the debate on the appropriation the whole question of the workings of the law is usually discussed, and those members who are opposed to it attack not only the law itself, but the commission which administers it. The occasion is, therefore, invariably seized as an opportunity for a pitched battle between the friends and foes of the system, the former trying to secure such an increase of appropriation as will permit the commission to extend its work, and the latter striving to abolish the law outright by refusing all appropriations. . . .

It is noteworthy that the men who have done most effective work for the law in Washington in the departments, and more especially in the House and Senate, are men of spotless character, who show by their whole course in public life that they are not only able and resolute, but also devoted to a high ideal. Much of what they have done has received little comment in public, because much of the work in committee, and some of the work in the House, such as making or combating points of order, and pointing out the danger or merit of certain bills, is not of a kind readily understood or appreciated by an outsider; yet no men have deserved better of the country, for there is in American public life no one other cause so fruitful of harm to the body politic as the spoils system, and the legislators and administrative officers who have done the best work toward its destruction merit a peculiar meed of praise from all well-wishes of the Republic.

I have spoken above of the good that would come from a thorough and intelligent knowledge as to who were the friends and who were the foes of the law in Washington. Departmental officers, the heads of bureaus, and, above all, the commissioners themselves should be carefully watched by all friends of the reform. They should be supported when they do well, and condemned when they do ill; and attention should be called not only to what they do, but to what they fail to do. To an even greater extent, of course, this applies to the president. As regards the senators and congressmen also there is urgent need of careful supervision by the friends of the law. We need criticism by those who are unable to do their part in action; but the criticism, to be useful, must be both honest and intelligent, and the critics must remember that the system has its staunch friends and bitter foes among both party men and men of no party—among Republicans, Democrats, and Independents. Each congressman should be made to feel that it is his duty to support the law, and that he will be held to account if he fails to support it. . . .

People sometimes grow a little downhearted about the reform. When they feel in this mood it would be well for them to reflect on what has actually been gained in the past six years. By the inclusion of the railway mail service, the smaller free-delivery offices, the Indian School service, the Internal Revenue Service, and other less important branches, the extent of the public service which is under the protection of the law has been more than doubled, and there are now nearly fifty thousand employees of the federal government who have been withdrawn from the degrading influences that rule under the spoils system. This of itself is a great success and a great advance, though, of course, it ought only to spur us on to renewed effort. In the fall of 1894 the people of the state of New York, by a popular vote, put into their constitution a provision providing for a merit system in the affairs of the state and its municipalities; and the following spring the great city of Chicago voted, by an overwhelming majority, in favor of applying in its municipal affairs the advanced and radical Civil Service Reform Law, which had already passed the Illinois legislature. Undoubtedly, after every success there comes a moment of reaction. The friends of the reform grow temporarily lukewarm, or, because it fails to secure everything they hoped, they neglect to lay proper stress upon all that it does secure. Yet, in spite of all rebuffs, in spite of all disappointments and opposition, the growth of the principle of civil service reform has been continually more rapid, and every year has taken us measurably nearer that ideal of pure and decent government which is dear to the heart of every honest American citizen.

THE ENFORCEMENT OF LAW

From the Forum, *September 1895*

The question at issue in New York City just at present is much more important than the question of a more or less liberal Sunday excise law. The question is as to whether public officials are to be true to their oaths of office, and see that the law is administered in good faith. The Police Board stands squarely in favor of the honest enforcement of the law. Our opponents of every grade and of every shade of political belief take the position that government officials, who have sworn to enforce the law, shall violate their oaths whenever they think it will please a sufficient number of the public to make the violation worthwhile. It seems almost incredible that in such a controversy it should be necessary to do more than state in precise terms both propositions. Yet it evidently is necessary. Not only have the wealthy brewers and liquor-sellers, whose illegal business was interfered with, venomously attacked the commissioners for enforcing the law; but they have been joined by the major portion of the New York press and by the very large mass of voters who put the gratification of appetite above all law. These men have not dared to meet the issue squarely and fairly. They have tried to befog it and to raise false issues. They have especially sought to change the fight from the simple principle of the enforcement of law into a contest as to the extent of the restrictions which should properly be placed on the sale of liquors. They do not deny that we have enforced the law with fairness and impartiality, but they insist that we ought to connive at lawbreaking.

Very many friends of the reform movement, and very many politicians of the party to which I belong, have become frightened at the issue thus raised; and the great bulk of the machine leaders of the Democracy profess to be exultant at it, and to see in it a chance for securing their own return to power. Senator Hill and Tammany in particular have loudly welcomed the contest. On the other hand, certain Republican politicians and certain Republican newspapers have contended that our action in honestly doing our duty as public officers of the municipality of New York will jeopardize the success of the Republican party, with which I, the president of the board, am identified. The implication is that for the sake of the Republican party, a party of which I am a very earnest member, I should violate my oath of office and connive at law breaking. To this I can only answer that I am far too good a Republican to be willing to believe that the honest enforcement of law by a Republican can redound to the discredit of the party to which he belongs. This applies as much to the weak-kneed municipal reformers who fear that we have hurt the cause of municipal reform as it does to the Republicans. I am not an impractical theorist; I am a practical politician. But I do not believe that practical politics and foul politics are necessarily synonymous terms. I never expect to get absolute perfection; and I have small sympathy with those people who are always destroying good men and good causes because they are not the best of all possible men and all possible causes; but on a naked issue of right and wrong, such as the performance or nonperformance of one's official duty, it is not possible to compromise. Indeed, according to the way we present commissioners feel, we have nothing to do with Republicanism or Democracy in the administration of the police force of the city of New York. Personally, I think I can best serve the Republican party by taking the police force absolutely out of politics. Our duty is to preserve order, to protect life and property, to arrest criminals, and to secure honest elections. In striving to attain these ends we recognize no party; we pay no heed to any man's political predilections, whether he is within or without the police force. In the past, "politics," in the base sense of the term, has been the curse of the police force of New York; and the present board has done away with such politics.

The position of Senator Hill and the Tammany leaders, when reduced to its simplest terms, is merely the expression of the conviction that it does not pay to be honest. They believe that advocacy of lawbreaking is a good card before the people. As one of their newspapers frankly put it, the machine Democratic leaders intend to bid for the support of the voters on the ground that their party "will not enforce laws" which are distasteful to any considerable section of the public. Senator Hill declaims against the board because it honestly enforces the law which was put on the statute book but three years ago by his legislature and his governor (for he owned them both). This is of course a mere frank avowal that Senator Hill and the Democratic leaders who think with him believe that a majority in the state can be built up out of the combined votes of the dishonest men, the stupid men, the timid weaklings, and the men who put appetite above principle—who declare, in the language of Scripture, that their god is their belly, and who rank every consideration of honor, justice, and public morality below the gratification of their desire to drink beer at times when it is prohibited by law.

When such are the fears of our friends and the hopes of our foes, it is worthwhile briefly to state exactly what the condition of affairs was when the present board of police commissioners in New York took office, and what that course of conduct was which has caused such violent excitement. The task is simple. On entering office we found—what indeed had long been a matter of common notoriety—that various laws, and notably the excise law, were enforced rigidly against people who had no political pull, but were not enforced at all against the men who had a political pull, or who possessed sufficient means to buy off the high officials who controlled, or had influence in, the Police Department. All that we did was to enforce these laws, not against some wrongdoers, but honestly and impartialy against all wrongdoers. We did not resurrect dead laws; we did not start a crusade to enforce blue laws. All that we did was to take a law which was very much alive, but which had been used only for purposes of blackmail, and to do away entirely with the blackmail feature by enforcing it equitably as regards all persons. Looked at soberly, this scarcely seems a revolutionary proceeding; and still less does it seem like one which needs an elaborate justification.

To show the nonsense of the talk that it was obsolete or a dead letter, I call attention to the following figures. In the year 1893 — 4,063 arrests were made in New York City for violation of the excise law on Sunday. This represented a falling off from previous years. In 1888, for instance, the arrests had numbered 5,830. In 1894, the year before we took office, when the Tammany board still had absolute power, the arrests rose to 8,464. On Sunday, September 30 of that year, they numbered 233; on October 14 — 230; on the following January 13, they rose to 254. During the time that the present board has been enforcing the law the top number of arrests which we have reached was but 223, a much smaller number than was reached again and again under the old regime. Nevertheless, by our arrests we actually closed the saloons, for we arrested men indiscriminately, and indeed paid particular attention to the worst offenders — the rich saloon-keepers with a pull; whereas under the old system the worst men were never touched at all, and all of them understood well that any display of energy by the police was merely spasmodic and done with some special purpose; so that always, after one or two dry Sundays, affairs were allowed to go back to their former condition. The real difference, the immense, the immeasurable difference between the old and the new methods of enforcing the law, is not one of severity, but of honesty. The old Tammany board was as ruthless in closing the saloons where the owners had no pull as we are in closing all saloons whether the owners have or have not a pull.

The corrupt and partial enforcement of the law under Tammany turned it into a gigantic implement for blackmailing a portion of the liquor-sellers, and for the wholesale corruption of the Police Department. The high Tammany officials and the police captains and patrolmen blackmailed and bullied the small liquor-sellers without a pull and turned them into abject slaves of Tammany Hall. On the other hand, the wealthy and politically influential liquor-sellers absolutely controlled the police, and made or marred captains, sergeants, and patrolmen at their pleasure. Many causes have tended to corrupt the police administration of New York, but no one cause was so potent as this.

When we entered office the law was really enforced at the will of the police officials. In some precincts most of the saloons were closed; in others almost all were open. In general, the poor man without political influence and without money had to shut up, while his rich rival who possessed a "pull" was never molested. Half of the liquor-sellers were allowed to violate the law. Half of them were not allowed to violate it. Under the circumstances we had one of two courses to follow. We could either instruct the police to allow all the saloon-keepers to become lawbreakers, or else we could instruct them to stop all lawbreaking. It is unnecessary to say that the latter course was the only one possible to officials who had respect for their oaths of office.

The clamor that followed our action was deafening; and it was also rather amusing in view of the fact that all we had done was to perform our obvious duty. At the outset the one invariable statement with which we were met was that we could not enforce the law. A hundred—aye, a thousand—times we were told by big politicians, by newspapers, by private individuals, that the excise law could not be enforced; that Mayor Hewitt had tried it and failed; that Superintendent Byrnes had tried it and failed; that nobody could succeed in such a task. Well, the answer is simple. We *have* enforced the law, so far. It is very badly drawn, so as to make it extremely difficult of enforcement; and some of the officials outside the Police Department hamper instead of aiding the police in their efforts to enforce it. However, we understand well that we must do the best we can with the tools actually at hand, if we cannot have the tools we wish. We cannot stop all illegal drinking on Sunday, any more than we can stop all theft; but so far we have succeeded in securing a substantial compliance with the law.

The next move of our opponents was to adopt the opposite tack, and to shriek that, in devoting our attention to enforcing the excise law, we were neglecting all other laws; and that in consequence crime was on the increase. We met this by publishing the comparative statistics of the felonies committed, and of the felons arrested, under our administration and under the previous administration. These showed that for a like period of time about one felony less a day occurred under our administration, while the number of arrests for felonies increased at the rate of nearly one a day. During our term of service fewer crimes were committed and more criminals were arrested. In the Sunday arrests for intoxication, and for disorderly conduct resulting from intoxication, the difference was more striking. Thus in the four Sundays of April 1895, the last month of the old regime, there were 341 arrests on charges of intoxication and of being drunk and disorderly. For the four Sundays beginning with June 30—the first day that we were able to rigidly enforce our policy of closing the saloons—the corresponding number of arrests was but 196. We put a stop to nearly half the violent drunkenness of the city.

The next argument advanced was that Americans of German origin demanded beer on Sundays, and that the popular sentiment was with them and must be heeded. To this we could only answer that we recognized popular sentiment only when embodied in law. To their discredit be it said, many men, who were themselves public officials, actually advocated our conniving at the violation of the law on this ground—of the alleged hostility of local sentiment. They took the view that as the law was passed by the state, for the entire state including the city, and was not (as they contended) upheld by public sentiment in the city, the officers of the law who are sworn to enforce it should connive at its violation. Such reasoning would justify any community in ignoring any law to which it objected. The income tax law was passed through Congress by the votes of the southerners and westerners, but it was collected (prior to the time it was declared to be unconstitutional) mainly in the Northeast. Any argument which would justify us in refusing to obey the excise law in New York would justify the whole Northeast in refusing to obey the income tax law.

The spirit shown by the men and the newspapers who denounce us for enforcing the law is simply one manifestation of the feeling which brings about and is responsible for lynchings, and for all the varieties of Whitecap outrages. The men who head a lynching party, and the officers who fail to protect criminals threatened with lynching, always advance as their excuse that public sentiment sanctions their action. The chief offenders often insist that they have taken such summary action because they fear lest the law be not enforced against the offender. In other words, they put public sentiment ahead of law in the first place; and in the second they offer, as a partial excuse for so doing, the fact that too often laws are not enforced by the men elected or appointed to enforce them. The only possible outcome of such an attitude is lawlessness, which gradually grows until it becomes mere anarchy. The one all-important element in good citizenship in our country is obedience to law. The greatest crimes that can be committed against our government are to put on the statute books, or to allow to remain there, laws that are not meant to be enforced, and to fail to enforce the laws that exist.

Mr. Jacob A. Riis, in a recent article, has put this in words so excellent that I cannot refrain from quoting them:

> That laws are made to break, not to obey, is a fact of which the street takes early notice, and shapes its conduct accordingly. Respect for the law is not going to spring from disregard of it. The boy who smokes his cigarette openly in defiance of one law carries the growler early and late on weekdays in defiance of another, and on Sunday of a third; observes fourteen saloons clustering about the door of his school in contempt of a fourth which expressly forbids their being there; plays hooky secure from arrest because nobody thinks of enforcing the compulsory-

education law; or slaves in the sweatshop under a perjured age-certificate bought for a quarter of a perjured notary; and so on to the end of the long register, while a shoal of offensive ordinances prohibit him from flying a kite, tossing a ball, or romping on the grass, where there is any, cannot be expected to grow up with a very exalted idea of law and order. The indifference or hypocrisy that makes dead letters of so many of our laws is one of the constantly active feeders of our jails. . . . The one breaks the law, the other has it broken for him. . . . The saloon is their ally, and the saloon is the boy's club as he grows into early manhood. It is not altogether his fault that he has no other. From it he takes his politics and gets his backing in his disputes with the police. That he knows it to be despised and denounced by the sentiment responsible for the laws he broke with impunity all his days, while to him it represents the one potent, practical force of life, is well calculated to add to his mental confusion as to the relationship of things, but hardly to increase his respect for the law or for the sentiment behind it. We need an era of enforcement of law—less of pretense—more of purpose.

The Police Board is doing its best to bring about precisely such an era.

Speech Before the Hamilton Club

Chicago, Illinois, April 10, 1899

The Strenuous Life*

In speaking to you, men of the greatest city of the West, men of the state which gave to the country Lincoln and Grant, men who preeminently and distinctly embody all that is most American in the American character, I wish to preach, not the doctrine of ignoble ease, but the doctrine of the strenuous life, the life of toil and effort, of labor and strife; to preach that highest form of success which comes, not to the man who desires mere easy peace, but to the man who does not shrink from danger, from hardship, or from bitter toil, and who out of these winds the splendid ultimate triumph.

A life of slothful ease, a life of that peace which springs merely from lack either of desire or of power to strive after great things, is as little worthy of a nation as of an individual. I ask only that what every self-respecting American demands from himself and from his sons shall be demanded of the American nation as a whole. Who among you would teach your boys that ease, that peace, is to be the first consideration in their eyes— to be the ultimate goal after which they strive? You men of Chicago have made this city great, you men of Illinois have done your share, and more than your share, in making America great, because you neither preach nor practice such a doctrine. You work yourselves, and you bring up your sons to work. If you are rich and are worth your salt, you will teach your sons that though they may have leisure, it is not to be spent in idleness; for wisely used leisure merely means that those who possess it,

*Published in *The Strenuous Life*, 1900.

being free from the necessity of working for their livelihood, are all the more bound to carry on some kind of nonremunerative work in science, in letters, in art, in exploration, in historical research—work of the type we most need in this country, the successful carrying out of which reflects most honor upon the nation. We do not admire the man of timid peace. We admire the man who embodies victorious effort; the man who never wrongs his neighbor, who is prompt to help a friend, but who has those virile qualities necessary to win in the stern strife of actual life. It is hard to fail, but it is worse never to have tried to succeed. In this life we get nothing save by effort. Freedom from effort in the present merely means that there has been stored up effort in the past. A man can be freed from the necessity of work only by the fact that he or his fathers before him have worked to good purpose. If the freedom thus purchased is used aright, and the man still does actual work, though of a different kind, whether as a writer or a general, whether in the field of politics or in the field of exploration and adventure, he shows he deserves his good fortune. But if he treats this period of freedom from the need of actual labor as a period, not of preparation, but of mere enjoyment, even though perhaps not of vicious enjoyment, he shows that he is simply a cumberer of the earth's surface, and he surely unfits himself to hold his own with his fellows if the need to do so should again arise. A mere life of ease is not in the end a very satisfactory life, and, above all, it is a life which ultimately unfits those who follow it for serious work in the world.

In the last analysis a healthy state can exist only when the men and women who make it up lead clean, vigorous, healthy lives; when the children are so trained that they shall endeavor, not to shirk difficulties, but to overcome them; not to seek ease, but to know how to wrest triumph from toil and risk. The man must be glad to do a man's work, to dare and endure and to labor; to keep himself, and to keep those dependent upon him. The woman must be the housewife, the helpmeet of the homemaker, the wise and fearless mother of many healthy children.

In one of Daudet's powerful and melancholy books he speaks of "the fear of maternity, the haunting terror of the young wife of the present day." When such words can be truthfully written of a nation, that nation is rotten to the heart's core. When men fear work or fear righteous war, when women fear motherhood, they tremble on the brink of doom; and well it is that they should vanish from the earth, where they are fit subjects for the scorn of all men and women who are themselves strong and brave and high-minded.

As it is with the individual, so it is with the nation. It is a base untruth to say that happy is the nation that has no history. Thrice happy is the nation that has a glorious history. Far better it is to dare mighty things, to win glorious triumphs, even though checkered by failure, than to take rank with those poor spirits who neither enjoy much nor suffer much, because they live in the gray twilight that knows not victory nor defeat. If in 1861 the men who loved the Union had believed that peace was the end of all things, and war and strife the worst of all things, and had acted up to their belief, we would have saved hundreds of thousands of lives, we would have saved hundreds of millions of dollars. Moreover, besides saving all the blood and treasure we then lavished, we would have prevented the heartbreak of many women, the dissolution of many homes, and we would have spared the country those months of gloom and shame when it seemed as if our armies marched only to defeat. We could have avoided all this suffering simply by shrinking from strife. And if we had thus avoided it, we would have shown that we were weaklings, and that we were unfit to stand among the great nations of the earth. Thank God for the iron in the blood of our fathers, the men who upheld the wisdom of Lincoln, and bore sword or rifle in the armies of Grant! Let us, the children of the men who proved themselves equal to the mighty days, let us, the children of the men who carried the great Civil War to a triumphant conclusion, praise the God of our fathers that the ignoble counsels of peace were rejected; that the suffering and loss, the blackness of sorrow and despair, were unflinchingly faced, and the years of strife endured; for in the end the slave was freed, the Union restored, and the mighty American Republic placed once more as a helmeted queen among nations.

We of this generation do not have to face a task such as that our fathers faced, but we have our tasks, and woe to us if we fail to perform them! We cannot, if we would, play the part of China, and be content to rot by inches in ignoble ease within our borders, taking no interest in what goes on beyond them, sunk in a scrambling commercialism; heedless of the higher life, the life of aspiration, of toil and risk, busying ourselves only with the wants of our bodies for the day, until suddenly we should find, beyond a shadow of question, what China has already found, that in this world the nation that has trained itself to a career of unwarlike and isolated ease is bound, in the end, to go down before other nations which have not lost the manly and adventurous qualities. If we are to be a really great people, we must strive in good faith to play a great part in the world. We cannot avoid meeting great issues. All that we can determine for ourselves is whether we shall meet them well or ill. In 1898 we could not help being brought face to face with the problem of war with Spain. All we could decide was whether we should shrink like cowards from the contest, or enter into it as beseemed a brave and high-spirited people; and, once in, whether failure or success should crown our banners. So it is now. We cannot avoid the responsibilities that confront us in Hawaii, Cuba, Puerto Rico, and the Philippines. All we can decide is whether we shall meet them in a way that will redound to the national credit, or whether we shall make of our dealings with these new problems a dark and shameful page in our history. To refuse to deal with them at all merely amounts to dealing with them badly. We have a given problem to solve. If we undertake the solution, there is, of course, always danger that we may not solve it aright; but to refuse to undertake the solution simply renders it certain that we cannot possibly solve it aright. The timid man, the lazy man, the man who distrusts his country, the overcivilized man, who has lost the great fighting, masterful virtues, the ignorant man, and the man of dull mind, whose soul is incapable of feeling the mighty lift that thrills "stern men with empires in their brains"—all these, of course, shrink from seeing the nation undertake its new duties; shrink from seeing us build a navy and an army adequate to our needs; shrink from seeing us do our share of the world's work, by bringing order out of chaos in the great, fair tropic islands from which the valor of our soldiers and sailors has driven the Spanish flag. These are the men who fear the strenuous life, who fear the only national life which is really worth leading. They believe in that cloistered life which saps the hardy virtues in a nation, as it saps them in the individual; or else they are wedded to that base spirit of gain and greed which recognizes in commercialism the be-all and end-all of national life, instead of realizing that, though an indispensable element, it is, after all, but one of the many elements that go to make up true national greatness. No country can long endure if its foundations are not laid deep in the material prosperity which comes from thrift, from business energy and enterprise, from hard, unsparing effort in the fields of industrial activity; but neither was any nation ever yet truly great if it relied upon material prosperity alone. All honor must be paid to the architects of our material prosperity, to the great captains of industry who have built our factories and our railroads, to the strong men who toil for wealth with brain or hand; for great is the debt of the nation to these and their kind. But our debt is yet greater to the men whose highest type is to be found in a statesman like Lincoln, a soldier like Grant. They showed by their lives that they recognized the law of work, the law of strife; they toiled to win a competence for themselves and those dependent upon them; but they recognized that there were yet other and even loftier duties—duties to the nation and duties to the race.

We cannot sit huddled within our own borders and avow ourselves merely an assemblage of well-to-do hucksters who care nothing for what happens beyond. Such a policy would

The Essential Theodore Roosevelt ★ 39

defeat even its own end; for as the nations grow to have ever wider and wider interests, and are brought into closer and closer contact, if we are to hold our own in the struggle for naval and commercial supremacy, we must build up our power without our own borders. We must build the Isthmian Canal, and we must grasp the points of vantage which will enable us to have our say in deciding the destiny of the oceans of the East and the West.

So much for the commercial side. From the standpoint of international honor the argument is even stronger. The guns that thundered off Manila and Santiago left us echoes of glory, but they also left us a legacy of duty. If we drove out a medieval tyranny only to make room for savage anarchy, we had better not have begun the task at all. It is worse than idle to say that we have no duty to perform, and can leave to their fates the islands we have conquered. Such a course would be the course of infamy. It would be followed at once by utter chaos in the wretched islands themselves. Some stronger, manlier power would have to step in and do the work, and we would have shown ourselves weaklings, unable to carry to successful completion the labors that great and high-spirited nations are eager to undertake.

The work must be done; we cannot escape our responsibility; and if we are worth our salt, we shall be glad of the chance to do the work—glad of the chance to show ourselves equal to one of the great tasks set modern civilization. But let us not deceive ourselves as to the importance of the task. Let us not be misled by vainglory into underestimating the strain it will put on our powers. Above all, let us, as we value our own self-respect, face the responsibilities with proper seriousness, courage, and high resolve. We must demand the highest order of integrity and ability in our public men who are to grapple with these new problems. We must hold to a rigid accountability those public servants who show unfaithfulness to the interests of the nation or inability to rise to the high level of the new demands upon our strength and our resources.

Of course we must remember not to judge any public servant by any one act, and especially should we beware of attacking the men who are merely the occasions and not the causes of disaster. Let me illustrate what I mean by the army and the navy. If twenty years ago we had gone to war, we should have found the navy as absolutely unprepared as the army. At that time our ships could not have encountered with success the fleets of Spain any more than nowadays we can put untrained soldiers, no matter how brave, who are armed with archaic black-powder weapons, against well-drilled regulars armed with the highest type of modern repeating rifle. But in the early eighties the attention of the nation became directed to our naval needs. Congress most wisely made a series of appropriations to build up a new navy, and under a succession of able and patriotic secretaries, of both political parties, the navy was gradually built up, until its material became equal to its splendid personnel, with the result that in the summer of 1898 it leaped to its proper place as one of the most brilliant and formidable fighting navies in the entire world. We rightly pay all honor to the men controlling the navy at the time it won these great deeds, honor to Secretary Long and Admiral Dewey, to the captains who handled the ships in action, to the daring lieutenants who braved death in the smaller craft, and to the heads of bureaus at Washington who saw that the ships were so commanded, so armed, so equipped, so well engined, as to insure the best results. But let us also keep ever in mind that all of this would not have availed if it had not been for the wisdom of the men who during the preceding fifteen years had built up the navy. Keep in mind the secretaries of the navy during those years; keep in mind the senators and congressmen who by their votes gave the money necessary to build and to armor the ships, to construct the great guns, and to train the crews; remember also those who actually did build the ships, the armor, and the guns; and remember the admirals and captains who handled battleship, cruiser, and torpedo-boat on the high seas, alone and in squadrons, developing the seamanship, the gunnery, and the power of acting together, which their successors utilized so gloriously at Manila and off Santiago. And, gentlemen, remember the converse, too. Remember that justice has two sides. Be just to those who built up the navy, and, for the sake of the future of the country, keep in mind those who opposed its building up. Read the *Congressional Record*. Find out the senators and congressmen who opposed the grants for building the new ships; who opposed the purchase of armor, without which the ships were worthless; who opposed any adequate maintenance for the Navy Department, and strove to cut down the number of men necessary to man our fleets. The men who did these things were one and all working to bring disaster on the country. They have no share in the glory of Manila, in the honor of Santiago. They have no cause to feel proud of the valor of our sea captains, of the renown of our flag. Their motives may or may not have been good, but their acts were heavily fraught with evil. They did ill for the national honor, and we won in spite of their sinister opposition.

Now, apply all this to our public men of today. Our army has never been built up as it should be built up. I shall not discuss with an audience like this the puerile suggestion that a nation of seventy millions of freemen is in danger of losing its liberties from the existence of an army of one hundred thousand men, three-fourths of whom will be employed in certain foreign islands, in certain coast fortresses, and on Indian reservations. No man of good sense and stout heart can take such a proposition seriously. If we are such weaklings as the proposition implies, then we are unworthy of freedom in any event. To no body of men in the United States is the country so much indebted as to the splendid officers and enlisted men of the regular army and navy. There is no body from which the country has less to fear, and none of which it should be prouder, none which it should be more anxious to upbuild.

Our army needs complete reorganization—not merely enlarging—and the reorganization can only come as the result of legislation. A proper general staff should be established, and the positions of ordnance, commissary, and quartermaster officers should be filled by detail from the line. Above all, the army must be given the chance to exercise in large bodies. Never again should we see, as we saw in the Spanish war, major-generals in command of divisions who had never before commanded three companies together in the field. Yet, incredible to relate, Congress has shown a queer inability to learn some of the lessons of the war. There were large bodies of men in both branches who opposed the declaration of war, who opposed the ratification of peace, who opposed the upbuilding of the army, and who even opposed the purchase of armor at a reasonable price for the battleships and cruisers, thereby putting an absolute stop to the building of any new fighting ships for the navy. If, during the years to come, any disaster should befall our arms, afloat or ashore, and thereby any shame come to the United States, remember that the blame will lie upon the men whose names appear upon the roll calls of Congress on the wrong side of these great questions. On them will lie the burden of any loss of our soldiers and sailors, of any dishonor to the flag; and upon you and the people of this country will lie the blame if you do not repudiate, in no unmistakable way, what these men have done. The blame will not rest upon the untrained commander of untried troops, upon the civil officers of a department the organization of which has been left utterly inadequate, or upon the admiral with an insufficient number of ships; but upon the public men who have so lamentably failed in forethought as to refuse to remedy these evils long in advance, and upon the nation that stands behind those public men.

So, at the present hour, no small share of the responsibility for the blood shed in the Philippines, the blood of our brothers, and the blood of their wild and ignorant foes, lies at the thresholds of those who so long delayed the adoption of the treaty of peace, and of those who by their worse than foolish words deliberately invited a savage people to plunge into a war fraught with sure disaster for them—a war, too, in which our own brave men who follow the flag must pay with their blood for the silly, mock humanitarianism of the prattlers who sit at home in peace.

The army and the navy are the sword and the shield which this nation must carry if she is to do her duty among the nations of the earth—if she is not to stand merely as the China of the Western Hemisphere. Our proper conduct toward the tropic islands we have wrested from Spain is merely the form which our duty has taken at the moment. Of course we are bound to handle the affairs of our own household well. We must see that there is civic honesty, civic cleanliness, civic good sense in our home administration of city, state, and nation. We must strive for honesty in office, for honesty toward the creditors of the nation and of the individual; for the widest freedom of individual initiative where possible, and for the wisest control of individual initiative where it is hostile to the welfare of the many. But because we set our own household in order we are not thereby excused from playing our part in the great affairs of the world. A man's first duty is to his own home, but he is not thereby excused from doing his duty to the state; for if he fails in this second duty it is under the penalty of ceasing to be a free man. In the same way, while a nation's first duty is within its own borders, it is not thereby absolved from facing its duties in the world as a whole; and if it refuses to do so, it merely forfeits its right to struggle for a place among the peoples that shape the destiny of mankind.

In the West Indies and the Philippines alike we are confronted by most difficult problems. It is cowardly to shrink from solving them in the proper way; for solved they must be, if not by us, then by some stronger and more manful race. If we are too weak, too selfish, or too foolish to solve them, some bolder and abler people must undertake the solution. Personally, I am far too firm a believer in the greatness of my country and the power of my countrymen to admit for one moment that we shall ever be driven to the ignoble alternative.

The problems are different for the different islands. Puerto Rico is not large enough to stand alone. We must govern it wisely and well, primarily in the interest of its own people. Cuba is, in my judgment, entitled ultimately to settle for itself whether it shall be an independent state or an integral portion of the mightiest of republics. But until order and stable liberty are secured, we must remain in the island to insure them, and infinite tact, judgment, moderation, and courage must be shown by our military and civil representatives in keeping the island pacified, in relentlessly stamping out brigandage, in protecting all alike, and yet in showing proper recognition to the men who have fought for Cuban liberty. The Philippines offer a yet graver problem. Their population includes half-caste and native Christians, warlike Moslems, and wild pagans. Many of their people are utterly unfit for self-government, and show no signs of becoming fit. Others may in time become fit but at present can only take part in self-gvoernment under a wise supervision, at once firm and beneficent. We have driven Spanish tyranny from the islands. If we now let it be replaced by savage anarchy, our work has been for harm and not for good. I have scant patience with those who fear to undertake the task of governing the Philippines, and who openly avow that they do fear to undertake it, or that they shrink from it because of the expense and trouble; but I have even scanter patience with those who make a pretense of humanitarianism to hide and cover their timidity, and who cant about "liberty" and the "consent of the governed," in order to excuse themselves for their unwillingness to play the part of men. Their doctrines, if carried out, would make it incumbent upon us to leave the Apaches of Arizona to work out their own salvation, and to decline to interfere in a single Indian reservation. Their doctrines condemn your forefathers and mine for ever having settled in these United States.

England's rule in India and Egypt has been of great benefit to England, for it has trained up generations of men accustomed to look at the larger and loftier side of public life. It has been of even greater benefit to India and Egypt. And finally, and most of all, it has advanced the cause of civilization. So, if we do our duty aright in the Philippines, we will add to that national renown which is the highest and finest part of national life, will greatly benefit the people of the Philippine Islands, and, above all, we will play our part well in the great work of uplifting mankind. But to do this work, keep ever in mind that we must show in a very high degree the qualities of courage, of honesty, and of good judgment. Resistance must be stamped out. The first and all-important work to be done is to establish the supremacy of our flag. We must put down armed resistance before we can accomplish anything else, and there should be no parleying, no faltering, in dealing with our foe. As for those in our own country who encourage the foe, we can afford contemptuously to disregard them; but it must be remembered that their utterances are not saved from being treasonable merely by the fact that they are despicable.

When once we have put down armed resistance, when once our rule is acknowledged, then an even more difficult task will begin, for then we must see to it that the islands are administered with absolute honesty and with good judgment. If we let the public service of the islands be turned into the prey of the spoils politician, we shall have begun to tread the path which Spain trod to her own destruction. We must send out there only good and able men, chosen for their fitness, and not because of their partisan service, and these men must not only administer impartial justice to the natives and serve their own government with honesty and fidelity, but must show the utmost tact and firmness, remembering that, with such people as those with whom we are to deal, weakness is the greatest of crimes, and that next to weakness comes lack of consideration for their principles and prejudices.

I preach to you, then, my countrymen, that our country calls not for the life of ease but for the life of strenuous endeavor. The twentieth century looms before us big with the fate of many nations. If we stand idly by, if we seek merely swollen, slothful ease and ignoble peace, if we shrink from the hard contests where men must win at hazard of their lives and at the risk of all they hold dear, then the bolder and stronger peoples will pass us by, and will win for themselves the domination of the world. Let us therefore boldly face the life of strife, resolute to do our duty well and manfully; resolute to uphold righteousness by deed and by word; resolute to be both honest and brave, to serve high ideals, yet to use practical methods. Above all, let us shrink from no strife, moral or physical, within or without the nation, provided we are certain that the strife is justified, for it is only through strife, through hard and dangerous endeavor, that we shall ultimately win the goal of true national greatness.

Raising the Regiment

From The Rough Riders, *1899*

During the year preceding the outbreak of the Spanish War I was assistant secretary of the navy. While my party was in opposition, I had preached, with all the fervor and zeal I possessed, our duty to intervene in Cuba, and to take this opportunity of driving the Spaniard from the Western world. Now that my party had come to power, I felt it incumbent on me, by word and deed, to do all I could to secure the carrying out of the policy in which I so heartily believed; and from the beginning I had determined that, if a war came, somehow or other, I was going to the front.

Meanwhile, there was any amount of work at hand in getting ready the navy, and to this I devoted myself.

Naturally, when one is intensely interested in a certain cause, the tendency is to associate particularly with those who take the same view. A large number of my friends felt very differently from the way I felt, and looked upon the possibility of war with sincere horror. But I found plenty of sympathizers, especially in the navy, the army, and the Senate Committee on Foreign Affairs. Commodore Dewey, Captain Evans, Captain Brownson, Captain Davis—with these and the various other naval officers on duty at Washington I used to hold long consultations, during which we went over and over not only every question of naval administration, but specifically everything necessary to do in order to put the navy in trim to strike quick and hard if, as we believed would be the case, we went to war with Spain. Sending an ample quantity of ammunition to the Asiatic squadron and providing it with coal; getting the battleships and the armored cruisers on the Atlantic into one squadron, both to train them in maneuvering together, and to have them ready to sail against either the Cuban or the Spanish coasts; gathering the torpedo-boats into a flotilla for practice; securing ample target exercise, so conducted as to raise the standard of our marksmanship; gathering in the small ships from European and South American waters; settling on the number and kind of craft needed as auxiliary cruisers—every one of these points was threshed over in conversations with officers who were present in Washington, or in correspondence with officers who, like Captain Mahan, were absent.

As for the senators, of course Senator Lodge and I felt precisely alike; for to fight in such a cause and with such an enemy was merely to carry out the doctrines we had both of us preached for many years. Senator Davis, Senator Proctor, Senator Foraker, Senator Chandler, Senator Morgan, Senator Frye, and a number of others also took just the right ground; and I saw a great deal of them, as well as of many members of the House, particularly those from the West, where the feeling for war was strongest.

Naval officers came and went, and senators were only in the city while the Senate was in session; but there was one friend who was steadily in Washington. This was an army surgeon, Dr. Leonard Wood. I only met him after I entered the navy department, but we soon found that we had kindred tastes and kindred principles. He had served in General Miles's inconceivably harassing campaigns against the Apaches, where he had displayed such courage that he won that most coveted of distinctions—the Medal of Honor; such extraordinary physical strength and endurance that he grew to be recognized as one of the two or three white men who could stand fatigue and hardship as well as an Apache; and such judgment that toward the close of the campaigns he was given, though a surgeon, the actual command of more than one expedition against the bands of renegade Indians. Like so many of the gallant fighters with whom it was later my good fortune to serve, he combined, in a very high degree, the qualities of entire manliness with entire uprightness and cleanliness of character. . . .

In the summer he and I took long walks together through

the beautiful broken country surrounding Washington. In winter we sometimes varied these walks by kicking a football in an empty lot, or, on the rare occasions when there was enough snow, by trying a couple of sets of skis or snow-skates, which had been sent me from Canada.

But always on our way out to and back from these walks and sport, there was one topic to which, in our talking, we returned, and that was the possible war with Spain. We both felt very strongly that such a war would be as righteous as it would be advantageous to the honor and the interests of the nation; and after the blowing up of the *Maine,* we felt that it was inevitable. We then at once began to try to see that we had our share in it. The president and my own chief, Secretary Long, were very firm against my going, but they said that if I was bent upon going they would help me. Wood was the medical adviser of both the president and the secretary of war, and could count upon their friendship. So we started with the odds in our favor.

At first we had great difficulty in knowing exactly what to try for. We could go on the staff of any one of several generals, but we much preferred to go in the line. Wood hoped he might get a commission in his native state of Massachusetts; but in Massachusetts, as in every other state, it proved there were ten men who wanted to go to the war for every chance to go. Then we thought we might get positions as field officers under an old friend of mine, Colonel—now General—Francis V. Greene, of New York, the colonel of the Seventy-first; but again there were no vacancies.

Our doubts were resolved when Congress authorized the raising of three cavalry regiments from among the wild riders and riflemen of the Rockies and the Great Plains. During Wood's service in the Southwest he had commanded not only regulars and Indian scouts, but also white frontiersmen. In the Northwest I had spent much of my time, for many years, either on my ranch or in long hunting trips, and had lived and worked for months together with the cowboy and the mountain hunter, faring in every way precisely as they did.

Secretary Alger offered me the command of one of these regiments. If I had taken it, being entirely inexperienced in military work, I should not have known how to get it equipped most rapidly, for I should have spent valuable weeks in learning its needs, with the result that I should have missed the Santiago campaign, and might not even have had the consolation prize of going to Puerto Rico. Fortunately, I was wise enough to tell the secretary that while I believed I could learn to command the regiment in a month, yet that it was just this very month which I could not afford to spare, and that therefore I would be quite content to go as lieutenant-colonel, if he would make Wood colonel.

This was entirely satisfactory to both the president and secretary, and, accordingly, Wood and I were speedily commissioned as colonel and lieutenant-colonel of the First United States Volunteer Cavalry. This was the official title of the regiment, but for some reason or other the public promptly christened us the Rough Riders. At first we fought against the use of the term, but to no purpose; and when finally the generals of division and brigade began to write in formal communications about our regiment as the Rough Riders, we adopted the term ourselves.

The mustering-places for the regiment were appointed in New Mexico, Arizona, Oklahoma, and Indian Territory. The difficulty in organizing was not in selecting but in rejecting men. Within a day or two after it was announced that we were to raise the regiment, we were literally deluged with applications from every quarter of the Union. Without the slightest trouble, so far as men went, we could have raised a brigade or even a division. The difficulty lay in arming, equipping, mounting, and disciplining the men we selected. Hundreds of regiments were being called into existence by the national government, and each regiment was sure to have innumerable wants to be satisfied. To a man who knew the ground as Wood did, and who was entirely aware of our national unpreparedness, it was evident that the ordnance and quartermaster's bureaus could not meet, for some time to come, one-tenth of the demands that would be made upon them; and it was all-important to get in first with our demands. Thanks to his knowledge of the situation and promptness, we immediately put in our requisitions for the articles indispensable for the equipment of the regiment; and then, by ceaseless worrying of excellent bureaucrats, who had no idea how to do things quickly or how to meet an emergency, we succeeded in getting our rifles, cartridges, revolvers, clothing, shelter-tents, and horse gear just in time to enable us to go on the Santiago expedition. Some of the state troops, who were already organized as National Guards, were, of course, ready, after a fashion, when the war broke out; but no other regiment which had our work to do was able to do it in anything like as quick time, and therefore no other volunteer regiment saw anything like the fighting which we did.

Wood thoroughly realized what the Ordnance Department failed to realize, namely, the inestimable advantage of smokeless powder; and, moreover, he was bent upon our having the weapons of the regulars, for this meant that we would be brigaded with them, and it was evident that they would do the bulk of the fighting if the war were short. Accordingly, by acting with the utmost vigor and promptness, he succeeded in getting our regiment armed with the Krag-Jorgensen carbine used by the regular cavalry.

It was impossible to take any of the numerous companies which were proffered to us from the various states. The only organized bodies we were at liberty to accept were those from the four territories. But owing to the fact that the number of men originally allotted to us, 780, was speedily raised to 1,000, we were given a chance to accept quite a number of eager volunteers who did not come from the territories, but who possessed precisely the same temper that distinguished our southwestern recruits, and whose presence materially benefited the regiment.

We drew recruits from Harvard, Yale, Princeton, and many another college; from clubs like the Somerset, of Boston, and

Knickerbocker, of New York; and from among the men who belonged neither to club nor to college, but in whose veins the blood stirred with the same impulse which once sent the Vikings over sea. Four of the policemen who had served under me, while I was president of the New York Police Board, insisted on coming—two of them to die, the other two to return unhurt after honorable and dangerous service. It seemed to me that almost every friend I had in every state had some one acquaintance who was bound to go with the Rough Riders, and for whom I had to make a place. . . .

Harvard being my own college, I had such a swarm of applicants from it that I could not take one in ten. What particularly pleased me, not only in the Harvard but the Yale and Princeton men, and, indeed, in these recruits from the older states generally, was that they did not ask for commissions. With hardly an exception they entered upon their duties as troopers in the spirit which they held to the end, merely endeavoring to show that no work could be too hard, too disagreeable, or too dangerous for them to perform, and neither asking nor receiving any reward in the way of promotion or consideration. The Harvard contingent was practically raised by Guy Murchie, of Maine. He saw all the fighting and did his duty with the utmost gallantry, and then left the service as he had entered it, a trooper, entirely satisfied to have done his duty—and no man did it better. So it was with Dudley Dean, perhaps the best quarterback who ever played on a Harvard eleven; and so with Bob Wrenn, a quarterback whose feats rivaled those of Dean's, and who, in addition, was the champion tennis player of America, and had, on two different years, saved this championship from going to an Englishman. So it was with Yale men like Waller, the high jumper, and Garrison and Girard; and with Princeton men like Devereux and Channing, the football players; with Larned, the tennis player; with Craig Wadsworth, the steeplechase rider; with Joe Stevens, the crack polo player; with Hamilton Fish, the ex-captain of the Columbia crew, and with scores of others whose names are quite as worthy of mention as any of those I have given. . . .

I felt many qualms at first in allowing men of this stamp to come in, for I could not be certain that they had counted the cost, and was afraid they would find it very hard to serve—not for a few days, but for months—in the ranks, while I, their former intimate associate, was a field officer; but they insisted that they knew their minds, and the events showed that they did. We enlisted about fifty of them from Virginia, Maryland, and the northeastern states, at Washington. Before allowing them to be sworn in, I gathered them together and explained that if they went in they must be prepared not merely to fight, but to perform the weary, monotonous labor incident to the ordinary routine of a soldier's life; that they must be ready to face fever exactly as they were to face bullets; that they were to obey unquestioningly, and to do their duty as readily if called upon to garrison a fort as if sent to the front. I warned them that work that was merely irksome and disagreeable must be faced as readily as work that was dangerous, and that no complaint of any kind must be made; and I told them that they were entirely at liberty not to go, but that after they had once signed there could then be no backing out.

Not a man of them backed out; not one of them failed to do his whole duty.

These men formed but a small fraction of the whole. They went down to San Antonio, where the regiment was to gather and where Wood preceded me, while I spent a week in Washington hurrying up the different bureaus and telegraphing my various railroad friends, so as to ensure our getting the carbines, saddles, and uniforms that we needed from the various armories and storehouses. Then I went down to San Antonio myself, where I found the men from New Mexico, Arizona, and Oklahoma already gathered, while those from Indian Territory came in soon after my arrival.

These were the men who made up the bulk of the regiment, and gave it its peculiar character. They came from the four territories which yet remained within the boundaries of the

United States; that is, from the lands that have been most recently won over to white civilization, and in which the conditions of life are nearest those that obtained on the frontier when
there still was a frontier. They were a splendid set of men, these
southwesterners—tall and sinewy, with resolute, weather-
beaten faces, and eyes that looked a man straight in the face
without flinching. They included in their ranks men of every
occupation; but the three types were those of the cowboy, the
hunter, and the mining prospector—the man who wandered
hither and thither, killing game for a living, and spending his life
in the quest for metal wealth.

In all the world there could be no better material for soldiers
than that afforded by these grim hunters of the mountains, these
wild rough riders of the plains. They were accustomed to handling wild and savage horses; they were accustomed to following the chase with the rifle, both for sport and as a means of
livelihood. Varied though their occupations had been, almost all
had, at one time or another, herded cattle and hunted big game.
They were hardened to life in the open, and to shifting for
themselves under adverse circumstances. They were used, for all
their lawless freedom, to the rough discipline of the roundup
and the mining company. Some of them came from the small
frontier towns; but most were from the wilderness, having left
their lonely hunters' cabins and shifting cow-camps to seek new
and more stirring adventures beyond the sea. . . .

The captains and lieutenants were sometimes men who
had campaigned in the regular army against Apache, Ute, and
Cheyenne, and who, on completing their term of service, had
shown their energy by settling in the new communities and
growing up to be men of mark. In other cases they were sher-
iffs, marshals, deputy-sheriffs, and deputy-marshals—men
who had fought Indians, and still more often had waged relentless war upon the bands of white desperadoes. There was
Bucky O'Neill, of Arizona, captain of Troop A, the mayor of
Prescott, a famous sheriff throughout the West for his feats of
victorious warfare against the Apache, no less than against the

white road-agents and man-killers. . . . He was a wild, reckless fellow, soft spoken, and of dauntless courage and boundless ambition; he was staunchly loyal to his friends, and cared for his men in every way. There was Captain Llewellen, of New Mexico, a good citizen, a political leader, and one of the most noted peace officers of the country; he had been shot four times in pitched fights with red marauders and white outlaws. There was Lieutenant Ballard, who had broken up the Black Jack gang of ill-omened notoriety, and his captain, Curry, another New Mexican sheriff of fame. . . .

Three of our higher officers had been in the regular army. One was Major Alexander Brodie, from Arizona, afterward lieutenant-colonel, who had lived for twenty years in the territory, and had become a thorough westerner without sinking the West Pointer—a soldier by taste as well as training, whose men worshiped him and would follow him anywhere, as they would Bucky O'Neill or any other of their favorites. Brodie was running a big mining business; but when the *Maine* was blown up, he abandoned everything and telegraphed right and left to bid his friends get ready for the fight he saw impending.

Then there was Micah Jenkins, the captain of Troop K, a gentle and courteous South Carolinian, on whom danger acted like wine. In action he was a perfect gamecock, and he won his majority for gallantry in battle.

Finally, there was Allyn Capron, who was, on the whole, the best soldier in the regiment. In fact, I think he was the ideal of what an American regular army officer should be. He was the fifth in descent from father to son who had served in the army of the United States, and in body and mind alike he was fitted to play his part to perfection. Tall and lithe, a remarkable boxer and walker, a first-class rider and shot, with yellow hair and piercing blue eyes, he looked what he was, the archetype of the fighting man. He had under him one of the two companies from the Indian Territory; and he so soon impressed himself upon the wild spirit of his followers that he got them ahead in discipline faster than any other troop in the regiment, while at the same time taking care of their bodily wants. . . .

The men in the ranks were mostly young; yet some were past their first youth. These had taken part in the killing of the great buffalo herds, and had fought Indians when the tribes were still on the warpath. The younger ones, too, had led rough lives; and the lines in their faces told of many a hardship endured, and many a danger silently faced with grim, unconscious philosophy. Some were originally from the East, and had seen strange adventures in different kinds of life, from sailing round the Horn to mining in Alaska. Others had been born and bred in the West, and had never seen a larger town than Santa Fe or a bigger body of water than the Pecos in flood. Some of them went by their own name; some had changed their names; and yet others possessed but half a name, colored by some adjective, like Cherokee Bill, Happy Jack of Arizona, Smoky Moore, the bronco-buster, so named because cowboys often call vicious horses "smoky" horses, and Rattlesnake Pete, who had lived among the Moquis and taken part in the snake-dances. Some were professional gamblers, and, on the other hand, no less than four were or had been Baptist or Methodist clergymen—and proved first-class fighters, too, by the way. . . .

There was one characteristic and distinctive contingent which could have appeared only in such a regiment as ours. From the Indian Territory there came a number of Indians— Cherokees, Chickasaws, Choctaws, and Creeks. Only a few were of pure blood. The others shaded off until they were absolutely indistinguishable from their white comrades; with whom, it may be mentioned, they all lived on terms of complete equality.

Not all of the Indians were from the Indian Territory. One of the gamest fighters and best soldiers in the regiment was Pollock, a full-blooded Pawnee. He had been educated, like most of the other Indians, at one of those admirable Indian schools which have added so much to the total of the small credit account with which the white race balances the very unpleasant debit account of its dealings with the red. Pollock was a silent, solitary fellow—an excellent penman, much given to drawing pictures. When we got down to Santiago he developed into the regimental clerk. . . .

Two of the young Cherokee recruits came to me with a most kindly letter from one of the ladies who had been teaching in the academy from which they were about to graduate. She and I had known one another in connection with governmental and philanthropic work on the reservations, and she wrote to commend the two boys to my attention. One was on the academy football team and the other in the glee club. Both were fine young fellows. The football player now lies buried with the other dead who fell in the fight at San Juan. The singer was brought to death's door by fever, but recovered and came back to his home.

There were other Indians of much wilder type, but their wildness was precisely like that of the cowboys with whom they were associated. One or two of them needed rough discipline; and they got it, too. Like the rest of the regiment, they were splendid riders. . . .

The life histories of some of the men who joined our regiment would make many volumes of thrilling adventure.

We drew a great many recruits from Texas; and from nowhere did we get a higher average, for many of them had served in that famous body of frontier fighters, the Texas Rangers. Of course, these rangers needed no teaching. They were already trained to obey and to take responsibility. They were splendid shots, horsemen, and trailers. They were accustomed to living in the open, to enduring great fatigue and hardship, and to encountering all kinds of danger.

Many of the Arizona and New Mexico men had taken part in warfare with the Apaches. . . . Of course, a man who had kept his nerve and held his own, year after year, while living where each day and night contained the threat of hidden death from a foe whose goings and comings were unseen, was not apt to lose courage when confronted with any other enemy. An experience in following in the trail of an enemy who might flee at one stretch through fifty miles of deathlike desert was a good school out of which to come with profound indifference for the ordinary hardships of campaigning.

As a rule, the men were more apt, however, to have had experience in warring against white desperadoes and lawbreakers than against Indians. Some of our best recruits came from Colorado. One, a very large, hawk-eyed man, Benjamin Franklin Daniels, had been marshal of Dodge City when that pleasing town was probably the toughest abode of civilized man to be found anywhere on the continent. In the course of the exercise of his rather lurid functions as peace officer he had lost half of one ear—"bitten off," it was explained to me. Naturally, he viewed the dangers of battle with philosophic calm. Such a man was, in reality, a veteran even in his first fight, and was a tower of strength to the recruits in his part of the line. . . .

The temptation is great to go on enumerating man after man who stood preeminent, whether as a killer of game, a tamer of horses, or a queller of disorder among his people, or who, mayhap, stood out with a more evil prominence as himself a dangerous man—one given to the taking of life on small provocation, or one who was ready to earn his living outside the law if the occasion demanded it. . . . There was many a skilled packer who had led and guarded his trains of laden mules through the Indian-haunted country surrounding some outpost of civilization. There were men who had won fame as Rocky Mountain stage-drivers, or who had spent endless days in guiding the slow wagon-trains across the grassy plains. There were miners who knew every camp from the Yukon to Leadville, and cow-punchers in whose memories were stored the brands carried by the herds from Chihuahua to Assiniboia. There were men who had roped wild steers in the mesquite brush of the Nueces, and who, year in and year out, had driven the trail herds northward over desolate wastes and across the fords of shrunken rivers to the fattening grounds of the Powder and the Yellowstone. . . .

Such were the men we had as recruits: soldiers ready made,

as far as concerned their capacity as individual fighters. What was necessary was to teach them to act together, and to obey orders. Our special task was to make them ready for action in the shortest possible time. We were bound to see fighting, and therefore to be with the first expedition that left the United States; for we could not tell how long the war would last.

I had been quite prepared for trouble when it came to enforcing discipline, but I was agreeably disappointed. There were plenty of hard characters who might by themselves have given trouble, and with one or two of whom we did have to take rough measures; but the bulk of the men thoroughly understood that without discipline they would be merely a valueless mob, and they set themselves hard at work to learn the new duties. . . . The men were singularly quick to respond to any appeal to their intelligence and patriotism. The faults they committed were those of ignorance merely. When Holderman, in announcing dinner to the colonel and the three majors, genially remarked, "If you fellars don't come soon, everything'll get cold," he had no thought of other than a kindly and respectful regard for their welfare, and was glad to modify his form of address on being told that it was not what could be described as conventionally military. When one of our sentinels, who had with much labor learned the manual of arms, saluted with great pride as I passed, and added, with a friendly nod, "Good evening, Colonel," this variation in the accepted formula on such occasions was meant, and was accepted, as mere friendly interest. In both cases the needed instruction was given and received in the same kindly spirit. . . .

It was astonishing how soon the men got over these little peculiarities. They speedily grew to recognize the fact that the observance of certain forms was essential to the maintenance of proper discipline. They became scrupulously careful in touching their hats, and always came to attention when spoken to. They saw that we did not insist upon the observance of these forms to humiliate them; that we were as anxious to learn our own duties as we were to have them learn theirs, and as scrupulous in paying respect to our superiors as we were in exacting the acknowledgment due our rank from those below us; moreover, what was very important, they saw that we were careful to look after their interests in every way, and were doing all that was possible to hurry up the equipment and drill of the regiment, so as to get into the war.

Rigid guard duty was established at once, and everyone was impressed with the necessity for vigilance and watchfulness. The policing of the camp was likewise attended to with the utmost rigor. As always with new troops, they were at first indifferent to the necessity for cleanliness in camp arrangements; but on this point Colonel Wood brooked no laxity, and in a very little while the hygienic conditions of the camp were as good as those of any regular regiment. Meanwhile the men were being drilled, on foot at first, with the utmost assiduity. Every night we had officers' school, the noncommissioned officers of each troop being given similar schooling by the captain or one of the lieutenants of the troop; and every day we practiced hard, by squad, by troop, by squadron, and battalion. The earnestness and intelligence with which the men went to work rendered the task of instruction much less difficult than would be supposed. . . . Skirmishing they took to naturally, which was fortunate, as practically all our fighting was done in open order.

Meanwhile we were purchasing horses. Judging from what I saw I do not think that we got heavy enough animals, and of those purchased certainly a half were nearly unbroken. It was no easy matter to handle them on the picket-lines, and to provide for feeding and watering; and the efforts to shoe and ride them were at first productive of much vigorous excitement. Of course, those that were wild from the range had to be thrown and tied down before they could be shod. Half the horses of the regiment bucked, or possessed some other of the amiable weaknesses incident to horse life on the great ranches; but we had abundance of men who were utterly unmoved by any antic a horse might commit. Every animal was speedily mastered, though a large number remained to the end mounts upon which an ordinary rider would have felt very uncomfortable. . . .

Mounted drill with such horses and men bade fair to offer opportunities for excitement; yet it usually went off smoothly enough. Before drilling the men on horseback they had all been drilled on foot, and having gone at their work with hearty zest, they knew well the simple movements to form any kind of line or column. Wood was busy from morning till night in hurrying the final details of the equipment, and he turned the drill of the men over to me. To drill perfectly needs long practice, but to drill roughly is a thing very easy to learn indeed. We were not always right about our intervals, our lines were somewhat irregular, and our more difficult movements were executed at times in rather a haphazard way; but the essential commands and the essential movements we learned without any difficulty, and the men performed them with great dash. When we put them on horseback, there was, of course, trouble with the horses; but the horsemanship of the riders was consummate. . . .

Our arms were the regular cavalry carbine, the Krag, a splendid weapon, and the revolver. A few carried their favorite Winchesters, using, of course, the new model, which took the government cartridge. We felt very strongly that it would be worse than a waste of time to try to train our men to use the saber —a weapon utterly alien to them; but with the rifle and revolver they were already familiar. Many of my cavalry friends in the past had insisted to me that the revolver was a better weapon than the sword. . . . Personally, I knew too little to decide as to the comparative merits of the two arms; but I did know that it was a great deal better to use the arm with which our men were already proficient. They were therefore armed with what might be called their natural weapon, the revolver. . . .

It was astonishing what a difference was made by two or three weeks' training. The mere thorough performance of guard and police duties helped the men very rapidly to become soldiers. The officers studied hard, and both officers and men worked hard in the drill-field. It was, of course, rough and ready drill; but it was very efficient, and it was suited to the men who made up the regiment. Their uniform also suited them. In their slouch hats, blue flannel shirts, brown trousers, leggings, and boots, with handkerchiefs knotted loosely around their necks, they looked exactly as a body of cowboy cavalry should look. The officers speedily grew to realize that they must not be overfamiliar with their men, and yet that they must care for them in every way. The men, in return, began to acquire those habits of attention to soldierly detail which mean so much in making a regiment. Above all, every man felt, and had constantly instilled into him, a keen pride of the regiment, and a resolute purpose to do his whole duty uncomplainingly, and, above all, to win glory by the way he handled himself in battle.

GUBERNATORIAL MESSAGE TO THE NEW YORK STATE LEGISLATURE

January 3, 1900

To the Legislature: It is a very genuine pleasure to congratulate the legislature upon the substantial sum of achievement in legislation and administration of the past year. Laws of the utmost usefulness to the community have been enacted, and there has been a steady betterment throughout the year in the methods and results of the administration of the government. . . .

The whole problem of taxation is now, as it has been at almost all times and in almost all places, one of extreme difficulty. It has become more and more evident in recent years that existing methods of taxation, which worked well enough in a simpler state of society, are not adequate to secure justice when applied to the conditions of our complex and highly specialized modern industrial development. At present the real estate owner is certainly bearing an excessive proportion of the tax burden. Men who have made a special study of the theory of taxation and men who have had long experience in its practical application are alike in conflict among themselves as to the best general system. Absolute equality, absolute justice in matters of taxation will probably never be realized; but we can approximate it much more closely than at present. The last legislature most wisely appointed a committee to consider the feasibility of a thorough and far-reaching change in our tax laws; and there is good reason to believe that their forthcoming report will present a scheme which will receive the support of substantially all classes of taxpayers, and which will be of such a character as to commend itself to the most careful consideration of your body upon broad lines.

The law must not only be correct in the abstract; it must work well in the concrete. Experience shows that certain classes or symbols of property which in theory ought to be taxed cannot under the present practice be reached. Some kinds of taxes are so fertile in tempting to perjury and sharp dealing that they amount to taxes on honesty—the last quality on which we should impose a needless burden. Moreover, where the conditions and complexity of life vary widely as between different communities, the desirability and possibility of certain taxes may seem or be so different that it is hard to devise a common system that will work. If possible the state tax should be levied on classes of property, and in a manner which will render it collectible with entire fairness in all sections of the community, as for instance the corporation or collateral inheritance tax is now collected. So far as possible we should divorce the state and municipal taxes, so as to render unnecessary the annual equalization of values between the several counties which has proved so fertile a source of friction between the city and the country.

There is a constant influx into New York State of capital ofttimes previously incorporated under the laws of other states, and an increasing number of men of means from other parts of the country, nonresidents of New York, come into this state to sojourn and to conduct and be at the head of various business enterprises which are drawn to New York as the financial center of the whole country. This calls for legislation which shall provide, in a broad and fair spirit, for taxing foreign capital in this state, whether in corporate or individual form, exactly as we tax domestic capital doing business along the same lines.

I call your attention to the fact that the great burden of taxation is local, not state. In the large cities the heavy local charges are mainly due to the action of the local authorities themselves. For this the local authorities are of course responsible. But sometimes taxation is added to by legislative enactment.

On certain points the failure of the tax laws has become so

evident that it is possible to provide more or less complete remedies without waiting for a general scheme of reorganization. Again and again in recent years this has been recognized, and through legislative enactment certain species of property which had escaped taxation have been made to pay their proper share of the public burdens. The collateral inheritance tax offers a case in point. The corporation tax offers another. In all these matters of taxation, however, it is necessary to proceed with extreme caution, the path never being so simple and clear as the advocates of any particular measure invariably believe. Every wealthy corporation that perpetrates or is allowed to perpetrate a wrong helps to produce or inflame a condition of angry excitement against all corporations, which in its turn may in the end harm alike the honest and the dishonest agents of public service and thereby do far-reaching damage to the whole body politic. Much of the outcry against wealth, against the men who acquire wealth, and against the means by which it is acquired, is blind, unreasoning and unjust; but in too many cases it has a basis in real abuses; and we must remember that every act of misconduct which affords any justification for this clamor is not only bad because of the wrong done but also because the justification thus given inevitably strengthens movements which are in reality profoundly antisocial and anticivic. Our laws should be so drawn as to protect and encourage corporations which do their honest duty by the public; and to discriminate sharply against those organized in a spirit of mere greed, or for improper speculative purposes.

There is plenty of misconduct, plenty of selfish disregard of the rights of others, and especially of the weak. There is also plenty of honorable and disinterested effort to prevent such misconduct or to minimize its effects. Any rational attempt to prevent or counteract the evils, by legislation or otherwise, is deserving of hearty support; but it cannot be too deeply impressed upon us that such attempts can result in permanent good only in proportion as they are made in a sane and wholesome spirit, as far removed as possible from whatever is hysterical or revolutionary. It is infinitely better when needed social and civic changes can be brought about as the result of natural and healthy growth than when they come with the violent dislocation and widespread wreck and damage inevitably attendant upon any movement which is revolutionary in its nature.

At the same time a change should never be shirked on the ground of its being radical, when the abuse has become flagrant and no other remedy appears possible. This was the case with the taxation of local franchises in this state. For years most of these franchises escaped paying their proper share of the public burdens. The last legislature placed on the statute book a law requiring them to be treated as real estate for the purposes of taxation, the tax to be assessed and collected by the state assessors for the benefit of the localities concerned. This marks an immense stride in advance. Of course, at first serious difficulties are sure to arise in enforcing it. The means for carrying it into effect are very inadequate. There may be delay before we get from it the substantial additions to the revenue which will finally accrue, and there may be disappointment to the enthusiasts who are so apt to hope too much from such legislation. But it will undoubtedly add largely to the public revenues as soon as it is fairly in operation, and the amount thus added will increase steadily year by year. The principle which this law establishes has come to stay. There will doubtless have to be additional legislation from time to time to perfect the system as its shortcomings are made evident in actual practice. But the corporations owning valuable public franchises must pay their full and proper share of the public burdens.

The franchise tax law is framed with the intent of securing exact and equal justice, no more and no less. It is not in any way intended as a means for persecuting or oppressing corporations. It is not intended to cut down legitimate dividends; still less to cut down wages or to prevent a just return for the far-sighted business skill of some captain of industry who has been able to establish a public service greatly to the advantage of the localities concerned, where before his time men of less business capacity had failed. But it is intended that property which derives its value from the grant of a privilege by the public shall be taxed proportionately to the value of the privilege granted. In enforcing this law, much tact, patience, resolution, and judgment will be needed. All these qualities the State Board of Tax Commissioners have thus far shown. Their salaries are altogether inadequate, for the new law has immensely increased not only their responsibilities, but their work. They should be given not only the needed increase for themselves, but also an appropriation for an additional number of clerks and experts.

During the year 1899 not a single corporation has received at the hands of the state of New York one privilege of any kind, sort or description, by law or otherwise, to which it was not entitled, and which was not in the public interest; nor has corporate influence availed against any measure which was in the public interest. At certain times, and in certain places, corporations have undoubtedly exerted a corrupting influence in political life; but in this state for this year it is absolutely true, as shown by the history of every measure that has come before the legislature from the franchise tax down, that no corporate influence has been able to prevail against the interests of the public.

It has become more and more evident of late years that the state will have to act in its collective capacity as regards certain subjects which we have been accustomed to treat as matters affecting the private citizen only, and that furthermore, it must exercise an increasing and more rigorous control over other matters which it is not desirable that it should directly manage. It is neither possible nor desirable to lay down a general hard and fast rule as to what this control should be in all cases. There is no possible reason in pure logic why a city, for instance, should supply its inhabitants with water, and allow private companies to supply them with gas, any more than there is why the general government should take charge of the delivery of letters but not of telegrams. On the other hand, pure logic has a very restricted application to actual social and civic life, and there is no possible reason for changing from one system to the other simply because the change would make our political system in theory more symmetrical. Obviously it is undesirable that the government should do anything that private individuals could do with better results to the community. Everything that tends to deaden individual initiative is to be avoided, and unless in a given case there is some very evident gain which will flow from state or municipal ownership, it should not be adopted. On the other hand, when private ownership entails grave abuses, and where the work is of a kind that can be performed with efficiency by the state or municipality acting in its collective capacity, no theory or tradition should interfere with our making the change. There is grave danger in attempting to establish invariable rules; indeed it may be that each case will have to be determined upon its own merits. In one instance a private corporation may be able to do the work best. In another the state or city may do it best. In yet a third, it may be to the advantage of everybody to give free scope to the power of some individual captain of industry.

On one point there must be no step backward. There is a consensus of opinion that New York must own its own water supply. Any legislation permitting private ownership should be annulled.

Nothing needs closer attention, nothing deserves to be treated with more courage, caution, and sanity, than the relations of the state to corporate wealth, and indeed to vast individual wealth. For almost every gain there is a penalty, and the great strides in the industrial upbuilding of the country, which have on the whole been attended with marked benefit, have also been attended by no little evil. Great fortunes are usually made under very complex conditions both of effort and of surrounding, and the mere fact of the complexity makes it difficult to deal with the new conditions thus created. The contrast offered in a highly specialized industrial community between the very rich and the very poor is exceedingly distressing, and while under normal conditions the acquirement of wealth by an individual is necessarily of great incidental benefit to the community as a whole, yet this is by no means always the case. In our great cities there is plainly in evidence much wealth contrasted with much poverty, and some of the wealth has been acquired, or is used, in a manner for which there is no moral justification. . . .

The true questions to be asked are: Has any given individual been injured by the acquisition of wealth by any man? Were the rights of that individual, if they have been violated, insufficiently protected by law? If so, these rights, and all similar rights, ought to be guaranteed by additional legislation. The point to be aimed at is the protection of the individual against wrong, not the attempt to limit and hamper the acquisition and output of wealth. . . .

It is well to remember on the one hand that the adoption of what is reasonable in the demands of reformers is the surest way to prevent the adoption of what is unreasonable; and on the other hand that many of the worst and most dangerous laws which have been put upon the statute books have been put there by zealous reformers with excellent intentions.

This problem has a hundred phases. The relation of the capitalist and the wage-worker makes one; the proper attitude of the state toward extreme poverty another; the proper attitude of the state toward the questions of the ownership and running of so-called "public utilities," a third. But among all these phases, the one which at this time has the greatest prominence is the question of what are commonly termed trusts, meaning by the name those vast combinations of capital, usually flourishing by virtue of some monopolistic element, which have become so startlingly common a feature in the industrial revolution which has progressed so rapidly during recent years.

Every new feature of this industrial revolution produces hardship because in its later stages it has been literally a revolution instead of an evolution. The new inventions and discoveries and the new methods of taking advantage of the business facilities afforded by the extraordinary development of our material civilization have caused the changes to proceed with such marvelous rapidity that at each stage some body of workers finds itself unable to accommodate itself to the new conditions with sufficient speed to escape hardship. In the end the accommodation of the class takes place; at times too late for the well-being of many individuals. The change which would be unaccompanied by hardship if it came slowly, may be fraught with severe suffering if it comes too fast, even when it is in the end beneficial. Occasionally, moreover, the change is positively deleterious, and very often, even when it is on the whole beneficial, it has features which are the reverse. In some cases, while recognizing the evil, it is impossible with our present knowledge to discover any remedy. In others, a remedy can be applied, but as yet only at a cost that would make it worse than the trouble itself. In yet others it is possible, by acting with wisdom, coolness, and fearlessness, to apply a remedy which will wholly or in great part remove the evil while leaving the good behind. We do not wish to discourage enterprise. We do not desire to destroy corporations; we do desire to put them fully at the service of the state and the people.

SPEECH AT THE
MINNESOTA STATE FAIR

St. Paul, September 2, 1901

THE BIG STICK

In his admirable series of studies of twentieth-century problems, Dr. Lyman Abbott has pointed out that we are a nation of pioneers; that the first colonists to our shores were pioneers, and that pioneers selected out from among the descendants of these early pioneers, mingled with others selected afresh from the Old World, pushed westward into the wilderness and laid the foundations for new commonwealths. They were men of hope and expectation, of enterprise and energy; for the men of dull content or more dull despair had no part in the great movement into and across the New World. Our country has been populated by pioneers, and therefore it has in it more energy, more enterprise, more expansive power than any other in the wide world.

You whom I am now addressing stand for the most part but one generation removed from these pioneers. You are typical Americans, for you have done the great, the characteristic, the typical work of our American life. In making homes and carving out careers for yourselves and your children, you have built up this state. Throughout our history the success of the home-maker has been but another name for the up-building of the nation. The men who with ax in the forests and pick in the mountains and plow on the prairies pushed to completion the dominion of our people over the American wilderness have given the definite shape to our nation. They have shown the qualities of daring, endurance, and far-sightedness, of eager desire for victory and stubborn refusal to accept defeat, which go to make up the essential manliness of the American character. Above all, they have recognized in practical form the fundamental law of success in American life—the law of worthy work, the law of high, resolute endeavor. We have but little room among our people for the timid, the irresolute, and the idle; and it is no less true that there is scant room in the world at large for the nation with mighty thews that dares not to be great.

Surely in speaking to the sons of the men who actually did the rough and hard and infinitely glorious work of making the great Northwest what it now is, I need hardly insist upon the righteousness of this doctrine. In your own vigorous lives you show by every act how scant is your patience with those who do not see in the life of effort the life supremely worth living. Sometimes we hear those who do not work spoken of with envy. Surely the willfully idle need arouse in the breast of a healthy man no emotion stronger than that of contempt—at the outside no emotion stronger than angry contempt. The feeling of envy would have in it an admission of inferiority on our part, to which the men who know not the sterner joys of life are not entitled. Poverty is a bitter thing; but it is not as bitter as the existence of restless vacuity and physical, moral, and intellectual flabbiness, to which those doom themselves who elect to spend all their years in that vainest of all vain pursuits—the pursuit of mere pleasure as a sufficient end in itself. The willfully idle man, like the willfully barren woman, has no place in a sane, healthy, and vigorous community. Moreover, the gross and hideous selfishness for which each stands defeats even its own miserable aims. Exactly as infinitely the happiest woman is she who has borne and brought up many healthy children, so infinitely the happiest man is he who has toiled hard and successfully in his life-work. The work may be done in a thousand different ways —with the brain or the hands, in the study, the field, or the workshop—if it is honest work, honestly done and well worth doing, that is all we have a right to ask. Every father and mother here, if they are wise, will bring up their children not to shirk difficulties, but to meet them and overcome them; not to strive after a life of ignoble ease, but to strive to do their duty, first to themselves and their families, and then to the whole state; and this duty must inevitably take the shape of work in some form or other. You, the sons of the pioneers, if you are true to your ancestry, must make your lives as worthy as they made theirs. They sought for true success, and therefore they did not seek ease. They knew that success comes only to those who lead the life of endeavor.

It seems to me that the simple acceptance of this fundamental fact of American life, this acknowledgment that the law of work is the fundamental law of our being, will help us to start aright in facing not a few of the problems that confront us from without and from within. As regards internal affairs, it should teach us the prime need of remembering that, after all has been said and done, the chief factor in any man's success or failure must be his own character—that is, the sum of his common sense, his courage, his virile energy and capacity. Nothing can take the place of this individual factor.

I do not for a moment mean that much cannot be done to supplement it. Besides each one of us working individually, all of us have got to work together. We cannot possibly do our best work as a nation unless all of us know how to act in combination as well as how to act each individually for himself. The acting in combination can take many forms, but of course its most effective form must be when it comes in the shape of law —that is, of action by the community as a whole through the lawmaking body.

But it is not possible ever to insure prosperity merely by law. Something for good can be done by law, and a bad law can do an infinity of mischief; but, after all, the best law can only prevent wrong and injustice, and give to the thrifty, the far-seeing, and the hard-working a chance to exercise to best advantage their special and peculiar abilities. No hard-and-fast rule can be laid down as to where our legislation shall stop in interfering between man and man, between interest and interest. All that can be said is that it is highly undesirable, on the one hand, to weaken individual initiative, and, on the other hand, that in a constantly increasing number of cases we shall find it necessary in the future to shackle cunning as in the past we have shackled force. It is not only highly desirable but necessary that there should be legislation which shall carefully shield the interests of wage-workers, and which shall discriminate in favor of the honest and humane employer by removing the disadvantage under which he stands when compared with unscrupulous competitors who have no conscience and will do right only under fear of punishment.

Nor can legislation stop only with what are termed labor questions. The vast individual and corporate fortunes, the vast combinations of capital, which have marked the development of our industrial system create new conditions, and necessitate a change from the old attitude of the state and the nation toward property. It is probably true that the large majority of the fortunes that now exist in this country have been amassed not by injuring our people, but as an incident to the conferring of great benefits upon the community; and this, no matter what may have been the conscious purpose of those amassing them. There is but the scantiest justification for most of the outcry against the men of wealth *as such;* and it ought to be unnecessary to state that any appeal which directly or indirectly leads to suspicion and hatred among ourselves, which tends to limit opportunity, and therefore to shut the door of success against poor men of talent, and, finally, which entails the possibility of lawlessness and violence, is an attack upon the fundamental properties of American citizenship. Our interests are at bottom common; in the long run we go up or go down together. Yet more and more it is evident that the state, and if necessary the nation, has got to possess the right of supervision and control as regards the great corporations which are its creatures; particularly as regards the great business combinations which derive a portion of their importance from the existence of some monopolistic tendency. The right should be exercised with caution and self-restraint; but it should exist, so that it may be invoked if the need arises.

So much for our duties, each to himself and each to his neighbor, within the limits of our own country. But our country, as it strides forward with ever-increasing rapidity to a foremost place among the world powers, must necessarily find, more and more, that it has world duties also. There are excellent people who believe that we can shirk these duties and yet retain our self-respect; but these good people are in error. Other good people seek to deter us from treading the path of hard but lofty duty by bidding us remember that all nations that have achieved greatness, that have expanded and played their part as world powers, have in the end passed away. So they have; and so have all others. The weak and the stationary have vanished as surely as, and more rapidly than, those whose citizens felt within them the lift that impels generous souls to great and noble effort. This is only another way of stating the universal law of death, which is itself part of the universal law of life. The man who works, the man who does great deeds, in the end dies as surely as the veriest idler who cumbers the earth's surface; but he leaves behind him the great fact that he has done his work well. So it is with nations. While the nation that has dared to be great, that has had the will and the power to change the destiny of the ages, in the end must die, yet no less surely the nation that has played the part of the weakling must also die; and whereas the nation that has done nothing leaves nothing behind it, the nation that has done a great work really continues, though in changed form, to live forevermore. The Roman has passed away exactly as all the nations of antiquity which did not expand when he expanded have passed away; but their very memory has vanished, while he himself is still a living force throughout the wide world in our entire civilization of today, and will so continue through countless generations, through untold ages.

It is because we believe with all our heart and soul in the greatness of this country, because we feel the thrill of hardy life in our veins, and are confident that to us is given the privilege of playing a leading part in the century that has just opened, that we hail with eager delight the opportunity to do whatever task Providence may allot us. We admit with all sincerity that our first duty is within our own household; that we must not merely talk, but act, in favor of cleanliness and decency and righteousness, in all political, social, and civic matters. No prosperity and no glory can save a nation that is rotten at heart. We must ever keep the core of our national being sound, and see to it that not only our citizens in private life, but, above all, our statesmen in public life, practice the old commonplace virtues which from time immemorial have lain at the root of all true national well-being. Yet while this is our first duty, it is not our whole duty. Exactly as each man, while doing first his duty to his wife and the children within his home, must yet, if he hopes to amount to much, strive mightily in the world outside his home, so our nation, while first of all seeing to its own domestic well-being, must not shrink from playing its part among the great nations without. Our duty may take many forms in the future as it has taken many forms in the past. Nor is it possible to lay down a hard-and-fast rule for all cases. We must ever face the fact of our shifting national needs, of the always-changing opportunities that present themselves. But we may be certain of one thing: whether we wish it or not, we cannot avoid hereafter having duties to do in the face of other nations. All that we can do is to settle whether we shall perform these duties well or ill.

Right here let me make as vigorous a plea as I know how in favor of saying nothing that we do not mean, and of acting without hesitation up to whatever we say. A good many of you are probably acquainted with the old proverb: "Speak softly and carry a big stick—you will go far." If a man continually blusters, if he lacks civility, a big stick will not save him from trouble; and neither will speaking softly avail, if back of the softness there does not lie strength, power. In private life there are few beings more obnoxious than the man who is always loudly boasting; and if the boaster is not prepared to back up his words his position becomes absolutely contemptible. So it is with the nation. It is both foolish and undignified to indulge in undue self-glorification, and, above all, in loose-tongued denunciation of other peoples. Whenever on any point we come in contact with a foreign power, I hope that we shall always strive to speak courteously and respectfully of that foreign power. Let us make it evident that we intend to do justice. Then let us make it equally evident that we will not tolerate injustice being done to us in return. Let us further make it evident that we use no words which we are not prepared to back up with deeds, and that while our speech is always moderate, we are ready and willing to make it good. Such an attitude will be the surest possible guarantee of that self-respecting peace, the attainment of which is and must ever be the prime aim of a self-governing people.

This is the attitude we should take as regards the Monroe Doctrine. There is not the least need of blustering about it. Still less should it be used as a pretext for our own aggrandizement at the expense of any other American state. But, most emphatically, we must make it evident that we intend on this point ever to maintain the old American position. Indeed, it is hard to understand how any man can take any other position, now that we are all looking forward to the building of the Isthmian Canal. The Monroe Doctrine is not international law; but there is no necessity that it should be. All that is needful is that it should continue to be a cardinal feature of American policy on this continent; and the Spanish-American states should, in their own interests, champion it as strongly as we do. We do not by this doctrine intend to sanction any policy of aggression by one American commonwealth at the expense of any other, nor any policy of commercial discrimination against any foreign power whatsoever. Commercially, as far as this doctrine is concerned, all we wish is a fair field and no favor; but if we are wise we shall strenuously insist that under no pretext whatsoever shall there be any territorial aggrandizement on American soil by any European power, and this, no matter what form the territorial aggrandizement may take.

We most earnestly hope and believe that the chance of our having any hostile military complication with any foreign power is very small. But that there will come a strain, a jar, here and there, from commercial and agricultural—that is, from industrial—competition is almost inevitable. Here again we have got to remember that our first duty is to our own people, and yet that we can best get justice by doing justice. We must continue the policy that has been so brilliantly successful in the past, and so shape our economic system as to give every advantage to the skill, energy, and intelligence of our farmers, merchants, manufacturers, and wage-workers; and yet we must also remember, in dealing with other nations, that benefits must be given where benefits are sought. It is not possible to dogmatize as to the exact way of attaining this end, for the exact conditions cannot be foretold. In the long run, one of our prime needs is stability and continuity of economic policy; and yet, through treaty or by direct legislation, it may, at least in certain cases, become advantageous to supplement our present policy by a system of reciprocal benefit and obligation.

Throughout a large part of our national career our history has been one of expansion, the expansion being of different kinds at different times. This expansion is not a matter of regret, but of pride. It is vain to tell a people as masterful as ours that the spirit of enterprise is not safe. The true American has never feared to run risks when the prize to be won was of sufficient value. No nation capable of self-government, and of developing by its own efforts a sane and orderly civilization, no matter how small it may be, has anything to fear from us. Our dealings with Cuba illustrate this, and should be forever a subject of just national pride. We speak in no spirit of arrogance when we state as a simple historic fact that never in recent times has any great nation acted with such disinterestedness as we have shown in Cuba. We freed the island from the Spanish yoke. We then earnestly did our best to help the Cubans in the establishment of free education, of law and order, of material prosperity, of the cleanliness necessary to sanitary well-being in their great cities. We did all this at great expense of treasure, at some expense of life; and now we are establishing them in a free and independent commonwealth, and have asked in return nothing whatever save that at no time shall their independence be prostituted to the advantage of some foreign rival of ours, or so as to menace our well-being. To have failed to ask this would have amounted to national stultification on our part.

In the Philippines we have brought peace, and we are at this moment giving them such freedom and self-government as they could never under any conceivable conditions have obtained had we turned them loose to sink into a welter of blood and confusion, or to become the prey of some strong tyranny without or within. The bare recital of the facts is sufficient to show that we did our duty; and what prouder title to honor can a nation have than to have done its duty? We have done our duty to ourselves, and we have done the higher duty of promoting the civilization of mankind. The first essential of civilization is law. Anarchy is simply the handmaiden and forerunner of tyranny and despotism. Law and order enforced with justice and by strength lie at the foundations of civilization. Law must be based upon justice, else it cannot stand, and it must be enforced with resolute firmness, because weakness in enforcing it means in the end that there is no justice and no law, nothing but the rule of disorderly and unscrupulous strength. Without the habit of orderly obedience to the law, without the stern enforcement of the laws at the expense of those who defiantly resist them, there can be no possible progress, moral or material, in civilization. There can be no weakening of the law-abiding spirit here at home, if we are permanently to succeed; and just as little can we afford to show weakness abroad. Lawlessness and anarchy were put down in the Philippines as a prerequisite to introducing the reign of justice.

Barbarism has, and can have, no place in a civilized world.

It is our duty toward the people living in barbarism to see that they are freed from their chains, and we can free them only by destroying barbarism itself. The missionary, the merchant, and the soldier may each have to play a part in this destruction, and in the consequent uplifting of the people. Exactly as it is the duty of a civilized power scrupulously to respect the rights of all weaker civilized powers and gladly to help those who are struggling toward civilization, so it is its duty to put down savagery and barbarism. As in such a work human instruments must be used, and as human instruments are imperfect, this means that at times there will be injustice; that at times merchant or soldier, or even missionary, may do wrong. Let us instantly condemn and rectify such wrong when it occurs, and if possible punish the wrongdoer. But shame, thrice shame to us, if we are so foolish as to make such occasional wrongdoing an excuse for failing to perform a great and righteous task. Not only in our own land, but throughout the world, throughout all history, the advance of civilization has been of incalculable benefit to mankind, and those through whom it has advanced deserve the highest honor. All honor to the missionary, all honor to the soldier, all honor to the merchant who now in our own day have done so much to bring light into the world's dark places.

Let me insist again, for fear of possible misconstruction, upon the fact that our duty is twofold, and that we must raise others while we are benefiting ourselves. In bringing order to the Philippines, our soldiers added a new page to the honor roll of American history, and they incalculably benefited the islanders themselves. Under the wise administration of Governor Taft the islands now enjoy a peace and liberty of which they have hitherto never even dreamed. But this peace and liberty under the law must be supplemented by material, by industrial development. Every encouragement should be given to their commercial development, to the introduction of American industries and products; not merely because this will be a good thing for our people, but infinitely more because it will be of incalculable benefit to the people in the Philippines.

We shall make mistakes; and if we let these mistakes frighten us from our work we shall show ourselves weaklings. Half a century ago Minnesota and the two Dakotas were Indian hunting-grounds. We committed plenty of blunders, and now and then worse than blunders, in our dealings with the Indians. But who does not admit at the present day that we were right in wresting from barbarism and adding to civilization the territory out of which we have made these beautiful states? And now we are civilizing the Indian and putting him on a level to which he could never have attained under the old conditions.

In the Philippines let us remember that the spirit and not the mere form of government is the essential matter. The Tagalogs have a hundredfold the freedom under us that they would have if we had abandoned the islands. We are not trying to subjugate a people; we are trying to develop them and make them a law-abiding, industrious, and educated people, and we hope ultimately a self-governing people. In short, in the work we have done we are but carrying out the true principles of our democracy. We work in a spirit of self-respect for ourselves and of goodwill toward others, in a spirit of love for and of infinite faith in mankind. We do not blindly refuse to face the evils that exist, or the shortcomings inherent in humanity; but across blundering and shirking, across selfishness and meanness of motive, across short-sightedness and cowardice, we gaze steadfastly toward the far horizon of golden triumph. If you will study our past history as a nation you will see we have made many blunders and have been guilty of many shortcomings, and yet that we have always in the end come out victorious because we have refused to be daunted by blunders and defeats, have recognized them, but have persevered in spite of them. So it must be in the future. We gird up our loins as a nation, with the stern purpose to play our part manfully in winning the ultimate triumph; and therefore we turn scornfully aside from the paths of mere ease and idleness, and with unfaltering steps tread the rough road of endeavor, smiting down the wrong and battling for the right, as Greatheart smote and battled in Bunyan's immortal story.

FIRST ANNUAL MESSAGE TO CONGRESS

December 3, 1901

To the Senate and House of Representatives: The Congress assembles this year under the shadow of a great calamity. On the sixth of September, President McKinley was shot by an anarchist while attending the Pan-American Exposition at Buffalo, and died in that city on the fourteenth of that month.

Of the last seven elected presidents, he is the third who has been murdered, and the bare recital of this fact is sufficient to justify grave alarm among all loyal American citizens. Moreover, the circumstances of this, the third assassination of an American president, have a peculiarily sinister significance. Both President Lincoln and President Garfield were killed by assassins of types unfortunately not uncommon in history; President Lincoln falling a victim to the terrible passions aroused by four years of civil war, and President Garfield to the revengeful vanity of a disappointed office-seeker. President McKinley was killed by an utterly depraved criminal belonging to that body of criminals who object to all governments, good and bad alike, who are against any form of popular liberty if it is guaranteed by even the most just and liberal laws, and who are as hostile to the upright exponent of a free people's sober will as to the tyrannical and irresponsible despot.

It is not too much to say that at the time of President McKinley's death he was the most widely loved man in all the United States; while we have never had any public man of his position who has been so wholly free from the bitter animosities incident to public life. His political opponents were the first to bear the heartiest and most generous tribute to the broad kindliness of nature, the sweetness and gentleness of character which so endeared him to his close associates. To a standard of lofty integrity in public life he united the tender affections and home virtues which are all-important in the makeup of national character. A gallant soldier in the great war for the Union, he also shone as an example to all our people because of his conduct in the most sacred and intimate of home relations. There could be no personal hatred of him, for he never acted with aught but consideration for the welfare of others. No one could fail to respect him who knew him in public or private life. The defenders of those murderous criminals who seek to excuse their criminality by asserting that it is exercised for political ends inveigh against wealth and irresponsible power. But for this assassination even this base apology cannot be urged.

President McKinley was a man of moderate means, a man whose stock sprang from the sturdy tillers of the soil, who had himself belonged among the wage-workers, who had entered the army as a private soldier. Wealth was not struck at when the president was assassinated, but the honest toil which is content with moderate gains after a lifetime of unremitting labor, largely in the service of the public. Still less was power struck at in the sense that power is irresponsible or centered in the hands of any one individual. The blow was not aimed at tyranny or wealth. It was aimed at one of the strongest champions the wage-worker has ever had; at one of the most faithful representatives of the system of public rights and representative government who has ever risen to public office. President McKinley filled that political office for which the entire people vote, and no president—not even Lincoln himself—was ever more earnestly anxious to represent the well-thought-out wishes of the people; his one anxiety in every crisis was to keep in closest touch with the people—to find out what they thought and to endeavor to give expression to their thought, after having endeavored to guide that thought aright. He had just been reelected to the presidency because the majority of our citizens, the majority of our farmers and wage-workers, believed that he had faithfully upheld their interests for four years. They felt themselves in close and intimate touch with him. They felt that he represented so well and so honorably all their ideals and aspirations that they wished him to continue for another four years to represent them.

And this was the man at whom the assassin struck! That there might be nothing lacking to complete the Judaslike infamy of his act, he took advantage of an occasion when the president was meeting the people generally; and advancing as if to take the hand outstretched to him in kindly and brotherly fellowship, he turned the noble and generous confidence of the victim into an opportunity to strike the fatal blow. There is no baser deed in all the annals of crime.

The shock, the grief of the country, are bitter in the minds of all who saw the dark days while the president yet hovered between life and death. At last the light was stilled in the kindly eyes and the breath went from the lips that even in mortal agony uttered no words save of forgiveness to his murderer, of love for his friends, and of unfaltering trust in the will of the Most High. Such a death, crowning the glory of such a life, leaves us with infinite sorrow, but with such pride in what he had accomplished and in his own personal character, that we feel the blow not as struck at him, but as struck at the nation. We mourn a good and great president who is dead; but while we mourn we are lifted up by the splendid achievements of his life and the grand heroism with which he met his death.

When we turn from the man to the nation, the harm done is so great as to excite our gravest apprehensions and to demand our wisest and most resolute action. This criminal was a professed anarchist, inflamed by the teachings of professed anarchists, and probably also by the reckless utterances of those who, on the stump and in the public press, appeal to the dark and evil spirits of malice and greed, envy and sullen hatred. The wind is sowed by the men who preach such doctrines, and they cannot escape their share of responsibility for the whirlwind that is reaped. This applies alike to the deliberate demagogue, to the exploiter of sensationalism, and to the crude and foolish visionary who, for whatever reason, apologizes for crime or excites aimless discontent.

The blow was aimed not at this president, but at all presidents; at every symbol of government. President McKinley was as emphatically the embodiment of the popular will of the nation expressed through the forms of law as a New England town meeting is in similar fashion the embodiment of the law-abiding purpose and practice of the people of the town. On no conceivable theory could the murder of the president be accepted as due to protest against "inequalities in the social order," save as the murder of all the freemen engaged in a town meeting could be accepted as a protest against that social inequality which puts a malefactor in jail. Anarchy is no more an expression of "social discontent" than picking pockets or wife-beating.

The anarchist, and especially the anarchist in the United States, is merely one type of criminal, more dangerous than any other because he represents the same depravity in a greater degree. The man who advocates anarchy directly or indirectly, in any shape or fashion, or the man who apologizes for anarchists and their deeds, makes himself morally accessory to murder before the fact. The anarchist is a criminal whose perverted instincts lead him to prefer confusion and chaos to the most beneficent form of social order. His protest of concern for workingmen is outrageous in its impudent falsity; for if the political institutions of this country do not afford opportunity to every honest and intelligent son of toil, then the door of hope is forever closed against him. The anarchist is everywhere not merely the enemy of system and of progress, but the deadly foe of liberty. If ever anarchy is triumphant, its triumph will last for but one red moment, to be succeeded for ages by the gloomy night of despotism.

For the anarchist himself, whether he preaches or practices his doctrines, we need not have one particle more concern than for any ordinary murderer. He is not the victim of social or political injustice. There are no wrongs to remedy in his case.

The cause of his criminality is to be found in his own evil passions and in the evil conduct of those who urge him on, not in any failure by others or by the state to do justice to him or his. He is a malefactor and nothing else. He is in no sense, in no shape or way, a "product of social conditions," save as a highwayman is "produced" by the fact that an unarmed man happens to have a purse. It is a travesty upon the great and holy names of liberty and freedom to permit them to be invoked in such a cause. No man or body of men preaching anarchistic doctrines should be allowed at large any more than if preaching the murder of some specified private individual. Anarchistic speeches, writings, and meetings are essentially seditious and treasonable.

I earnestly recommend to the Congress that in the exercise of its wise discretion it should take into consideration the coming to this country of anarchists or persons professing principles hostile to all government and justifying the murder of those placed in authority. Such individuals as those who not long ago gathered in open meeting to glorify the murder of King Humbert of Italy perpetrate a crime, and the law should ensure their rigorous punishment. They and those like them should be kept out of this country; and if found here they should be promptly deported to the country whence they came; and far-reaching provisions should be made for the punishment of those who stay. No matter calls more urgently for the wisest thought of the Congress.

The federal courts should be given jurisdiction over any man who kills or attempts to kill the president or any man who by the Constitution or by law is in line of succession for the presidency, while the punishment for an unsuccessful attempt should be proportioned to the enormity of the offense against our institutions.

Anarchy is a crime against the whole human race; and all mankind should band against the anarchist. His crime should be made an offense against the law of nations, like piracy and that form of man-stealing known as the slave trade; for it is of far blacker infamy than either. It should be so declared by treaties among all civilized powers. Such treaties would give to the federal government the power of dealing with the crime.

A grim commentary upon the folly of the anarchist position was afforded by the attitude of the law toward this very criminal who had just taken the life of the president. The people would have torn him limb from limb if it had not been that the law he defied was at once invoked in his behalf. So far from his deed being committed on behalf of the people against the government, the government was obliged at once to exert its full police power to save him from instant death at the hands of the people. Moreover, his deed worked not the slightest dislocation in our governmental system, and the danger of a recurrence of such deeds, no matter how great it might grow, would work only in the direction of strengthening and giving harshness to the forces of order. No man will ever be restrained from becoming president by any fear as to his personal safety. If the risk to the president's life became great, it would mean that the office would more and more come to be filled by men of a spirit which would make them resolute and merciless in dealing with every friend of disorder. This great country will not fall into anarchy, and if anarchists should ever become a serious menace to its institutions, they would not merely be stamped out, but would involve in their own ruin every active or passive sympathizer with their doctrines. The American people are slow to wrath, but when their wrath is once kindled it burns like a consuming flame.

During the last five years business confidence has been restored and the nation is to be congratulated because of its present abounding prosperity. Such prosperity can never be created by law alone, although it is easy enough to destroy it by mischievous laws. If the hand of the Lord is heavy upon any country, if flood or drought comes, human wisdom is powerless to avert the calamity. Moreover, no law can guard us against the consequences of our own folly. The men who are idle or credulous, the men who seek gains not by genuine work with head or hand but by gambling in any form, are always a source of menace not only to themselves but to others. If the business world loses its head, it loses what legislation cannot supply. Fundamentally the welfare of each citizen, and therefore the welfare of the aggregate of citizens which makes the nation, must rest upon individual thrift and energy, resolution and intelligence. Nothing can take the place of this individual capacity; but wise legislation and honest and intelligent administration can give it the fullest scope, the largest opportunity to work to good effect.

The tremendous and highly complex industrial development which went on with ever accelerated rapidity during the latter half of the nineteenth century brings us face to face, at the beginning of the twentieth, with very serious social problems. The old laws, and the old customs which had almost the binding force of law, were once quite sufficient to regulate the accumulation and distribution of wealth. Since the industrial changes which have so enormously increased the productive power of mankind, they are no longer sufficient.

The growth of cities has gone on beyond comparison faster than the growth of the country, and the upbuilding of the great industrial centers has meant a startling increase, not merely in the aggregate of wealth, but in the number of very large individual, and especially of very large corporate, fortunes. The creation of these great corporate fortunes has not been due to the tariff nor to any other governmental action, but to natural causes in the business world, operating in other countries as they operate in our own.

The process has aroused much antagonism, a great part of which is wholly without warrant. It is not true that as the rich have grown richer the poor have grown poorer. On the contrary, never before has the average man, the wage-worker, the farmer, the small trader, been so well off as in this country and at the present time. There have been abuses connected with the accumulation of wealth; yet it remains true that a fortune accumulated in legitimate business can be accumulated by the person specially benefited only on condition of conferring immense incidental benefits upon others. Successful enterprise, of the type which benefits all mankind, can only exist if the conditions are such as to offer great prizes as the rewards of success.

The captains of industry who have driven the railway systems across this continent, who have built up our commerce, who have developed our manufactures, have on the whole done great good to our people. Without them the material development of which we are so justly proud could never have taken place. Moreover, we should recognize the immense importance to this material development of leaving as unhampered as is compatible with the public good the strong and forceful men upon whom the success of business operations inevitably rests. The slightest study of business conditions will satisfy anyone capable of forming a judgment that the personal equation is the most important factor in a business operation; that the business ability of the man at the head of any business concern, big or little, is usually the factor which fixes the gulf between striking success and hopeless failure.

An additional reason for caution in dealing with corporations is to be found in the international commercial conditions of today. The same business conditions which have produced the great aggregations of corporate and individual wealth have made them very potent factors in international commercial competition. Business concerns which have the largest means at their disposal and are managed by the ablest men are naturally those which take the lead in the strife for commercial supremacy among the nations of the world. America has only just begun to assume that commanding position in the international business world which we believe will more and more be hers. It is of the utmost importance that this position be not jeoparded, especially at a time when the overflowing abundance of our own natural resources and the skill, business energy, and mechanical aptitude of our people make foreign markets essential. Under such conditions it would be most unwise to cramp or to fetter the youthful strength of our nation.

Moreover, it cannot too often be pointed out that to strike with ignorant violence at the interests of one set of men almost inevitably endangers the interests of all. The fundamental rule in our national life—the rule which underlies all others—is that, on the whole, and in the long run, we shall go up or down together. There are exceptions; and in times of prosperity some will prosper far more, and in times of adversity some will suffer far more, than others; but speaking generally, a period of good times means that all share more or less in them, and in a period of hard times all feel the stress to a greater or less degree. It surely ought not to be necessary to enter into any proof of this statement; the memory of the lean years which began in 1893 is still vivid, and we can contrast them with the conditions in this very year which is now closing. Disaster to great business enterprises can never have its effects limited to the men at the top. It spreads throughout, and while it is bad for everybody, it is worst for those furthest down. The capitalist may be shorn of his luxuries; but the wage-worker may be deprived of even bare necessities.

The mechanism of modern business is so delicate that extreme care must be taken not to interfere with it in a spirit of rashness or ignorance. Many of those who have made it their vocation to denounce the great industrial combinations which are popularly, although with technical inaccuracy, known as trusts, appeal especially to hatred and fear. These are precisely the two emotions, particularly when combined with ignorance, which unfit men for the exercise of cool and steady judgment. In facing new industrial conditions, the whole history of the world shows that legislation will generally be both unwise and ineffective unless undertaken after calm inquiry and with sober self-restraint. Much of the legislation directed at the trusts would have been exceedingly mischievous had it not also been entirely ineffective. In accordance with a well-known sociological law, the ignorant or reckless agitator has been the really effective friend of the evils which he has been nominally opposing. In dealing with business interests, for the government to undertake by crude and ill-considered legislation to do what may turn out to be bad, would be to incur the risk of such far-reaching national disaster that it would be preferable to undertake nothing at all. The men who demand the impossible or the undesirable serve as the allies of the forces with which they are nominally at war, for they hamper those who would endeavor to find out in rational fashion what the wrongs really are and to what extent and in what manner it is practicable to apply remedies.

All this is true; and yet it is also true that there are real and grave evils, one of the chief being overcapitalization because of its many baleful consequences; and a resolute and practical effort must be made to correct these evils.

There is widespread conviction in the minds of the American people that the great corporations known as trusts are in certain of their features and tendencies hurtful to the general welfare. This springs from no spirit of envy or uncharitableness, nor lack of pride in the great industrial achievements that have placed this country at the head of the nations struggling for commercial supremacy. It does not rest upon a lack of intelligent appreciation of the necessity of meeting changing and changed conditions of trade with new methods, nor upon ignorance of the fact that combination of capital in the effort to accomplish great things is necessary when the world's progress demands that great things be done. It is based upon sincere conviction that combination and concentration should be, not prohibited, but supervised and within reasonable limits controlled; and in my judgment this conviction is right.

It is no limitation upon property rights or freedom of contract to require that when men receive from government the privilege of doing business under corporate form, which frees them from individual responsibility, and enables them to call into their enterprises the capital of the public, they shall do so upon absolutely truthful representations as to the value of the property in which the capital is to be invested. Corporations engaged in interstate commerce should be regulated if they are found to exercise a license working to the public injury. It should be as much the aim of those who seek for social betterment to rid the business world of crimes of cunning as to rid the entire body politic of crimes of violence. Great corporations exist only because they are created and safeguarded by our institutions; and it is therefore our right and our duty to see that they work in harmony with these institutions.

The first essential in determining how to deal with the great industrial combinations is knowledge of the facts—publicity. In the interest of the public, the government should have the right to inspect and examine the workings of the great corporations engaged in interstate business. Publicity is the only sure remedy which we can now invoke. What further remedies are needed in the way of governmental regulation, or taxation, can only be determined after publicity has been obtained, by process of law, and in the course of administration. The first requisite is knowledge, full and complete—knowledge which may be made public to the world.

Artificial bodies, such as corporations and joint stock or other associations, depending upon any statutory law for their existence or privileges, should be subject to proper governmental supervision, and full and accurate information as to their operations should be made public regularly at reasonable intervals.

The large corporations, commonly called trusts, though organized in one state, always do business in many states, often doing very little business in the state where they are incorporated. There is utter lack of uniformity in the state laws about them; and as no state has any exclusive interest in or power over their acts, it has in practice proved impossible to get adequate regulation through state action. Therefore, in the interest of the whole people, the nation should, without interfering with the power of the states in the matter itself, also assume power of supervision and regulation over all corporations doing an interstate business. This is especially true where the corporation derives a portion of its wealth from the existence of some monopolistic element or tendency in its business. There would be no hardship in such supervision; banks are subject to it, and in their case it is now accepted as a simple matter of course. Indeed, it is probable that supervision of corporations by the national government need not go so far as is now the case with the supervision exercised over them by so conservative a state as Massachusetts, in order to produce excellent results.

When the Constitution was adopted, at the end of the eighteenth century, no human wisdom could foretell the sweeping changes, alike in industrial and political conditions, which were to take place by the beginning of the twentieth century. At that time it was accepted as a matter of course that the several states were the proper authorities to regulate, so far as was then necessary, the comparatively insignificant and strictly localized corporate bodies of the day. The conditions are now wholly different and wholly different action is called for. I believe that a law can be framed which will enable the national government to exercise control along the lines above indicated, profiting by the experience gained through the passage and administration of the Interstate Commerce Act. If, however, the judgment of the Congress is that it lacks the constitutional power to pass such an act, then a constitutional amendment should be submitted to confer the power. . . .

The most vital problem with which this country, and for that matter the whole civilized world, has to deal is the problem which has for one side the betterment of social conditions, oral and physical, in large cities, and for another side the effort to deal with that tangle of far-reaching questions which we group together when we speak of "labor." The chief factor in the success of each man—wage-worker, farmer, and capitalist alike—must ever be the sum total of his own individual qualities and abilities. Second only to this comes the power of acting in combination or association with others. Very great good has been and will be accomplished by associations or unions of wage-workers, when managed with forethought, and when they combine insistence upon their own rights with law-abiding respect for the rights of others. The display of these qualities in such bodies is a duty to the nation no less than to the associations themselves. Finally, there must also in many cases be action by the government in order to safeguard the rights and interests of all. Under our Constitution there is much more scope for such action by the state and the municipality than by the nation. But on points such as those touched on above the national government can act. . . .

Our present immigration laws are unsatisfactory. We need every honest and efficient immigrant fitted to become an American citizen, every immigrant who comes here to stay, who brings here a strong body, a stout heart, a good head, and a resolute purpose to do his duty well in every way and to bring up his children as law-abiding and God-fearing members of the community. But there should be a comprehensive law enacted with the object of working a threefold improvement over our present system. First, we should aim to exclude absolutely not only all persons who are known to be believers in anarchistic principles or members of anarchistic societies, but also all persons who are of a low moral tendency or of unsavory reputation. This means that we should require a more thorough system of inspection abroad and a more rigid system of examination at our immigration ports, the former being especially necessary.

The second object of a proper immigration law ought to be to secure by a careful and not merely perfunctory educational test some intelligent capacity to appreciate American institutions and act sanely as American citizens. This would not keep out all anarchists, for many of them belong to the intelligent criminal class. But it would do what is also in point, that is, tend to decrease the sum of ignorance, so potent in producing the envy, suspicion, malignant passion, and hatred of order, out of which anarchistic sentiment inevitably springs. Finally, all persons should be excluded who are below a certain standard of economic fitness to enter our industrial field as competitors with American labor. There should be proper proof of personal capacity to earn an American living and enough money to ensure a decent start under American conditions. This would stop the influx of cheap labor, and the resulting competition which gives rise to so much of bitterness in American industrial life; and it would dry up the springs of the pestilential social conditions in our great cities, where anarchistic organizations have their greatest possibility of growth. . . .

There is general acquiescence in our present tariff system as a national policy. The first requisite to our prosperity is the continuity and stability of this economic policy. Nothing could be more unwise than to disturb the business interests of the country by any general tariff change at this time. Doubt, apprehension, uncertainty are exactly what we most wish to avoid in the interest of our commercial and material well-being. Our experience in the past has shown that sweeping revisions of the tariff are apt to produce conditions closely approaching panic in the business world. Yet it is not only possible, but eminently desirable, to combine with the stability of our economic system a supplementary system of reciprocal benefit and obligation with other nations. Such reciprocity is an incident and result of the firm establishment and preservation of our present economic policy. It was specially provided for in the present tariff law. . . .

It is most important that we should maintain the high level of our present prosperity. We have now reached the point in the development of our interests where we are not only able to supply our own markets but to produce a constantly growing surplus for which we must find markets abroad. To secure these markets we can utilize existing duties in any case where they are no longer needed for the purpose of protection, or in any case where the article is not produced here and the duty is no longer necessary for revenue, as giving us something to offer in exchange for what we ask. The cordial relations with other nations which are so desirable will naturally be promoted by the course thus required by our own interests. . . .

The Act of March 14, 1900, intended unequivocally to establish gold as the standard money and to maintain at a parity therewith all forms of money medium in use with us, has been shown to be timely and judicious. The price of our government bonds in the world's market, when compared with the price of similar obligations issued by other nations, is a flattering tribute to our public credit. This condition it is evidently desirable to maintain.

In many respects the National Banking law furnishes sufficient liberty for the proper exercise of the banking function; but there seems to be need of better safeguards against the deranging influence of commercial crises and financial panics. Moreover, the currency of the country should be made responsive to the demands of our domestic trade and commerce. . . .

I call special attention to the need of strict economy in expenditures. The fact that our national needs forbid us to be niggardly in providing whatever is actually necessary to our well-being, should make us doubly careful to husband our national resources, as each of us husbands his private resources, by scrupulous avoidance of anything like wasteful or reckless expenditure. Only by avoidance of spending money on what is needless or unjustifiable can we legitimately keep our income to the point required to meet our needs that are genuine.

In 1887 a measure was enacted for the regulation of interstate railways, commonly known as the Interstate Commerce Act. The cardinal provisions of that act were that railway rates should be just and reasonable and that all shippers, localities, and commodities should be accorded equal treatment. A commission was created and endowed with what were supposed to be the necessary powers to execute the provisions of this act.

That law was largely an experiment. Experience has shown the wisdom of its purposes, but has also shown, possibly that some of its requirements are wrong, certainly that the means devised for the enforcement of its provisions are defective. Those who complain of the management of the railways allege that established rates are not maintained; that rebates and similar devices are habitually resorted to; that these preferences are usually in favor of the large shipper; that they drive out of business the smaller competitor; that while many rates are too low, many others are excessive; and that gross preferences are made, affecting both localities and commodities. Upon the other hand, the railways assert that the law by its very terms tends to produce many of these illegal practices by depriving carriers of that right of concerted action which they claim is necessary to establish and maintain nondiscriminating rates.

The act should be amended. The railway is a public servant. Its rates should be just to and open to all shippers alike. The government should see to it that within its jurisdiction this is so and should provide a speedy, inexpensive, and effective remedy to that end. At the same time it must not be forgotten that our railways are the arteries through which the commercial lifeblood of this nation flows. Nothing could be more foolish than the enactment of legislation which would unnecessarily interfere with the development and operation of these commercial agencies. The subject is one of great importance and calls for the earnest attention of the Congress. . . .

Public opinion throughout the United States has moved steadily toward a just appreciation of the value of forests, whether planted or of natural growth. The great part played by them in the creation and maintenance of the national wealth is now more fully realized than ever before.

Wise forest protection does not mean the withdrawal of forest resources, whether of wood, water, or grass, from contributing their full share to the welfare of the people, but, on the contrary, gives the assurance of larger and more certain supplies. The fundamental idea of forestry is the perpetuation of forests by use. Forest protection is not an end of itself; it is a means to increase and sustain the resources of our country and the industries which depend upon them. The preservation of our forests is an imperative business necessity. We have come to see clearly that whatever destroys the forest, except to make way for agriculture, threatens our well-being.

The practical usefulness of the national forest reserves to the mining, grazing, irrigation, and other interests of the regions in which the reserves lie has led to a widespread demand by the people of the West for their protection and extension. The forest reserves will inevitably be of still greater use in the future than in the past. Additions should be made to them whenever practicable, and their usefulness should be increased by a thoroughly businesslike management.

At present the protection of the forest reserves rests with the General Land Office, the mapping and description of their timber with the United States Geological Survey, and the preparation of plans for their conservative use with the Bureau of Forestry, which is also charged with the general advancement of practical forestry in the United States. These various functions should be united in the Bureau of Forestry, to which they properly belong. The present diffusion of responsibility is bad from every standpoint. It prevents that effective cooperation between the government and the men who utilize the resources of the reserves, without which the interests of both must suffer. The scientific bureaus generally should be put under the Department of Agriculture. The president should have by law the power of transferring lands for use as forest reserves to the Department of Agriculture. He already has such power in the case of lands needed by the departments of War and the Navy.

The wise administration of the forest reserves will be not less helpful to the interests which depend on water than to those which depend on wood and grass. The water supply itself depends upon the forest. In the arid region it is water, not land, which measures production. The western half of the United States would sustain a population greater than that of our whole country today if the waters that now run to waste were saved and used for irrigation. The forest and water problems are perhaps the most vital internal questions of the United States.

Certain of the forest reserves should also be made preserves for the wild forest creatures. All of the reserves should be better protected from fires. Many of them need special protection because of the great injury done by livestock, above all by sheep. The increase in deer, elk, and other animals in the Yellowstone Park shows what may be expected when other mountain forests are properly protected by law and properly guarded. Some of these areas have been so denuded of surface vegetation by over-grazing that the ground breeding birds, including grouse and quail, and many mammals, including deer, have been exterminated or driven away. At the same time the water-storing capacity of the surface has been decreased or destroyed, thus promoting floods in times of rain and diminishing the flow of streams between rains.

In cases where natural conditions have been restored for a few years, vegetation has again carpeted the ground, birds and deer are coming back, and hundreds of persons, especially from the immediate neighborhood, come each summer to enjoy the privilege of camping. Some at least of the forest reserves should afford perpetual protection to the native fauna and flora, safe havens of refuge to our rapidly diminishing wild animals of the larger kinds, and free camping grounds for the ever-increasing numbers of men and women who have learned to find rest, health, and recreation in the splendid forests and flower-clad meadows of our mountains. The forest reserves should be set apart forever for the use and benefit of our people as a whole and not sacrificed to the shortsighted greed of a few.

The forests are natural reservoirs. By restraining the streams in flood and replenishing them in drought they make possible the use of waters otherwise wasted. They prevent the soil from washing, and so protect the storage reservoirs from filling up with silt. Forest conservation is therefore an essential condition of water conservation.

The forests alone cannot, however, fully regulate and conserve the waters of the arid region. Great storage works are necessary to equalize the flow of streams and to save the flood waters. Their construction has been conclusively shown to be an undertaking too vast for private effort. Nor can it be best accomplished by the individual states acting alone. Far-reaching interstate problems are involved; and the resources of single states would often be inadequate. It is properly a national function, at least in some of its features. It is as right for the national government to make the streams and rivers of the arid region useful by engineering works for water storage as to make useful the rivers and harbors of the humid region by engineering works of another kind. The storing of the floods in reservoirs at the headwaters of our rivers is but an enlargement of our present policy of river control, under which levees are built on the lower reaches of the same streams.

The government should construct and maintain these reservoirs as it does other public works. Where their purpose is to regulate the flow of streams, the water should be turned freely into the channels in the dry season to take the same course under the same laws as the natural flow.

The reclamation of the unsettled arid public lands presents a different problem. Here it is not enough to regulate the flow of streams. The object of the government is to dispose of the land to settlers who will build homes upon it. To accomplish this object water must be brought within their reach.

The pioneer settlers on the arid public domain chose their homes along streams from which they could themselves divert the water to reclaim their holdings. Such opportunities are practically gone. There remain, however, vast areas of public land which can be made available for homestead settlement, but only by reservoirs and main-line canals impracticable for private enterprise. These irrigation works should be built by the national government. The lands reclaimed by them should be reserved by the government for actual settlers, and the cost of construction should so far as possible be repaid by the land reclaimed. The distribution of the water, the division of the streams among irrigators, should be left to the settlers themselves in conformity with state laws and without interference with those laws or with vested rights. The policy of the national government should be to aid irrigation in the several states and territories in such manner as will enable the people in the local communities to help themselves, and as will stimulate needed reforms in the state laws and regulations governing irrigation. . . .

Our aim should be not simply to reclaim the largest area of land and provide homes for the largest number of people, but to create for this new industry the best possible social and industrial conditions; and this requires that we not only understand the existing situation, but avail ourselves of the best experience of the time in the solution of its problems. A careful study should be made, both by the nation and the states, of the irrigation laws and conditions here and abroad. Ultimately it will probably be necessary for the nation to cooperate with the several arid states in proportion as these states by their legislation and administration show themselves fit to receive it.

In Hawaii our aim must be to develop the territory on the traditional American lines. We do not wish a region of large estates tilled by cheap labor; we wish a healthy American community of men who themselves till the farms they own. All our legislation for the islands should be shaped with this end in view; the well-being of the average home-maker must afford the true test of the healthy development of the islands. The land policy should as nearly as possible be modeled on our homestead system.

It is a pleasure to say that it is hardly more necessary to report as to Puerto Rico than as to any state or territory within our continental limits. The island is thriving as never before, and it is being administered efficiently and honestly. Its people are now enjoying liberty and order under the protection of the United States, and upon this fact we congratulate them and ourselves. Their material welfare must be as carefully and jealously considered as the welfare of any other portion of our country. We have given them the great gift of free access for their products to the markets of the United States. I ask the attention of the Congress to the need of legislation concerning the public lands of Puerto Rico.

In Cuba such progress has been made toward putting the independent government of the island upon a firm footing that before the present session of the Congress closes this will be an accomplished fact. Cuba will then start as her own mistress; and to the beautiful Queen of the Antilles, as she unfolds this new page of her destiny, we extend our heartiest greetings and good wishes. Elsewhere I have discussed the question of reciprocity. In the case of Cuba, however, there are weighty reasons of morality and of national interest why the policy should be held to have a peculiar application, and I most earnestly ask your attention to the wisdom, indeed to the vital need, of providing for a substantial reduction in the tariff duties on cuban imports into the United States. Cuba has in her constitution affirmed what we desired, that she should stand, in international matters, in closer and more friendly relations with us than with any other power; and we are bound by every consideration of honor and expediency to pass commercial measures in the interest of her material well-being.

In the Philippines our problem is larger. They are very rich tropical islands, inhabited by many varying tribes, representing widely different stages of progress toward civilization. Our earnest effort is to help these people upward along the stony and difficult path that leads to self-government. We hope to make our administration of the islands honorable to our nation by making it of the highest benefit to the Filipinos themselves; and as an earnest of what we intend to do, we point to what we have done. Already a greater measure of material prosperity and of governmental honesty and efficiency has been attained in the Philippines than ever before in their history.

It is no light task for a nation to achieve the temperamental qualities without which the institutions of free government are but an empty mockery. Our people are now successfully governing themselves, because for more than a thousand years they have been slowly fitting themselves, sometimes consciously, sometimes unconsciously, toward this end. What has taken us thirty generations to achieve we cannot expect to see another race accomplish out of hand, especially when large portions of that race start very far behind the point which our ancestors had reached even thirty generations ago. In dealing with the Philippine people we must show both patience and strength, forbearance and steadfast resolution. Our aim is high. We do not desire to do for the islanders merely what has elsewhere been done for tropic peoples by even the best foreign governments. We hope to do for them what has never before been done for any people of the tropics—to make them fit for self-government after the fashion of the really free nations.

History may safely be challenged to show a single instance in which a masterful race such as ours, having been forced by the exigencies of war to take possession of an alien land, has behaved to its inhabitants with the disinterested zeal for their progress that our people have shown in the Philippines. To leave the islands at this time would mean that they would fall into a welter of murderous anarchy. Such desertion of duty on our part would be a crime against humanity. The character of Governor Taft and of his associates and subordinates is a proof, if such be needed, of the sincerity of our effort to give the islanders a constantly increasing measure of self-government, exactly as fast as they show themselves fit to exercise it. Since the civil government was established not an appointment has been made in the islands with any reference to considerations of political influence, or to aught else save the fitness of the man and the needs of the service.

In our anxiety for the welfare and progress of the Philippines, it may be that here and there we have gone too rapidly in giving them local self-government. It is on this side that our error, if any, has been committed. No competent observer, sincerely desirous of finding out the facts and influenced only by a desire for the welfare of the natives, can assert that we have not gone far enough. We have gone to the very verge of safety in hastening the process. To have taken a single step further or faster in advance would have been folly and weakness, and might well have been crime. We are extremely anxious that the natives shall show the power of governing themselves. We are anxious, first for their sakes, and next, because it relieves us of a great burden. There need not be the slightest fear of our not continuing to give them all the liberty for which they are fit.

The only fear is lest in our overanxiety we give them a degree of independence for which they are unfit, thereby inviting reaction and disaster. As fast as there is any reasonable hope that in a given district the people can govern themselves, self-government has been given in that district. There is not a locality fitted for self-government which has not received it. But it may well be that in certain cases it will have to be withdrawn because the inhabitants show themselves unfit to exercise it; such instances have already occurred. In other words, there is not the slightest chance of our failing to show a sufficiently humanitarian spirit. The danger comes in the opposite direction. . . .

The time has come when there should be additional legislation for the Philippines. Nothing better can be done for the islands than to introduce industrial enterprises. Nothing would benefit them so much as throwing them open to industrial development. The connection between idleness and mischief is proverbial, and the opportunity to do remunerative work is one of the surest preventives of war. Of course no businessman will go into the Philippines unless it is to his interest to do so, and it is immensely to the interest of the islands that he should go in. It is therefore necessary that the Congress should pass laws by which the resources of the islands can be developed; so that franchises (for limited terms of years) can be granted to companies doing business in them, and every encouragement be given to the incoming of businessmen of every kind.

Not to permit this is to do a wrong to the Philippines. The

franchises must be granted and the business permitted only under regulations which will guarantee the islands against any kind of improper exploitation. But the vast natural wealth of the islands must be developed, and the capital willing to develop it must be given the opportunity. . . .

No single great material work which remains to be undertaken on this continent is of such consequence to the American people as the building of a canal across the Isthmus connecting North and South America. Its importance to the nation is by no means limited merely to its material effects upon our business prosperity; and yet with view to these effects alone it would be to the last degree important for us immediately to begin it. While its beneficial effects would perhaps be most marked upon the Pacific Coast and the Gulf and South Atlantic states, it would also greatly benefit other sections. It is emphatically a work which it is for the interest of the entire country to begin and complete as soon as possible; it is one of those great works which only a great nation can undertake with prospects of success, and which when done are not only permanent assets in the nation's material interests, but standing monuments to its constructive ability.

I am glad to be able to announce to you that our negotiations on this subject with Great Britain, conducted on both sides in a spirit of friendliness and mutual goodwill and respect, have resulted in my being able to lay before the Senate a treaty which if ratified will enable us to begin preparations for an Isthmian Canal at any time, and which guarantees to this nation every right that it has ever asked in connection with the canal. In this treaty, the old Clayton-Bulwer Treaty, so long recognized as inadequate to supply the base for the construction and maintenance of a necessarily American ship canal, is abrogated. It specifically provides that the United States alone shall do the work of building and assume the responsibility of safeguarding the canal and shall regulate its neutral use by all nations on terms of equality without the guarantee or interference of any outside nation from any quarter. The signed treaty will at once be laid before the Senate, and if approved the Congress can then proceed to give effect to the advantages it secures us by providing for the building of the canal.

The true end of every great and free people should be self-respecting peace; and this nation most earnestly desires sincere and cordial friendship with all others. Over the entire world, of recent years, wars between the great civilized powers have become less and less frequent. Wars with barbarous or semibarbarous peoples come in an entirely different category, being merely a most regrettable but necessary international police duty which must be performed for the sake of the welfare of mankind. Peace can only be kept with certainty where both sides wish to keep it; but more and more the civilized peoples are realizing the wicked folly of war and are attaining that condition of just and intelligent regard for the rights of others which will in the end, as we hope and believe, make worldwide peace possible. The peace conference at The Hague gave definite expression to this hope and belief and marked a stride toward their attainment.

This same peace conference acquiesced in our statement of the Monroe Doctrine as compatible with the purposes and aims of the conference.

The Monroe Doctrine should be the cardinal feature of the foreign policy of all the nations of the two Americas, as it is of the United States. Just seventy-eight years have passed since President Monroe in his Annual Message announced that "the American continents are henceforth not to be considered as subjects for future colonization by any European power." In other words, the Monroe Doctrine is a declaration that there must be no territorial aggrandizement by any non-American power at the expense of any American power on American soil. It is in no wise intended as hostile to any nation in the Old World. Still less is it intended to give cover to any aggression by one New World power at the expense of any other. It is simply a step, and a long step, toward assuring the universal peace of the world by securing the possibility of permanent peace on this hemisphere.

During the past century other influences have established the permanence and independence of the smaller states of Europe. Through the Monroe Doctrine we hope to be able to safeguard like independence and secure like permanence for the lesser among the New World nations. . . .

The work of upbuilding the navy must be steadily continued. No one point of our policy, foreign or domestic, is more important than this to the honor and material welfare, and above all to the peace, of our nation in the future. Whether we desire it or not, we must henceforth recognize that we have international duties no less than international rights. Even if our flag were hauled down in the Philippines and Puerto Rico, even if we decided not to build the Isthmian Canal, we should need a thoroughly trained navy of adequate size, or else be prepared definitely and for all time to abandon the idea that our nation is among those whose sons go down to the sea in ships. Unless our commerce is always to be carried in foreign bottoms, we must have war craft to protect it.

Inasmuch, however, as the American people have no thought of abandoning the path upon which they have entered, and especially in view of the fact that the building of the Isthmian Canal is fast becoming one of the matters which the whole people are united in demanding, it is imperative that our navy should be put and kept in the highest state of efficiency, and should be made to answer to our growing needs. So far from being in any way a provocation to war, an adequate and highly trained navy is the best guarantee against war, the cheapest and most effective peace insurance. The cost of building and maintaining such a navy represents the very lightest premium for insuring peace which this nation can possibly pay.

Probably no other great nation in the world is so anxious for peace as we are. There is not a single civilized power which has anything whatever to fear from aggressiveness on our part. All we want is peace; and toward this end we wish to be able to secure the same respect for our rights from others which we are eager and anxious to extend to their rights in return, to insure fair treatment to us commercially, and to guarantee the safety of the American people.

Our people intend to abide by the Monroe Doctrine and to insist upon it as the one sure means of securing the peace of the Western Hemisphere. The navy offers us the only means of making our insistence upon the Monroe Doctrine anything but a subject of derision to whatever nation chooses to disregard it. We desire the peace which comes as of right to the just man armed; not the peace granted on terms of ignominy to the craven and the weakling. . . .

The American people must either build and maintain an adequate navy or else make up their minds definitely to accept a secondary position in international affairs, not merely in political, but in commercial, matters. It has been well said that there is no surer way of courting national disaster than to be "opulent, aggressive, and unarmed."

It is not necessary to increase our army beyond its present size at this time. But it is necessary to keep it at the highest point of efficiency. The individual units who as officers and enlisted men compose this army, are, we have good reason to believe, at least as efficient as those of any other army in the entire world. It is our duty to see that their training is of a kind to insure the highest possible expression of power to these units when acting in combination.

The conditions of modern war are such as to make an infinitely heavier demand than ever before upon the individual character and capacity of the officer and the enlisted man, and to make it far more difficult for men to act together with effect. At present the fighting must be done in extended order, which means that each man must act for himself and at the same time act in combination with others with whom he is no longer in the old-fashioned elbow-to-elbow touch. Under such conditions a few men of the highest excellence are worth more than many men without the special skill which is only found as the result of special training applied to men of exceptional physique and morale. But nowadays the most valuable fighting man and the most difficult to perfect is the rifleman who is also a skillful and daring rider.

The proportion of our cavalry regiments has wisely been increased. The American cavalryman, trained to maneuver and fight with equal facility on foot and on horseback, is the best type of soldier for general purposes now to be found in the world. The ideal cavalryman of the present day is a man who can fight on foot as effectively as the best infantryman, and who is in addition unsurpassed in the care and management of his horse and in his ability to fight on horseback.

A general staff should be created. As for the present staff and supply departments, they should be filled by details from the line, the men so detailed returning after a while to their line duties. It is very undesirable to have the senior grades of the army composed of men who have come to fill the positions by the mere fact of seniority. A system should be adopted by which there shall be an elimination grade by grade of those who seem unfit to render the best service in the next grade. Justice to the veterans of the Civil War who are still in the army would seem to require that in the matter of retirements they be given by law the same privileges accorded to their comrades in the navy.

The process of elimination of the least fit should be conducted in a manner that would render it practically impossible to apply political or social pressure on behalf of any candidate, so that each man may be judged purely on his own merits. Pressure for the promotion of civil officials for political reasons is bad enough, but it is tenfold worse where applied on behalf of officers of the army or navy. Every promotion and every detail under the War Department must be made solely with regard to the good of the service and to the capacity and merit of the man himself. No pressure, political, social, or personal, of any kind, will be permitted to exercise the least effect in any question of promotion or detail; and if there is reason to believe that such pressure is exercised at the instigation of the officer concerned, it will be held to militate against him. In our army we cannot afford to have rewards or duties distributed save on the simple ground that those who by their own merits are entitled to the rewards get them, and that those who are peculiarly fit to do the duties are chosen to perform them. . . .

A great debt is owing from the public to the men of the army and navy. They should be so treated as to enable them to reach the highest point of efficiency, so that they may be able to respond instantly to any demand made upon them to sustain the interests of the nation and the honor of the flag. The individual American enlisted man is probably on the whole a more formidable fighting man than the regular of any other army. Every consideration should be shown him, and in return the highest standard of usefulness should be exacted from him. It is well worthwhile for the Congress to consider whether the pay of enlisted men upon second and subsequent enlistments should not be increased to correspond with the increased value of the veteran soldier. . . .

The merit system of making appointments is in its essence as democratic and American as the common school system itself. It simply means that in clerical and other positions where the duties are entirely nonpolitical, all applicants should have a fair field and no favor, each standing on his merits as he is able to show them by practical test. Written competitive examinations offer the only available means in many cases for applying this system. In other cases, as where laborers are employed, a system of registration undoubtedly can be widely extended. There are, of course, places where the written competitive examination cannot be applied, and others where it offers by no means an ideal solution, but where under existing political conditions it is, though an imperfect means, yet the best present means of getting satisfactory results.

Wherever the conditions have permitted the application of the merit system in its fullest and widest sense, the gain to the government has been immense. The navy yards and postal service illustrate, probably better than any other branches of the government, the great gain in economy, efficiency, and honesty due to the enforcement of this principle.

I recommend the passage of a law which will extend the classified service to the District of Columbia, or will at least enable the president thus to extend it. In my judgment all laws providing for the temporary employment of clerks should hereafter contain a provision that they be selected under the Civil Service Law.

It is important to have this system obtain at home, but it is even more important to have it applied rigidly in our insular possessions. Not an office should be filled in the Philippines or Puerto Rico with any regard to the man's partisan affiliations or services, with any regard to the political, social, or personal influence which he may have at his command; in short, heed should be paid to absolutely nothing save the man's own character and capacity and the needs of the service. . . .

In my judgment the time has arrived when we should definitely make up our minds to recognize the Indian as an individual and not as a member of a tribe. The General Allotment Act is a mighty pulverizing engine to break up the tribal mass. It acts directly upon the family and the individual. Under its provisions some sixty thousand Indians have already become citizens of the United States. We should now break up the tribal funds, doing for them what allotment does for the tribal lands; that is, they should be divided into individual holdings. There will be a transition period during which the funds will in many cases have to be held in trust. This is the case also with the lands. A stop should be put upon the discriminate permission to Indians to lease their allotments. The effort should be steadily to make the Indian work like any other man on his own ground. The marriage laws of the

Indians should be made the same as those of the whites.

In the schools the education should be elementary and largely industrial. The need of higher education among the Indians is very, very limited. On the reservations care should be taken to try to suit the teaching to the needs of the particular Indian. There is no use in attempting to induce agriculture in a country suited only for cattle raising, where the Indian should be made a stock grower. The ration system, which is merely the corral and the reservation system, is highly detrimental to the Indians. It promotes beggary, perpetuates pauperism, and stifles industry. It is an effectual barrier to progress. It must continue to a greater or less degree as long as tribes are herded on reservations and have everything in common. The Indian should be treated as an individual—like the white man. During the change of treatment inevitable hardships will occur; every effort should be made to minimize these hardships; but we should not because of them hesitate to make the change. There should be a continuous reduction in the number of agencies.

In dealing with the aboriginal races few things are more important than to preserve them from the terrible physical and moral degradation resulting from the liquor traffic. We are doing all we can to save our own Indian tribes from this evil. Wherever by international agreement this same end can be attained as regards races where we do not possess exclusive control, every effort should be made to bring it about. . . .

The advancement of the highest interests of national science and learning and the custody of objects of art and of the valuable results of scientific expeditions conducted by the United States have been committed to the Smithsonian Institution. In furtherance of its declared purpose—for the "increase and diffusion of knowledge among men"—the Congress has from time to time given it other important functions. Such trusts have been executed by the Institution with notable fidelity. There should be no halt in the work of the Institution, in accordance with the plans which its secretary has presented, for the preservation of the vanishing races of great North American animals in the National Zoological Park. The urgent needs of the national museum are recommended to the favorable consideration of the Congress.

Perhaps the most characteristic educational movement of the past fifty years is that which has created the modern public library and developed it into broad and active service. There are now over five thousand public libraries in the United States, the product of this period. In addition to accumulating material, they are also striving by organization, by improvement in method, and by cooperation, to give greater efficiency to the material they hold, to make it more widely useful, and by avoidance of unnecessary duplication in process to reduce the cost of its administration.

In these efforts they naturally look for assistance to the federal library, which, though still the Library of Congress, and so entitled, is the one national library of the United States. Already the largest single collection of books on the Western Hemisphere, and certain to increase more rapidly than any other through purchase, exchange, and the operation of the copyright law, this library has a unique opportunity to render to the libraries of this country—to American scholarship—service of the highest importance. It is housed in a building which is the largest and most magnificent yet erected for library uses. Resources are now being provided which will develop the collection properly, equip it with the apparatus and service necessary to its effective use, render its bibliographic work widely available, and enable it to become, not merely a center of research, but the chief factor in great cooperative efforts for the diffusion of knowledge and the advancement of learning. . . .

The remarkable growth of the postal service is shown in the fact that its revenues have doubled and its expenditures have nearly doubled within twelve years. Its progressive development compels constantly increasing outlay, but in this period of business energy and prosperity its receipts grow so much faster than its expenses that the annual deficit has been steadily reduced from $11,411,779 in 1897 to $3,923,727 in 1901. Among recent postal advances the success of rural free delivery wherever established has been so marked, and actual experience has made its benefits so plain, that the demand for its extension is general and urgent.

It is just that the great agricultural population should share in the improvement of the service. The number of rural routes now in operation is 6,009, practically all established within three years, and there are 6,000 applications awaiting action. It is expected that the number in operation at the close of the current fiscal year will reach 8,600. The mail will then be daily carried to the doors of 5,700,000 of our people who have heretofore been dependent upon distant offices, and one-third of all that portion of the country which is adapted to it will be covered by this kind of service. . . .

Owing to the rapid growth of our power and our interests on the Pacific, whatever happens in China must be of the keenest national concern to us.

The general terms of the settlement of the questions growing out of the antiforeign uprisings in China of 1900, having been formulated in a joint note addressed to China by the representatives of the injured powers in December last, were promptly accepted by the Chinese government. After protracted conferences the plenipotentiaries of the several powers were able to sign a final protocol with the Chinese plenipotentiaries on the seventh of last September, setting forth the measures taken by China in compliance with the demands of the joint note, and expressing their satisfaction therewith. . . .

The agreement reached disposes in a manner satisfactory to the powers of the various grounds of complaint, and will contribute materially to better future relations between China and the powers. Reparation has been made by China for the murder of foreigners during the uprising and punishment has been inflicted on the officials, however high in rank, recognized as responsible for or having participated in the outbreak. Official examinations have been forbidden for a period of five years in all cities in which foreigners have been murdered or cruelly treated, and edicts have been issued making all officials directly responsible for the future safety of foreigners and for the suppression of violence against them.

Provisions have been made for ensuring the future safety of the foreign representatives in Peking by setting aside for their exclusive use a quarter of the city which the powers can make defensible and in which they can if necessary maintain permanent military guards; by dismantling the military works between the capital and the sea; and by allowing the temporary maintenance of foreign military posts along this line. An edict has been issued by the emperor of China prohibiting for two years the importation of arms and ammunition into China. China has agreed to pay adequate indemnities to the states, societies, and individuals for the losses sustained by them and for the expenses of the military expeditions sent by the various powers to protect life and restore order.

Under the provisions of the joint note of December 1900, China has agreed to revise the treaties of commerce and navigation and to take such other steps for the purpose of facilitating foreign trade as the foreign powers may decide to be needed.

The Chinese government has agreed to participate financially in the work of bettering the water approaches to Shanghai and to Tien-tsin, the centers of foreign trade in central and northern China, and an international conservancy board, in which the Chinese government is largely represented, has been provided for the improvement of the Shanghai River and the control of its navigation. . . .

During these troubles our government has unswervingly advocated moderation, and has materially aided in bringing about an adjustment which tends to enhance the welfare of China and to lead to a more beneficial intercourse between the empire and the modern world; while in the critical period of revolt and massacre we did our full share in safeguarding life and property, restoring order, and vindicating the national interest and honor. It behooves us to continue in these paths, doing what lies in our power to foster feelings of goodwill, and leaving no effort untried to work out the great policy of full and fair intercourse between China and the nations, on a footing of equal rights and advantages to all. We advocate the "open door" with all that it implies; not merely the procurement of enlarged commercial opportunities on the coasts, but access to the interior by the waterways with which China has been so extraordinarily favored. Only by bringing the people of China into peaceful and friendly community of trade with all the peoples of the earth can the work now auspiciously begun be carried to fruition. In the attainment of this purpose we necessarily claim parity of treatment, under the conventions, throughout the empire for our trade and our citizens with those of all other powers.

We view with lively interest and keen hopes of beneficial results the proceedings of the Pan-American Congress, convoked at the invitation of Mexico, and now sitting at the Mexican capital. The delegates of the United States are under the most liberal instructions to cooperate with their colleagues in all matters promising advantage to the great family of American commonwealths, as well in their relations among themselves as in their domestic advancement and in their intercourse with the world at large. . . .

The death of Queen Victoria caused the people of the United States deep and heartfelt sorrow, to which the government gave full expression. When President McKinley died, our nation in turn received from every quarter of the British Empire expressions of grief and sympathy no less sincere. The death of the Empress Dowager Frederick of Germany also aroused the genuine sympathy of the American people; and this sympathy was cordially reciprocated by Germany when the president was assassinated. Indeed, from every quarter of the civilized world we received, at the time of the president's death, assurances of such grief and regard as to touch the hearts of our people. In the midst of our affliction we reverently thank the Almighty that we are at peace with the nations of mankind; and we firmly intend that our policy shall be such as to continue unbroken these international relations of mutual respect and goodwill.

Speech at Yellowstone National Park

Gardiner, Montana, April 24, 1903

Mr. Mayor, Mr. Superintendent, and My Fellow Citizens: I wish to thank the people of Montana generally, those of Gardiner and Cinnabar especially, and more especially still all those employed in the park, whether in civil or military capacity, for my very enjoyable two weeks' holiday.

It is a pleasure now to say a few words to you at the laying of the cornerstone of the beautiful road which is to mark the entrance to this park. The Yellowstone Park is something absolutely unique in the world, so far as I know. Nowhere else in any civilized country is there to be found such a tract of veritable wonderland made accessible to all visitors, where at the same time not only the scenery of the wilderness but the wild creatures of the park are scrupulously preserved; the only change being that these same wild creatures have been so carefully protected as to show a literally astounding tameness. The creation and preservation of such a great natural playground in the interest of our people as a whole is a credit to the nation; but above all a credit to Montana, Wyoming, and Idaho. It has been preserved with wise foresight. The scheme of its preservation is noteworthy in its essential democracy. Private game preserves, though they may be handled in such a way as to be not only good things for themselves, but good things for the surrounding community, can yet never be more than poor substitutes, from the standpoint of the public, for great national playgrounds such as this Yellowstone Park. This park was created, and is now administered, for the benefit and enjoyment of the people. The government must continue to appropriate for it especially in the direction of completing and perfecting an excellent system of driveways. But already its beauties can be seen with great comfort in a short space of time and at an astoundingly small cost, and with the sense on the part of every visitor that it is in part his property, that it is the property of Uncle Sam and therefore of all of us. The only way that the people as a whole can secure to themselves and their children the enjoyment in perpetuity of what the Yellowstone Park has to give is by assuming the ownership in the name of the nation and by jealously safeguarding and preserving the scenery, the forests, and the wild creatures. When we have a good system of carriage roads throughout the park—for of course it would be very unwise to allow either steam or electric roads in the park—we shall have a region as easy and accessible to travel in as it is already every whit as interesting as any similar territory of the Alps or the Italian Riviera. The geysers, the extraordinary hot springs, the lakes, the mountains, the canyons, and cataracts unite to make this region something not wholly to be paralleled elsewhere on the globe. It must be kept for the benefit and enjoyment of all of us; and I hope to see a steadily increasing number of our people take advantage of its attractions. At present it is rather singular that a greater number of people come from Europe to see it than come from our own eastern states. The people nearby seem awake to its beauties; and I hope that more and more of our people who dwell far off will appreciate its really marvelous character. Incidentally, I should like to point out that some time people will surely awake to the fact that the park has special beauties to be seen in winter; and any hardy man who can go through it in that season on skis will enjoy himself as he scarcely could elsewhere.

I wish especially to congratulate the people of Montana, Wyoming, and Idaho, and notably you of Gardiner and Cinnabar and the immediate outskirts of the park, for the way in which you heartily cooperate with the superintendent to prevent acts of vandalism and destruction. Major Pitcher has explained to me how much he owes to your cooperation and your lively appreciation of the fact that the park is simply being kept in the interest of all of us, so that everyone may have the chance to see its wonders with ease and comfort at the minimum of expense. I have always thought it was a liberal education to any man of the East to come West, and he can combine profit with pleasure if he will incidentally visit this park, the Grand Canyon of the Colorado, and the Yosemite, and take the sea voyage to Alaska. Major Pitcher reports to me, by the way, that he has received invaluable assistance from the game wardens of Montana and Wyoming, and that the present game warden of Idaho has also promised his hearty aid.

The preservation of the forests is of course the matter of prime importance in every public reserve of this character. In this region of the Rocky Mountains and the Great Plains the problem of the water supply is the most important which the home-maker has to face. Congress has not of recent years done anything wiser than in passing the irrigation bill; and nothing is more essential to the preservation of the water supply than the preservation of the forests. Montana has in its water power a source of development which has hardly yet been touched. This water power will be seriously impaired if ample protection is not given the forests. Therefore this park, like the forest reserves generally, is of the utmost advantage to the country around from the merely utilitarian side. But of course this park, also because of its peculiar features, is to be preserved as a beautiful natural playground. Here all the wild creatures of the old days are being preserved, and their overflow into the surrounding country means that the people of the surrounding country, so long as they see that the laws are observed by all, will be able to ensure to themselves and to their children and to their children's children much of the old-time pleasure of the hardy life of the wilderness and of the hunter in the wilderness. This pleasure, moreover, can under such conditions be kept for all who have the love of adventure and the hardihood to take advantage of it, with small regard for what their fortune may be. I cannot too often repeat that the essential feature in the present management of the Yellowstone Park, as in all similar places, is its essential democracy—it is the preservation of the scenery, of the forests, of the wilderness life and the wilderness game for the people as a whole, instead of leaving the enjoyment thereof to be confined to the very rich who can control private reserves. I have been literally astounded at the enormous quantities of elk and at the number of deer, antelope, and mountain sheep which I have seen on their wintering grounds; and the deer and sheep in particular are quite as tame as range stock. A few buffalo are being preserved. I wish very much that the government could somewhere provide for an experimental breeding station of crossbreeds between buffalo and the common cattle. If these crossbreeds could be successfully perpetuated we should have animals which would produce a robe quite as good as the old buffalo robe with which twenty years ago everyone was familiar, and animals moreover which would be so hardy that I think they would have a distinct commercial importance. They would, for instance, be admirably suited for Alaska, a territory which I look to see develop astoundingly within the next decade or two, not only because of its furs and fisheries, but because of its agricultural and pastoral possibilities.

SPEECH AT THE
NEW YORK STATE FAIR

Syracuse, September 7, 1903

A SQUARE DEAL

Governor Higgins, My Fellow Citizens: In speaking on Labor Day at the annual fair of the New York State Agricultural Association, it is natural to keep especially in mind the two bodies who compose the majority of our people and upon whose welfare depends the welfare of the entire state. If circumstances are such that thrift, energy, industry, and forethought enable the farmer, the tiller of the soil, on the one hand, and the wage-worker, on the other, to keep themselves, their wives, and their children in reasonable comfort, then the state is well off, and we can be assured that the other classes in the community will likewise prosper. On the other hand, if there is in the long run a lack of prosperity among the two classes named, then all other prosperity is sure to be more seeming than real. It has been our profound good fortune as a nation that hitherto, disregarding exceptional periods of depression and the normal and inevitable fluctuations, there has been on the whole from the beginning of our government to the present day a progressive betterment alike in the condition of the tiller of the soil and in the condition of the man who, by his manual skill and labor, supports himself and his family, and endeavors to bring up his children so that they may be at least as well off as, and if possible better off than, he himself has been. There are, of course, exceptions, but as a whole the standard of living among the farmers of our country has risen from generation to generation, and the wealth represented on the farms has steadily increased, while the wages of labor have likewise risen, both as regards to actual money paid and as regards the purchasing power which that money represents.

Side by side with this increase in the prosperity of the wage-worker and the tiller of the soil has gone on a great increase in prosperity among the businessmen and among certain classes of professional men; and the prosperity of these men has been partly the cause and partly the consequence of the prosperity of farmer and wage-worker. It cannot be too often repeated that in this country, in the long run, we all of us tend to go up or go down together. If the average of well-being is high, it means that the average wage-worker, the average farmer, and the average businessman are all alike well off. If the average shrinks, there is not one of these classes which will not feel the shrinkage. Of course there are always some men who are not affected by good times, just as there are some men who are not affected by bad times. But speaking broadly, it is true that if prosperity comes all of us tend to share more or less therein, and that if adversity comes each of us, to a greater or less extent, feels the tension. Unfortunately, in this world the innocent frequently find themselves obliged to pay some of the penalty for the misdeeds of the guilty; and so if hard times come, whether they be due to our own fault or to our misfortune, whether they be due to some burst of speculative frenzy that has caused a portion of the business world to lose its head—a loss which no legislation can possibly supply—or whether they be due to any lack of wisdom in a portion of the world of labor—in each case the trouble once started is felt more or less in every walk of life.

It is all-essential to the continuance of our healthy national life that we should recognize this community of interest among our people. The welfare of each of us is dependent fundamentally upon the welfare of all of us, and therefore in public life that man is the best representative of each of us who seeks to do good to each by doing good to all; in other words, whose endeavor it is not to represent any special class and promote merely that class's selfish interests, but to represent all true and honest men of all sections and all classes and to work for their interests by working for our common country.

We can keep our government on a sane and healthy basis, we can make and keep our social system what it should be, only on condition of judging each man, not as a member of a class, but on his worth as a man. It is an infamous thing in our American life, and fundamentally treacherous to our institutions, to apply to any man any test save that of his personal worth, or to draw between two sets of men any distinction save the distinction of conduct, the distinction that marks off those who do well and wisely from those who do ill and foolishly. There are good citizens and bad citizens in every class as in every locality, and the attitude of decent people toward great public and social questions should be determined, not by the accidental questions of employment or locality, but by those deep-set principles which represent the innermost souls of men.

The failure in public and in private life thus to treat each man on his own merits, the recognition of this government as being either for the poor as such or for the rich as such, would prove fatal to our Republic, as such failure and such recognition have always proved fatal in the past to other republics. A healthy republican government must rest upon individuals, not upon classes or sections. As soon as it becomes government by a class or by a section it departs from the old American ideal.

It is, of course, the merest truism to say that free institutions are of avail only to people who possess the high and peculiar characteristics needed to take advantage of such institutions. The century that has just closed has witnessed many and lamentable instances in which people have seized a government free in form, or have had it bestowed upon them, and yet have permitted it under the forms of liberty to become some species of despotism or anarchy, because they did not have in them the power to make this seeming liberty one of deed instead of one merely of word. Under such circumstances the seeming liberty may be supplanted by a tyranny or despotism in the first place, or it may reach the road of despotism by the path of license and anarchy. It matters but little which road is taken. In either case the same goal is reached. People show themselves just as unfit for liberty whether they submit to anarchy or to tyranny; and class government, whether it be the government of a plutocracy or the government of a mob, is equally incompatible with the principles established in the days of Washington and perpetuated in the days of Lincoln.

Many qualities are needed by a people which would preserve the power of self-government in fact as well as in name. Among these qualities are forethought, shrewdness, self-restraint, the courage which refuses to abandon one's own rights, and the disinterested and kindly good sense which enables one to do justice to the rights of others. Lack of strength and lack of courage unfit men for self-government on the one hand; and on the other, brutal arrogance, envy, in short, any manifestation of the spirit of selfish disregard, whether of one's own duties or of the rights of others, are equally fatal.

In the history of mankind many republics have risen, have flourished for a less or greater time, and then have fallen because their citizens lost the power of governing themselves and thereby of governing their state; and in no way has this loss of power been so often and so clearly shown as in the tendency to turn the government into a government primarily for the benefit of one class instead of a government for the benefit of the people as a whole.

Again and again in the republics of ancient Greece, in those of medieval Italy and medieval Flanders, this tendency was shown, and wherever the tendency became a habit it invariably and inevitably proved fatal to the state. In the final result it mattered not one whit whether the movement was in favor of one class or of another. The outcome was equally fatal, whether the country fell into the hands of a wealthy oligarchy which exploited the poor or whether it fell under the domination of a turbulent mob which plundered the rich. In both cases there resulted violent alternations between tyranny and disorder, and a final complete loss of liberty to all citizens—destruction in the end overtaking the class which had for the moment been victorious as well as that which had momentarily been defeated. The death knell of the republic had rung as soon as the active power became lodged in the hands of those who sought, not to do justice to all citizens, rich and poor alike, but to stand for one special class and for its interests as opposed to the interests of others.

The reason why our future is assured lies in the fact that our people are genuinely skilled in and fitted for self-government and therefore will spurn the leadership of those who seek to excite this ferocious and foolish class antagonism. The average American knows not only that he himself intends to do about what is right, but that his average fellow countryman has the same intention and the same power to make his intention effective. He knows, whether he be businessman, professional man, farmer, mechanic, employer, or wage-worker, that the welfare of each of these men is bound up with the welfare of all the others; that each is neighbor to the other, is actuated by the same hopes and fears, has fundamentally the same ideals, and that all alike have much the same virtues and the same faults. Our average fellow citizen is a sane and healthy man, who believes in decency and has a wholesome mind. He therefore feels an equal scorn alike for the man of wealth guilty of the mean and base spirit of arrogance toward those who are less well off, and for the man of small means who in his turn either feels, or seeks to excite in others the feeling of, mean and base envy for those who are better off. The two feelings, envy and arrogance, are but opposite sides of the same shield, but different developments of the same spirit. Fundamentally, the unscrupulous rich man who seeks to exploit and oppress those who are less well off is in spirit not opposed to, but identical with, the unscrupulous poor man who desires to plunder and oppress those who are better off. The courtier and the demagogue are but developments of the same type under different conditions, each manifesting the same servile spirit, the same desire to rise by pandering to base passions; though one panders to power in the shape of a single man and the other to power in the shape of a multitude. So likewise the man who wishes to rise by wronging others must by right be contrasted, not with the man who likewise wishes to do wrong, though to a different set of people, but with the man who wishes to do justice to all people and to wrong none.

The line of cleavage between good and bad citizenship lies not between the man of wealth who acts squarely by his fellows and the man who seeks each day's wage by that day's work, wronging no one and doing his duty by his neighbor; nor yet does this line of cleavage divide the unscrupulous wealthy man, who exploits others in his own interest, from the demagogue or from the sullen and envious being who wishes to attack all men of property, whether they do well or ill. On the contrary, the line of cleavage between good citizenship and bad citizenship separates the rich man who does well from the rich man who does ill, the poor man of good conduct from the poor man of bad conduct. This line of cleavage lies at right angles to any such arbitrary line of division as that separating one class from another, one locality from another, or men with a certain degree of property from those of a less degree of property.

The good citizen is the man who, whatever his wealth or his poverty, strives manfully to do his duty to himself, to his family, to his neighbor, to the state; who is incapable of the baseness which manifests itself either in arrogance or in envy, but who while demanding justice for himself is no less scrupulous to do justice to others. It is because the average American citizen, rich or poor, is of just this type that we have cause for our profound faith in the future of the Republic.

Ours is a government of liberty, by, through, and under the law. Lawlessness and connivance at lawbreaking—whether the lawbreaking take the form of a crime of greed and cunning or of a crime of violence—are destructive not only of order, but of the true liberties which can only come through order. If alive to their true interests rich and poor alike will set their faces like flint against the spirit which seeks personal advantage by overriding the laws, without regard to whether this spirit shows itself in the form of bodily violence by one set of men or in the form of vulpine cunning by another set of men.

Let the watchwords of all our people be the old familiar watchwords of honesty, decency, fair-dealing, and common sense. The qualities denoted by these words are essential to all of us, as we deal with the complex industrial problems of today, the problems affecting not merely the accumulation but even more the wise distribution of wealth. We ask no man's permission when we require him to obey the law; neither the permission of the poor man nor yet of the rich man. Least of all can the man of great wealth afford to break the law, even for his own financial advantage; for the law is his prop and support, and it is both foolish and profoundly unpatriotic for him to fail in giving hearty support to those who show that there is in very fact one law, and one law only, alike for the rich and the poor, for the great and the small.

Men sincerely interested in the due protection of property, and men sincerely interested in seeing that the just rights of labor are guaranteed, should alike remember not only that in the long run neither the capitalist nor the wage-worker can be helped in healthy fashion save by helping the other; but also that to require either side to obey the law and do its full duty toward the community is emphatically to that side's real interest.

There is no worse enemy of the wage-worker than the man who condones mob violence in any shape or who preaches class hatred; and surely the slightest acquaintance with our industrial history should teach even the most short-sighted that the times of most suffering for our people as a whole, the times when business is stagnant, and capital suffers from shrinkage and gets no return from its investments, are exactly the times of hardship, and want, and grim disaster among the poor. If all the existing instrumentalities of wealth could be abolished, the first and severest suffering would come among those of us who are least well off at present. The wage-worker is well off only when the rest of the country is well off;

and he can best contribute to this general well-being by showing sanity and a firm purpose to do justice to others.

In his turn the capitalist who is really a conservative, the man who has forethought as well as patriotism, should heartily welcome every effort, legislative or otherwise, which has for its object to secure fair dealing by capital, corporate or individual, toward the public and toward the employee. Such laws as the franchise-tax law in this state, which the court of appeals recently unanimously decided constitutional—such a law as that passed in Congress last year for the purpose of establishing a Department of Commerce and Labor, under which there should be a bureau to oversee and secure publicity from the great corporations which do an interstate business—such a law as that passed at the same time for the regulation of the great highways of commerce so as to keep these roads clear on fair terms to all producers in getting their goods to market—these laws are in the interest not merely of the people as a whole, but of the propertied classes. For in no way is the stability of property better assured than by making it patent to our people that property bears its proper share of the burdens of the state; that property is handled not only in the interest of the owner, but in the interest of the whole community.

In other words, legislation to be permanently good for any class must also be good for the nation as a whole, and legislation which does injustice to any class is certain to work harm to the nation. Take our currency system, for example. This nation is on a gold basis. The treasury of the public is in excellent condition. Never before has the per capita of circulation been as large as it is this day; and this circulation, moreover, is of money every dollar of which is at par with gold. Now, our having this sound currency system is of benefit to banks, of course, but it is of infinitely more benefit to the people as a whole, because of the healthy effect on business conditions.

In the same way, whatever is advisable in the way of remedial or corrective currency legislation—and nothing revolutionary is advisable under present conditions—must be undertaken only from the standpoint of the business community as a whole, that is, of the American body politic as a whole. Whatever is done, we cannot afford to take any step backward or to cast any doubt upon the certain redemption in standard coin of every circulating note.

Among ourselves we differ in many qualities of body, head, and heart; we are unequally developed, mentally as well as physically. But each of us has the right to ask that he shall be protected from wrongdoing as he does his work and carries his burden through life. No man needs sympathy because he has to work, because he has a burden to carry. Far and away the best prize that life offers is the chance to work hard at work worth doing; and this is a prize open to every man, for there can be no work better worth doing than that done to keep in health and comfort and with reasonable advantages those immediately dependent upon the husband, the father, or the son.

There is no room in our healthy American life for the mere idler, for the man or the woman whose object it is throughout life to shirk the duties which life ought to bring. Life can mean nothing worth meaning, unless its prime aim is the doing of duty, the achievement of results worth achieving. A recent writer has finely said: "After all, the saddest thing that can happen to a man is to carry no burdens. To be bent under too great a load is bad; to be crushed by it is lamentable; but even in that, there are possibilities that are glorious. But to carry no load at all—there is nothing in that. No one seems to arrive at any goal really worth reaching in this world who does not come to it heavy laden."

Surely from our own experience each one of us knows that this is true. From the greatest to the smallest, happiness and usefulness are largely found in the same soul, and the joy of life is won in its deepest and truest sense only by those who have not shirked life's burdens. The men whom we most delight to honor in all this land are those who, in the iron years from '61 to '65, bore on their shoulders the burden of saving the Union. They did not choose the easy task. They did not shirk the difficult duty. Deliberately and of their own free will they strove for an ideal, upward and onward across the stony slopes of greatness. They did the hardest work that was then to be done; they bore the heaviest burden that any generation of Americans ever had to bear; and because they did this they have won such proud joy as it has fallen to the lot of no other men to win, and have written their names forevermore on the golden honor roll of the nation. As it is with the soldier, so it is with the civilian. To win success in the business world, to become a first-class mechanic, a successful farmer, an able lawyer or doctor, means that the man has devoted his best energy and power through long years to the achievement of his ends. So it is in the life of the family, upon which in the last analysis the whole welfare of the nation rests. The man or woman who as breadwinner and home-maker, or as wife and mother, has done all that he or she can do, patiently and uncomplainingly, is to be honored, and is to be envied by all those who have never had the good fortune to feel the need and duty of doing such work. The woman who has borne, and who has reared as they should be reared, a family of children, has in the most emphatic manner deserved well of the Republic. Her burden has been heavy, and she has been able to bear it worthily only by the possession of resolution, of good sense, of conscience, and of unselfishness. But if she has borne it well, then to her shall come the supreme blessing, for in the words of the oldest and greatest of books, "Her children shall rise up and call her blessed"; and among the benefactors of the land her place must be with those who have done the best and the hardest work, whether as lawgivers or as soldiers, whether in public or private life.

This is not a soft and easy creed to preach. It is a creed willingly learned only by men and women who, together with the softer virtues, possess also the stronger; who can do, and dare, and die at need, but who while life lasts will never flinch from their allotted task. You farmers, and wage-workers, and businessmen of this great state, of this mighty and wonderful nation, are gathered together today, proud of your state and still prouder of your nation, because your forefathers and predecessors have lived up to just this creed. You have received from their hands a great inheritance, and you will leave an even greater inheritance to your children and your children's children, provided only that you practice alike in your private and your public lives the strong virtues that have given us as a people greatness in the past. It is not enough to be well-meaning and kindly, but weak; neither is it enough to be strong, unless morality and decency go hand in hand with strength. We must possess the qualities which make us do our duty in our homes and among our neighbors, and in addition we must possess the qualities which are indispensable to the makeup of every great and masterful nation—the qualities of courage and hardihood, of individual initiative and yet of power to combine for a common end, and above all, the resolute determination to permit no man and no set of men to sunder us one from the other by lines of caste or creed or section. We must act upon the motto of all for each and each for all. There must be ever present in our minds the fundamental truth that in a republic such as ours the only safety is to stand neither for nor against any man because he is rich or because he is poor, because he is engaged in one occupation or another, because he works with his brains or because he works with his hands. We must treat each man on his worth and merits as a man. We must see that each is given a square deal, because he is entitled to no more and should receive no less. Finally we must keep ever in mind that a republic such as ours can exist only by virtue of the orderly liberty which comes through the equal domination of the law over all men alike, and through its administration in such resolute and fearless fashion as shall teach all that no man is above it and no man below it.

MESSAGE TO CONGRESS ON THE PANAMA CANAL

January 4, 1904

To the Senate and House of Representatives: I lay before the Congress for its information a statement of my action up to this time in executing the act entitled "An Act to Provide for the Construction of a Canal Connecting the Waters of the Atlantic and Pacific Oceans," approved June 28, 1902.

By the said act the president was authorized to secure for the United States the property of the Panama Canal Company and the perpetual control of a strip six miles wide across the Isthmus of Panama. It was further provided that "should the president be unable to obtain for the United States a satisfactory title to the property of the New Panama Canal Company and the control of the necessary territory of the Republic of Colombia . . . within a reasonable time and upon reasonable terms, then the president" should endeavor to provide for a canal by the Nicaragua route. The language quoted defines with exactness and precision what was to be done, and what as a matter of fact has been done. The president was authorized to go to the Nicaragua route only if within a reasonable time he could not obtain "control of the necessary territory of the Republic of Colombia." This control has now been obtained; the provision of the act has been complied with; it is no longer possible under existing legislation to go to the Nicaragua route as an alternative.

This act marked the climax of the effort on the part of the United States to secure, so far as legislation was concerned, an interoceanic canal across the Isthmus. The effort to secure a treaty for this purpose with one of the Central American republics did not stand on the same footing with the effort to secure a treaty under any ordinary conditions. The proper position for the United States to assume in reference to this canal, and therefore to the governments of the Isthmus, had been clearly set forth by Secretary Cass in 1858. In my Annual Message I have already quoted what Secretary Cass said; but I repeat the quotation here, because the principle it states is fundamental:

> While the rights of sovereignty of the states occupying this region (Central America) should always be respected, we shall expect that these rights be exercised in a spirit befitting the occasion and the wants and circumstances that have arisen. Sovereignty has its duties as well as its rights, and none of these local governments, even if administered with more regard to the just demands of other nations than they have been, would be permitted, in a spirit of Eastern isolation, to close the gates of intercourse on the great highways of the world, and justify the act by the pretension that these avenues of trade and travel belong to them and that they choose to shut them, or, what is almost equivalent, to encumber them with such unjust relations as would prevent their general use.

The principle thus enunciated by Secretary Cass was sound then and it is sound now. The United States has taken the position that no other government is to build the canal. In 1889, when France proposed to come to the aid of the French Panama Company by guaranteeing their bonds, the Senate of the United States in executive session, with only some three votes dissenting, passed a resolution as follows:

> That the government of the United States will look with serious concern and disapproval upon any connection of any European government with the construction or control of any ship canal across the Isthmus of Darien or across Central America, and must regard any such connection or control as injurious to the just rights and interests of the United States and as a menace to their welfare.

Under the Hay-Pauncefote Treaty it was explicitly provided that the United States should control, police, and protect the canal which was to be built, keeping it open for the vessels of all nations on equal terms. The United States thus assumed the position of guarantor of the canal and of its peaceful use by all the world. The guarantee included as a matter of course the building of the canal. The enterprise was recognized as responding to an international need; and it would be the veriest travesty on right and justice to treat the governments in possession of the Isthmus as having the right, in the language of Mr. Cass, "to close the gates of intercourse on the great highways of the world, and justify the act by the pretension that these avenues of trade and travel belong to them and that they choose to shut them."

When this government submitted to Colombia the Hay-Herran Treaty three things were, therefore, already settled.

One was that the canal should be built. The time for delay, the time for permitting the attempt to be made by private enterprise, the time for permitting any government of antisocial spirit and of imperfect development to bar the work was past. The United States had assumed in connection with the canal certain responsibilities not only to its own people, but to the civilized world, which imperatively demanded that there should no longer be delay in beginning the work.

Second. While it was settled that the canal should be built without unnecessary or improper delay, it was no less clearly shown to be our purpose to deal not merely in a spirit of justice but in a spirit of generosity with the people through whose land we might build it. The Hay-Herran Treaty, if it erred at all, erred in the direction of an overgenerosity toward the Colombian government. In our anxiety to be fair we had gone to the very verge in yielding to a weak nation's demands what that nation was helplessly unable to enforce from us against our will. The only criticisms made upon the administration for the terms of the Hay-Herran Treaty were for having granted too much to Colombia, not for failure to grant enough. Neither in the Congress nor in the public press, at the time that this treaty was formulated, was there complaint that it did not in the fullest and amplest manner guarantee to Colombia everything that she could by any color of title demand.

Nor is the fact to be lost sight of that the rejected treaty, while generously responding to the pecuniary demands of Colombia, in other respects merely provided for the construction of the canal in conformity with the express requirements of the act of the Congress of June 28, 1902. By that act, as heretofore quoted, the president was authorized to acquire from Colombia, for the purposes of the canal, "perpetual control" of a certain strip of land; and it was expressly required that the "control" thus to be obtained should include "jurisdiction" to make police and sanitary regulations and to establish such judicial tribunals as might be agreed on for their enforcement. These were conditions precedent prescribed by the Congress; and for their fulfillment suitable stipulations were embodied in the treaty. . . . During all the years of negotiation and discussion that preceded the conclusion of the Hay-Herran Treaty, Colombia never intimated that the requirement by the United States of control over the canal strip would render unattainable the construction of a canal by way of the Isthmus of Panama; nor were we advised, during the months when legislation of 1902 was pending before the Congress, that the terms which it embodied would render negotiations with Colombia impracticable. It is plain that no nation could construct and guarantee the neutrality of the canal with a less degree of control than was stipulated for in the Hay-Herran Treaty. A refusal to grant such degree of control was necessarily a refusal to make any practicable treaty at all. Such refusal therefore squarely raised the question whether Colombia was entitled to bar the transit of the world's traffic across the Isthmus.

That the canal itself was eagerly demanded by the people of the locality through which it was to pass, and that the people of this locality no less eagerly longed for its construction under American control, are shown by the unanimity of action in the new Panama Republic. Furthermore, Colombia, after having rejected the treaty in spite of our protests and warnings when it was in her power to accept it, has since shown the utmost eagerness to accept the same treaty if only the status quo could be restored. One of the men standing highest in the official circles of Colombia, on November 6, addressed the American minister at Bogota, saying that if the government of the United States would land troops to preserve Colombian sovereignty and the transit, the Colombian government would "declare martial law; and, by virtue of vested constitutional authority, when public order is disturbed, [would] approve by decree the ratification of the canal treaty as signed; or, if the government of the United States prefers, [would] call extra session of the Congress—with new and friendly members—next May to approve the treaty." Having these facts in view, there is no shadow of question that the government of the United States proposed a treaty which was not merely just, but generous to Colombia, which our people regarded as erring, if at all, on the side of overgenerosity; which was hailed with delight by the people of the immediate locality through which the canal was to pass, who were most concerned as to the new order of things; and which the Colombia authorities now recognize as being so good that they are willing to promise its unconditional ratification if only we will desert those who have shown themselves our friends and restore to those who have shown themselves unfriendly the power to undo what they did. . . .

Third. Finally the Congress definitely settled where the canal was to be built. It was provided that a treaty should be made for building the canal across the Isthmus of Panama; and if, after reasonable time, it proved impossible to secure such treaty, that then we should go to Nicaragua. The treaty has been made; for it needs no argument to show that the intent of the Congress was to ensure a canal across Panama, and that whether the republic granting the title was called New Granada, Colombia, or Panama mattered not one whit. As events turned out, the question of "reasonable time" did not enter into the matter at all. Although, as the months went by, it became increasingly improbable that the Colombian Congress would ratify the treaty or take steps which would be equivalent thereto, yet all chance for such action on their part did not vanish until the Congress closed at the end of October; and within three days thereafter the revolution in Panama had broken out. Panama became an independent state, and the control of the territory necessary for building the canal then became obtainable. The condition under which alone we could have gone to Nicaragua thereby became impossible of fulfillment. If the pending treaty with Panama should not be ratified by the Senate this would not alter the fact that we could not go to Nicaragua. The Congress has decided the route, and there is no alternative under existing legislation.

When in August it began to appear probable that the Colombia legislature would not ratify the treaty, it became incumbent upon me to consider well what the situation was and to be ready to advise the Congress as to what were the various alternatives of action open to us. There were several possibilities. One was that Colombia would at the last moment see the unwisdom of her position. . . .

A second alternative was that by the close of the session of the last day of October, without the ratification of the treaty by Colombia and without any steps taken by Panama, the American Congress on assembling early in November would be confronted with a situation in which there had been a failure to come to terms as to building the canal along the Panama route, and yet there had not been a lapse of a reasonable time—using the word reasonable in any proper sense—such as would justify the administration going to the Nicaraguan route. . . .

It was the opinion of eminent international jurists that in view of the fact that the great design of our guarantee under the treaty of 1846 was to dedicate the Isthmus to the purposes of interoceanic transit, and above all to secure the construction of an interoceanic canal, Colombia could not under existing conditions refuse to enter into a proper arrangement with the United States to that end, without violating the spirit and substantially repudiating the obligations of a treaty the full benefits of which she had enjoyed for over fifty years. . . .

A third possibility was that the people of the Isthmus, who had formerly constituted an independent state, and who until recently were united to Colombia only by a loose tie of federal relationship, might take the protection of their own vital interests into their own hands, reassert their former rights, declare their independence upon just grounds, and establish a government competent and willing to do its share in this great work for civilization. This third possibility is what actually occurred. Everyone knew that it was a possibility, but it was not until toward the end of October that it appeared to be an imminent probability. Although the administration, of course, had special means of knowledge, no such means were necessary in order to appreciate the possibility, and toward the end the likelihood of such a revolutionary outbreak and of its success. It was a matter of common notoriety. Quotations from the daily papers could be indefinitely multiplied to show this state of affairs; a very few will suffice. From Costa Rica on August 31 a special was sent to the Washington *Post,* running as follows:

> *San Jose, Costa Rica, August 31*
>
> Travelers from Panama report the Isthmus alive with fires of a new revolution. It is inspired, it is believed, by men who, in Panama and Colon, have systematically engendered the pro-American feeling to secure the building of the Isthmian Canal by the United States.
>
> The Indians have risen, and the late followers of General Benjamin Herrera are mustering in the mountain villages, preparatory to joining in an organized revolt, caused by the rejection of the canal treaty.
>
> Hundreds of stacks of arms, confiscated by the Colombian government at the close of the late revolution, have reappeared from some mysterious source, and thousands of rifles that look suspiciously like the Mausers the United States captured in Cuba are issuing to the gathering forces from central points of distri-

bution. With the arms goes ammunition, fresh from factories, showing the movement is not spasmodic, but is carefully planned. . . .

The government forces in Panama and Colon, numbering less than 1,500 men, are reported to be a little more than friendly to the revolutionary spirit. They have been ill-paid since the revolution closed, and their only hope of prompt payment is another war.

General Huertes, commander of the forces, who is ostensibly loyal to the Bogota government, is said to be secretly friendly to the proposed revolution. At least, all his personal friends are open in denunciation of the Bogota government and the failure of the Colombian Congress to ratify the canal treaty.

The consensus of opinion gathered from late arrivals from the Isthmus is that the revolution is coming, and that it will succeed.

A special dispatch to the Washington *Post,* under date of New York, September 1, runs as follows:

B. G. Duque, editor and proprietor of the Panama *Star and Herald,* a resident of the Isthmus during the past twenty-seven years, who arrived today in New York, declared that if the canal treaty fell through a revolution would be likely to follow.

"There is a very strong feeling in Panama," said Mr. Duque, "that Colombia, in negotiating the sale of a canal concession in Panama, is looking for profits that might just as well go to Panama herself.

"The Colombian government, only the other day, suppressed a newspaper that dared to speak of independence for Panama. A while ago there was a secret plan afoot to cut loose from Colombia and seek the protection of the United States."

In the New York *Herald* of September 10 the following statement appeared:

Representatives of strong interests on the Isthmus of Panama, who make their headquarters in this city, are considering a plan of action to be undertaken in cooperation with men of similar views in Panama and Colon to bring about a revolution and form an independent government in Panama opposed to that in Bogota.

There is much indignation on the Isthmus on account of the failure of the canal treaty, which is ascribed to the authorities at Bogota. This opinion is believed to be shared by a majority of the Isthmians of all shades of political belief, and they think it is to their best interest for a new republic to be formed on the Isthmus, which may negotiate directly with the United States a new treaty which will permit the digging of the Panama Canal under favorable conditions.

In the New York *Times,* under date of September 13, there appeared from Bogota the following statement:

> A proposal made by Señor Perez y Sotos to ask the executive to appoint an antisecessionist governor in Panama has been approved by the Senate. . . .
> Señor Deroux, representative for a Panama constituency, recently delivered a sensational speech in the House. Among other things he said:
> "In Panama the bishops, governors, magistrates, military chiefs, and their subordinates have been and are foreign to the department. It seems that the government, with surprising tenacity, wishes to exclude the Isthmus from all participation in public affairs. As regards international dangers in the Isthmus, all I can say is that if these dangers exist they are due to the conduct of the national government, which is in the direction of reaction.
> "If the Colombian government will not take action with a view to preventing disaster, the responsibility will rest with it alone."

In the New York *Herald* of October 26 it was reported that a revolutionary expedition of about seventy men had actually landed on the Isthmus. In the Washington *Post* of October 29 it was reported from Panama that in view of the impending trouble on the Isthmus the Bogota government had gathered troops in sufficient numbers to at once put down an attempt at secession. In the New York *Herald* of October 30 it was announced from Panama that Bogota was hurrying troops to the Isthmus to put down the projected revolt. In the New York *Herald* of November 2 it was announced that in Bogota the Congress had endorsed the energetic measures taken to meet the situation on the Isthmus and that six thousand men were about to be sent thither.

Quotations like the above could be multiplied indefinitely. Suffice it to say that it was notorious that revolutionary trouble of a serious nature was impending upon the Isthmus. But it was not necessary to rely exclusively upon such general means of information. On October 15 Commander Hubbard, of the navy, notified the Navy Department that, though things were quiet on the Isthmus, a revolution had broken out in the state of Cauca. On October 16, at the request of Lieutenant-General Young, I saw Captain C. B. Humphrey and Lieutenant Grayson Mallet-Prevost Murphy, who had just returned from a four months' tour through the northern portions of Venezuela and Colombia. They stopped in Panama on their return in the latter part of September. At the time they were sent down there had been no thought of their going to Panama, and their visit to the Isthmus was but an unpremeditated incident of their return journey; nor had they been spoken to by anyone at Washington regarding the possibility of a revolt. Until they landed at Colon they had no knowledge that a revolution was impending, save what they had gained from the newspapers. What they saw in Panama so impressed them that they reported thereon to Lieutenant-General Young, according to his memorandum, that

> while on the Isthmus they became satisfied beyond question that, owing largely to the dissatisfaction because of the failure of Colombia to ratify the Hay-Herran Treaty, a revolutionary party was in course of organization having for its object the separation of the state of Panama from Colombia, the leader being Dr. Richard Arango, a former governor of Panama; that when they were on the Isthmus arms and ammunition were being smuggled into the city of Colon in piano boxes, merchandise crates, etc., the small arms received being principally the

Gras French rifle, the Remington, and the Mauser; that nearly every citizen in Panama had some sort of rifle or gun in his possession, with ammunition therefor; that in the city of Panama there had been organized a fire brigade which was really intended for a revolutionary military organization; that there were representatives of the revolutionary organization at all important points on the Isthmus; that in Panama, Colon, and the other principal places of the Isthmus police forces had been organized which were in reality revolutionary forces; that the people on the Isthmus seemed to be unanimous in their sentiment against the Bogota government, and their disgust over the failure of that government to ratify the treaty providing for the construction of the canal, and that a revolution might be expected immediately upon the adjournment of the Colombian Congress without ratification of the treaty.

Lieutenant-General Young regarded their report as of such importance as to make it advisable that I should personally see these officers. They told me what they had already reported to the lieutenant-general, adding that on the Isthmus the excitement was seething, and that the Colombian troops were reported to be disaffected. In response to a question of mine they informed me that it was the general belief that the revolution might break out at any moment, and if it did not happen before, would doubtless take place immediately after the closing of the Colombian Congress (at the end of October) if the canal treaty were not ratified. . . .

In view of all these facts I directed the Navy Department to issue instructions such as would ensure our having ships within easy reach of the Isthmus in the event of need arising. Orders were given on October 19 to the *Boston* to proceed to San Juan del Sur, Nicaragua; to the *Dixie* to prepare to sail from League Island; and to the *Atlanta* to proceed to Guantanamo. On October 30 the *Nashville* was ordered to proceed to Colon. On November 2, when, the Colombian Congress having adjourned, it was evident that the outbreak was imminent, and when it was announced that both sides were making ready forces whose meeting would mean bloodshed and disorder, the Colombian troops having been embarked on vessels, the following instructions were sent to the commanders of the *Boston, Nashville,* and *Dixie:*

> Maintain free and uninterrupted transit. If interruption is threatened by armed force, occupy the line of railroad. Prevent landing of any armed force with hostile intent, either government or insurgent, at any point within fifty miles of Panama. Government force reported approaching the Isthmus in vessels. Prevent their landing if, in your judgment, the landing would precipitate a conflict.

These orders were delivered in pursuance of the policy on which our government had repeatedly acted. This policy was exhibited in the following orders, given under somewhat similar circumstances last year, and the year before, and the year before that. The first two telegrams are from the Department of State to the consul at Panama:

> *July 25, 1900*
>
> You are directed to protest against any act of hostility which may involve or imperil the safe and peaceful transit of persons or property across the Isthmus of Panama. The bombardment of Panama would have this effect, and the United States must insist upon the neutrality of the Isthmus as guaranteed by the treaty.

> *November 20, 1901*
>
> Notify all parties molesting or interfering with free transit across the Isthmus that such interference must cease and that the United States will prevent the interruption of traffic upon the railroad. Consult with captain of the *Iowa,* who will be instructed to land marines, if necessary, for the protection of the railroad, in accordance with the treaty rights and obligations of the United States. Desirable to avoid bloodshed, if possible.

The next three telegrams are from and to the secretary of the navy:

September 12, 1902

Ranger, Panama:

United States guarantees perfect neutrality of Isthmus and that a free transit from sea to sea be not interrupted or embarrassed. . . . Any transportation of troops which might contravene these provisions of treaty should not be sanctioned by you nor should use of road be permitted which might convert the line of transit into theater of hostility.

MOODY

Colon, September 20, 1902

Secretary Navy, Washington:

Everything is conceded. The United States guards and guarantees traffic and the line of transit. Today I permitted the exchange of Colombian troops from Panama to Colon, about one thousand men each way, the troops without arms in train guarded by American naval force in the same manner as other passengers; arms and ammunition in separate train, guarded also by naval force in the same manner as other freight.

McLEAN

Panama, October 3, 1902

Secretary Navy, Washington, D.C.:

Have sent this communication to the American consul at Panama:

"Inform governor while trains running under United States protection I must decline transportation any combatants, ammunition, arms, which might cause interruption traffic or convert line of transit into theater hostilities."

CASEY

On November 3 Commander Hubbard responded to the above-quoted telegram of November 2, 1903, saying that before the telegram had been received four hundred Colombian troops from Cartagena had landed at Colon; that there had been no revolution on the Isthmus, but that the situation was most critical if the revolutionary leaders should act. On this same date the Associated Press in Washington received a bulletin stating that a revolutionary outbreak had occurred. When this was brought to the attention of the assistant secretary of state, Mr. Loomis, he prepared the following cablegram to the consul general at Panama and the consul at Colon:

> Uprising on Isthmus reported. Keep department promptly and fully informed.

Before this telegram was sent, however, one was received from Consul Malmros at Colon, running as follows:

> Revolution imminent. Government force on the Isthmus about 500 men. Their official promised support revolution. Fire department, Panama, 441, are well organized and favor revolution. Government vessel, *Cartagena,* with about 400 men, arrived early today with new commander-in-chief, Tobar. Was not expected until November 10. Tobar's arrival is not probable to stop revolution.

This cablegram was received at 2:35 P.M., and at 3:40 P.M. Mr. Loomis sent the telegram which he had already prepared to both Panama and Colon. Apparently, however, the consul general at Panama had not received the information embodied in the Associated Press bulletin, upon which the assistant secretary of state based his dispatch; for his answer was that there was no uprising, although the situation was critical, this answer being received at 8:15 P.M. Immediately afterward he sent another dispatch, which was received at 9:50 P.M., saying that the uprising had occurred, and had been successful, with no bloodshed. The Colombian gunboat *Bogota* next day began to shell the city of Panama, with the result of killing one Chinaman. The consul general was directed to notify her to stop firing. Meanwhile, on November 4, Commander Hubbard notified the department that he had landed a force to protect the lives and property of American citizens against the threats of the Colombian soldiery.

Before any step whatever had been taken by the United States troops to restore order, the commander of the newly landed Colombian troops had indulged in wanton and violent threats against American citizens, which created serious apprehension. As Commander Hubbard reported in his letter of November 5, this officer and his troops practically began war against the United States, and only the forbearance and coolness of our officers and men prevented bloodshed. The letter of Commander Hubbard is of such interest that it deserves quotation in full, and runs as follows:

> USS *Nashville, Third Rate,*
> *Colon, U. S. Colombia, November 5, 1903*

Sir:

Pending a complete report of the occurrences of the last three days in Colon, Colombia, I most respectfully invite the department's attention to those of the date of Wednesday, November 4, which amounted to practically the making of war against the United States by the officer in command of the Colombian troops in Colon. At 1 o'clock P.M. on that date I was summoned on shore by a preconcerted signal, and on landing met the United States consul, vice-consul, and Colonel Shaler, the general superintendent of the Panama Railroad. The consul informed me that he had received notice from the officer commanding the Colombian troops, Colonel Torres, through the prefect of Colon, to the effect that if the Colombian officers, Generals Tobar and Amaya, who had been seized in Panama on the evening of the third of November by the Independents and held as prisoners, were not released by 2 o'clock P.M., he, Torres, would open fire on the town of Colon and kill every United States citizen in the place, and my advice and action were requested. I advised that all the United States citizens should take refuge in the shed of the Panama Railroad Company, a stone building susceptible of being put into good state for defense, and that I would immediately land such body of men with extra arms for arming the citizens, as the complement of the ship would permit. This was agreed to, and I immediately returned on board, arriving at 1:15 P.M. The order for landing was immediately given, and at 1:30 P.M.

the boats left the ship with a party of forty-two men under the command of Lieutenant-Commander H. M. Witzel, with Midshipman J. P. Jackson as second in command. Time being pressing I gave verbal orders to Mr. Witzel to take the building above referred to, to put it into the best state of defense possible, and protect the lives of the citizens assembled there—not firing unless fired upon. The women and children took refuge on the German steamer *Marcomania* and Panama Railroad steamer *City of Washington,* both ready to haul out from dock if necessary. The *Nashville* I got under way and patrolled with her along the water front close in and ready to use either small-arm or shrapnel fire. The Colombians surrounded the building of the railroad company almost immediately after we had taken possession, and for about one and a half hours their attitude was most threatening, it being seemingly their purpose to provoke an attack. Happily our men were cool and steady, and, while the tension was very great, no shot was fired. At about 3:15 P.M. Colonel Torres came into the building for an interview and expressed himself as most friendly to Americans, claiming that the whole affair was a misapprehension and that he would like to send the alcalde of Colon to Panama to see General Tobar and have him direct the discontinuance of the show of force. A special train was furnished and safe conduct guaranteed. At about 5:30 P.M. Colonel Torres made the proposition of withdrawing his troops to Monkey Hill, if I would withdraw the *Nashville*'s force and leave the town in possession of the police until the return of the alcalde on the morning of the fifth. After an interview with the United States consul and Colonel Shaler as to the probability of good faith in the matter, I decided to accept the proposition and brought my men on board, the disparity in numbers between my force and that of the Colombians, nearly ten to one, making me desirous of avoiding a conflict so long as the object in view, the protection of American citizens, was not imperiled.

I am positive that the determined attitude of our men, their coolness and evident intention of standing their ground, had a most salutary and decisive effect on the immediate situation, and was the initial step in the ultimate abandoning of Colon by these troops and their return to Cartagena the following day. Lieutenant-Commander Witzel is entitled to much praise for his admirable work in command on the spot.

I feel that I cannot sufficiently strongly represent to the department the grossness of this outrage and the insult to our dignity, even apart from the savagery of the threat.

Very respectfully,

JOHN HUBBARD,
Commander, U.S. Navy, Commanding

The Secretary of the Navy,
Navy Department, Washington, D.C.

In his letter of November 8 Commander Hubbard sets forth the facts more in detail. . . .

This plain official account of the occurrences of November 4 shows that, instead of there having been too much prevision by the American government for the maintenance of order and the protection of life and property on the Isthmus, the orders for the movement of the American warships had been too long delayed; so long, in fact, that there were but forty-two marines and sailors available to land and protect the lives of American men and women. It was only the coolness and gallantry with which this little band of men wearing the American uniform faced ten times their number of armed foes, bent on carrying out the atrocious threat of the Colombian commander, that prevented a murderous catastrophe. At Panama, when the revolution broke out, there was no American man-of-war and no American troops or sailors. At Colon, Commander Hubbard acted with entire impartiality toward both sides, preventing any movement, whether by the Colombians or the Panamans, which would tend to produce bloodshed. On November 9 he prevented a body of the revolutionists from landing at Colon. Throughout he behaved in the most creditable manner. In the New York *Evening Post,* under date of Panama, December 8, there is an article from a special correspondent, which sets forth in detail the unbearable oppression of the Colombian government in

Panama. In this article is an interesting interview with a native Panaman, which runs in part as follows:

> We looked upon the building of the canal as a matter of life or death to us. We wanted that because it meant, with the United States in control of it, peace and prosperity for us. President Marroquin appointed an Isthmian to be governor of Panama; and we looked upon that as of happy augury. Soon we heard that the canal treaty was not likely to be approved at Bogota; next we heard that our Isthmian governor, Obaldía, who had scarcely assumed power, was to be superseded by a soldier from Bogota. . . .
> Notwithstanding all that Colombia has drained us of in the way of revenues, she did not bridge for us a single river, nor make a single roadway, nor erect a single college where our children could be educated, nor do anything at all to advance our industries. . . . Well, when the new generals came we seized them, arrested them, and the town of Panama was in joy. Not a protest was made, except the shots fired from the Colombian gunboat *Bogota,* which killed one Chinese lying in his bed. We were willing to encounter the Colombian troops at Colon and fight it out; but the commander of the United States cruiser *Nashville* forbade Superintendent Shaler to allow the railroad to transport troops for either party. That is our story.

I call especial attention to the concluding portion of this interview, which states the willingness of the Panama people to fight the Colombian troops and the refusal of Commander Hubbard to permit them to use the railroad and therefore to get into a position where the fight could take place. It thus clearly appears that the fact that there was no bloodshed on the Isthmus was directly due—and only due—to the prompt and firm enforcement by the United States of its traditional policy. During the past forty years revolutions and attempts at revolution have succeeded one another with monotonous regularity on the Isthmus, and again and again United States sailors and marines have been landed as they were landed in this instance and under similar instructions to protect the transit. One of these revolutions resulted in three years of warfare; and the aggregate of bloodshed and misery caused by them has been incalculable. The fact that in this last revolution not a life was lost, save that of the man killed by the shells of the Colombian gunboat, and no property destroyed, was due to the action which I have described. We, in effect, policed the Isthmus in the interest of its inhabitants and of our own national needs, and for the good of the entire civilized world. Failure to act as the administration acted would have meant great waste of life, great suffering, great destruction of property; all of which was avoided by the firmness and prudence with which Commander Hubbard carried out his orders and prevented either party from attacking the other. Our action was for the peace both of Colombia and of Panama. It is earnestly to be hoped that there will be no unwise conduct on our part which may encourage Colombia to embark on a war which cannot result in her regaining control of the Isthmus, but which may cause much bloodshed and suffering.

I hesitate to refer to the injurious insinuations which have been made of complicity by this government in the revolutionary movement in Panama. They are as destitute of foundation as of propriety. The only excuse for my mentioning them is the fear lest unthinking persons might mistake for acquiescence the silence of mere self-respect. I think proper to say, therefore, that no one connected with this government had any part in preparing, inciting, or encouraging the late revolution on the Isthmus of Panama, and that save from the reports of our military and naval officers, given above, no one connected with this government had any previous knowledge of the revolution except such as was accessible to any person of ordinary intelligence who read the newspapers and kept up a current acquaintance with public affairs. . . .

Long before the conclusion of the Hay-Herran Treaty the course of events had shown that a canal to connect the Atlantic and Pacific oceans must be built by the United States or not at all. Experience had demonstrated that private enterprise was utterly inadequate for the purpose; and a fixed policy, declared by the United States on many memorable occasions, and supported by the practically unanimous voice of American opinion, had rendered it morally impossible that the work should be undertaken by European powers, either singly or in combination. Such were the universally recognized conditions on which the legislation of the Congress was based, and on which the late negotiations with Colombia were begun and concluded. Nevertheless, when the well-considered agreement was rejected by Colombia and the revolution on the Isthmus ensued, one of Colombia's first acts was to invoke the intervention of the United States; nor does her invitation appear to have been confined to this government alone. By a telegram from Mr. Beaupré, our minister at Bogota, of the seventh of November last, we were informed that General Reyes would soon leave Panama invested with full powers; that he had telegraphed the president of Mexico to ask the government of the United States and all countries represented at the Pan-American Conference "to aid Colombia to preserve her integrity"; and that he had requested that the government of the United States should meanwhile "preserve the neutrality and transit of the Isthmus" and should "not recognize the new government." In another telegram from Mr. Beaupré, which was sent later in the day, this government was asked whether it would take action "to maintain Colombian right and sovereignty on the Isthmus in accordance with article 35 [of] the treaty of 1846" in case the Colombian government should be "entirely unable to suppress the secession movement there." Here was a direct solicitation to the United States to intervene for the purpose of suppressing, contrary to the treaty of 1846 as this government has uniformly construed it, a new revolt against Colombia's authority brought about by her own refusal to permit the fulfillment of the great design for which that treaty was made. It was under these circumstances that the United States, instead of using its forces to destroy those who sought to make the engagements of the treaty a reality, recognized them as the proper custodians of the sovereignty of the Isthmus.

This recognition was, in the second place, further justified by the highest considerations of our national interests and safety. In all the range of our international relations I do not hesitate to affirm that there is nothing of greater or more pressing importance than the construction of an interoceanic canal. Long acknowledged to be essential to our commercial development, it has become, as the result of the recent extension of our territorial dominion, more than ever essential to our national self-defense. . . .

In the third place, I confidently maintain that the recognition of the Republic of Panama was an act justified by the interests of collective civilization. If ever a government could be said to have received a mandate from civilization to effect an object the accomplishment of which was demanded in the interest of mankind, the United States holds that position with regard to the interoceanic canal. Since our purpose to build the canal was definitely announced, there have come from all quarters assurances of approval and encouragement, in which even Colombia herself at one time participated; and to general assurances were added specific acts and declarations. In order that no obstacle might stand in our way, Great Britain renounced important rights under the Clayton-Bulwer Treaty and agreed to its abrogation, receiving in return nothing but our honorable pledge to build the canal and protect it as an open highway. It was in view of this pledge, and of the proposed enactment by the Congress of the United States of legislation to give it immediate effect, that the Second Pan-American Conference, at the City of Mexico, on January 22, 1902, adopted the following resolution:

> The republics assembled at the International Conference of Mexico applaud the purpose of the United States government to construct an interoceanic canal, and acknowledge that this work will not only be worthy of the greatness of the American people, but also in the highest sense a work of civilization, and to the greatest degree beneficial to the development of commerce between the American states and the other countries of the world.

Among those who signed this resolution on behalf of their respective governments was General Reyes, the delegate of Colombia. Little could it have been foreseen that two years later the Colombian government, led astray by false allurements of selfish advantage, and forgetful alike of its international obligations and of the duties and responsibilities of sovereignty, would thwart the efforts of the United States to enter upon and complete a work which the nations of America, reechoing the sentiment of the nations of Europe, had pronounced to be not only "worthy of the greatness of the American people," but also "in the highest sense a work of civilization."

That our position as the mandatory of civilization has been by no means misconceived is shown by the promptitude with which the powers have, one after another, followed our lead in recognizing Panama as an independent state. Our action in recognizing the new republic has been followed by like recognition on the part of France, Germany, Denmark, Russia, Sweden, and Norway, Nicaragua, Peru, China, Cuba, Great Britain, Italy, Costa Rica, Japan, and Austria-Hungary. . . .

Instead of using our forces, as we were invited by Colombia to do, for the twofold purpose of defeating our own rights and interests and the interests of the civilized world, and of compelling the submission of the people of the Isthmus to those whom they regarded as oppressors, we shall, as in duty bound, keep the transit open and prevent its invasion. Meanwhile, the only question now before us is that of the ratification of the treaty. For it is to be remembered that a failure to ratify the treaty will not undo what has been done, will not restore Panama to Colombia, and will not alter our obligation to keep the transit open across the Isthmus, and to prevent any outside power from menacing this transit. . . .

In conclusion let me repeat that the question actually before this government is not that of the recognition of Panama as an independent republic. That is already an accomplished fact. The question, and the only question, is whether or not we shall build an Isthmian Canal. . . .

Fourth Annual Message
to Congress

December 6, 1904

To the Senate and House of Representatives: The nation continues to enjoy noteworthy prosperity. Such prosperity is of course primarily due to the high individual average of our citizenship, taken together with our great natural resources; but an important factor therein is the working of our long-continued governmental policies. The people have emphatically expressed their approval of the principles underlying these policies, and their desire that these principles be kept substantially unchanged, although of course applied in a progressive spirit to meet changing conditions.

The enlargement of scope of the functions of the national government required by our development as a nation involves, of course, increase of expense; and the period of prosperity through which the country is passing justifies expenditures for permanent improvements far greater than would be wise in hard times. Battleships and forts, public buildings, and improved waterways are investments which should be made when we have the money; but abundant revenues and a large surplus always invite extravagance, and constant care should be taken to guard against unnecessary increase of the ordinary expenses of government. The cost of doing government business should be regulated with the same rigid scrutiny as the cost of doing a private business.

In the vast and complicated mechanism of our modern civilized life the dominant note is the note of industrialism; and the relations of capital and labor, and especially of organized capital and organized labor, to each other and to the public at large come second in importance only to the intimate questions of family life. Our peculiar form of government, with its sharp division of authority between the nation and the several states, has been on the whole far more advantageous to our development than a more strongly centralized government. But it is undoubtedly responsible for much of the difficulty of meeting with adequate legislation the new problems presented by the total change in industrial conditions on this continent during the last half century. In actual practice it has proved exceedingly difficult, and in many cases impossible, to get unanimity of wise action among the various states on these subjects. From the very nature of the case this is especially true of the laws affecting the employment of capital in huge masses.

With regard to labor the problem is no less important, but it is simpler. As long as the states retain the primary control of the police power, the circumstances must be altogether extreme which require interference by the federal authorities, whether in the way of safeguarding the rights of labor or in the way of seeing that wrong is not done by unruly persons who shield themselves behind the name of labor. If there is resistance to the federal courts, interference with the mails or interstate commerce, or molestation of federal property, or if the state authorities in some crisis which they are unable to face call for help, then the federal government may interfere; but though such interference may be caused by a condition of things arising out of trouble connected with some question of labor, the interference itself simply takes the form of restoring order without regard to the questions which have caused the breach of order —for to keep order is a primary duty and in a time of disorder and violence all other questions sink into abeyance until order has been restored. In the District of Columbia and in the territories the federal law covers the entire field of government; but the labor question is only acute in populous centers of commerce, manufactures, or mining. Nevertheless, both in the enactment and in the enforcement of law the federal government within its

restricted sphere should set an example to the state governments, especially in a matter so vital as this affecting labor. I
believe that under modern industrial conditions it is often necessary, and even where not necessary it is yet often wise, that there
should be organization of labor in order better to secure the
rights of the individual wage-worker. All encouragement should
be given to any such organization, so long as it is conducted
with a due and decent regard for the rights of others. There are
in this country some labor unions which have habitually, and
other labor unions which have often, been among the most
effective agents in working for good citizenship and for uplifting
the condition of those whose welfare should be closest to our
hearts. But when any labor union seeks improper ends, or seeks
to achieve proper ends by improper means, all good citizens and
more especially all honorable public servants must oppose the
wrongdoing as resolutely as they would oppose the wrongdoing
of any great corporation. Of course any violence, brutality, or
corruption should not for one moment be tolerated. Wage-
workers have an entire right to organize and by all peaceful and
honorable means to endeavor to persuade their fellows to join
with them in organizations. They have a legal right, which,
according to circumstances, may or may not be a moral right,
to refuse to work in company with men who decline to join their
organizations. They have under no circumstances the right to
commit violence upon those, whether capitalists or wage-workers, who refuse to support their organizations, or who side with
those with whom they are at odds; for mob rule is intolerable
in any form.

The wage-workers are peculiarly entitled to the protection and
the encouragement of the law. From the very nature of their
occupation railroad men, for instance, are liable to be maimed
in doing the legitimate work of their profession, unless the
railroad companies are required by law to make ample provision for their safety. The administration has been zealous in
enforcing the existing law for this purpose. That law should be

amended and strengthened. Wherever the national government has power there should be a stringent employers'-liability law, which should apply to the government itself where the government is an employer of labor.

In my Message to the Fifty-seventh Congress, at its second session, I urged the passage of an employers'-liability law for the District of Columbia. I now renew that recommendation, and further recommend that the Congress appoint a commission to make a comprehensive study of employers' liability with the view of extending the provisions of a great and constitutional law to all employments within the scope of federal power. . . .

Much can be done by the government in labor matters merely by giving publicity to certain conditions. The Bureau of Labor has done excellent work of this kind in many different directions. I shall shortly lay before you in a special message the full report of the investigation of the Bureau of Labor into the Colorado mining strike, as this is a strike in which certain very evil forces, which are more or less at work everywhere under the conditions of modern industrialism, became startling prominent. It is greatly to be wished that the Department of Commerce and Labor, through the Labor Bureau, should compile and arrange for the Congress a list of the labor laws of the various states, and should be given the means to investigate and report to the Congress upon the labor conditions in the manufacturing and mining regions throughout the country, both as to wages, as to hours of labor, as to the labor of women and children, and as to the effect in the various labor centers of immigration from abroad. In this investigation especial attention should be paid to the conditions of child labor and child-labor legislation in the several states. Such an investigation must necessarily take into account many of the problems with which this question of child labor is connected. These problems can be actually met, in most cases, only by the states themselves; but the lack of proper legislation in one state in such a matter as child labor often renders it excessively difficult to establish protective restriction upon the work in another state having the same industries, so that the worst tends to drag down the better. For this reason, it would be well for the nation at least to endeavor to secure comprehensive information as to the conditions of labor of children in the different states. Such investigation and publication by the national government would tend toward the securing of approximately uniform legislation of the proper character among the several states.

When we come to deal with great corporations the need for the government to act directly is far greater than in the case of labor, because great corporations can become such only by engaging in interstate commerce, and interstate commerce is peculiarly the field of the general government. It is an absurdity to expect to eliminate the abuses in great corporations by state action. It is difficult to be patient with an argument that such matters should be left to the states, because more than one state pursues the policy of creating on easy terms corporations which are never operated within that state at all, but in other states whose laws they ignore. The national government alone can deal adequately with these great corporations. To try to deal with them in an intemperate, destructive, or demagogic spirit would, in all probability, mean that nothing whatever would be accomplished, and, with absolute certainty, that if anything were accomplished it would be of a harmful nature. The American people need to continue to show the very qualities that they have shown—that is, moderation, good sense, the earnest desire to avoid doing any damage, and yet the quiet determination to proceed, step by step, without halt and without hurry, in eliminating or at least in minimizing whatever of mischief or of evil there is to interstate commerce in the conduct of great corporations. They are acting in no spirit of hostility to wealth, either individual or corporate. They are not against the rich man any more than against the poor man. On the contrary, they are friendly alike toward rich man and toward poor man, provided only that each acts in a spirit of justice and decency toward his fellows. Great corporations are necessary, and only men of great and singular mental power can manage such corporations successfully, and such men must have great rewards. But these corporations should be managed with due regard to the interests of the public as a whole. Where this can be done under the present laws it must be done. Where these laws come short others should be enacted to supplement them. . . .

In pursuing the set plan to make the city of Washington an example to other American municipalities several points should be kept in mind by the legislators. In the first place, the people of this country should clearly understand that no amount of industrial prosperity, and above all no leadership in international industrial competition, can in any way atone for the sapping of the vitality of those who are usually spoken of as the working classes. The farmers, the mechanics, the skilled and unskilled laborers, the small shopkeepers make up the bulk of the population of any country; and upon their well-being, generation after generation, the well-being of the country and the race depends. Rapid development in wealth and industrial leadership is a good thing, but only if it goes hand in hand with improvement, and not deterioration, physical and moral. The overcrowding of cities and the draining of country districts are unhealthy and even dangerous symptoms in our modern life. We should not permit overcrowding in cities. In certain European cities it is provided by law that the population of towns shall not be allowed to exceed a very limited density for a given area, so that the increase in density must be continually pushed back into a broad zone around the center of the town, this zone having great avenues or parks within it. The death-rate statistics show a terrible increase in mortality, and especially in infant mortality, in overcrowded tenements. The poorest families in tenement houses live in one room, and it appears that in these one-room tenements the average death rate for a number of given cities at home and abroad is about twice what it is in a two-room tenement, four times what it is in a three-room tenement, and eight times what it is in a tenement consisting of four rooms or over. These figures vary somewhat for different cities, but they approximate in each city those given above; and in all cases the increase of mortality, and especially of infant mortality, with the decrease in the number of rooms used by the family and with the consequent overcrowding is startling. The slum exacts a heavy total of deaths from those who dwell therein; and this is the case not merely in the great crowded slums of high buildings in New York and Chicago, but in the alley slums of Washington. In Washington people cannot afford to ignore the harm that this causes. No Christian and civilized community can afford to show a happy-go-lucky lack of concern for the youth of today; for, if so, the community will have to pay a terrible penalty of financial burden and social degradation in the tomorrow. There should be severe child-labor and factory-inspection laws. It is very desirable that married women should not work in factories. The prime duty of the man is to work, to be the bread-winner; the prime duty of the woman is to be the mother, the housewife. All questions of tariff and finance sink into utter insignificance when compared with the tremendous, the vital importance of trying to shape conditions so that these two duties of the man and of the woman can be fulfilled under reasonably favorable circumstances. If a race does not have plenty of children, or if the children do not grow up, or if when they grow up they are unhealthy in body and stunted or vicious in mind, then that race is decadent, and no heaping up of wealth, no splendor of momentary material prosperity, can avail in any degree as offsets.

The Congress has the same power of legislation for the District of Columbia which the state legislatures have for the various states. The problems incident to our highly complex modern industrial civilization, with its manifold and perplexing tendencies both for good and for evil, are far less sharply accentuated in the city of Washington than in most other cities. For this very reason it is easier to deal with the various phases of these problems in Washington, and the District of Columbia

government should be a model for the other municipal governments of the nation, in all such matters as supervision of the
housing of the poor, the creation of small parks in the districts
inhabited by the poor, in laws affecting labor, in laws providing
for the taking care of the children, in truant laws, and in providing schools.

In the vital matter of taking care of children, much advantage could be gained by a careful study of what has been accomplished in such states as Illinois and Colorado by the juvenile
courts. The work of the juvenile court is really a work of
character building. It is now generally recognized that young
boys and young girls who go wrong should not be treated as
criminals, not even necessarily as needing reformation, but
rather as needing to have their characters formed, and for this
end to have them tested and developed by a system of probation.
Much admirable work has been done in many of our commonwealths by earnest men and women who have made a special
study of the needs of those classes of children which furnish the
greatest number of juvenile offenders, and therefore the greatest
number of adult offenders; and by their aid, and by profiting by
the experiences of the different states and cities in these matters,
it would be easy to provide a good code for the District of
Columbia.

Several considerations suggest the need for a systematic
investigation into and improvement of housing conditions in
Washington. The hidden residential alleys are breeding grounds
of vice and disease, and should be opened into minor streets. For
a number of years influential citizens have joined with the District commissioners in the vain endeavor to secure laws permitting the condemnation of unsanitary dwellings. The local death
rates, especially from preventable diseases, are so unduly high as
to suggest that the exceptional wholesomeness of Washington's
better sections is offset by bad conditions in her poorer neigh-
borhoods. A special Commission on Housing and Health Conditions in the national capital would not only bring about the
reformation of existing evils, but would also formulate an ap-

propriate building code to protect the city from mammoth brick tenements and other evils which threaten to develop here as they have in other cities. . . .

It is mortifying to remember that Washington has no compulsory school-attendance law and that careful inquiries indicate the habitual absence from school of some 20 percent of all children between the ages of eight and fourteen. It must be evident to all who consider the problems of neglected child life, or the benefits of compulsory education in other cities, that one of the most urgent needs of the national capital is a law requiring the school attendance of all children, this law to be enforced by attendance agents directed by the Board of Education.

Public playgrounds are necessary means for the development of wholesome citizenship in modern cities. It is important that the work inaugurated here through voluntary efforts should be taken up and extended through congressional appropriation of funds sufficient to equip and maintain numerous convenient small playgrounds upon land which can be secured without purchase or rental. It is also desirable that small vacant places be purchased and reserved as small-park playgrounds in densely settled sections of the city which now have no public open spaces and are destined soon to be built up solidly. . . .

There are certain offenders, whose criminality takes the shape of brutality and cruelty toward the weak, who need a special type of punishment. The wife-beater, for example, is inadequately punished by imprisonment; for imprisonment may often mean nothing to him, while it may cause hunger and want to the wife and children who have been the victims of his brutality. Probably some form of corporal punishment would be the most adequate way of meeting this kind of crime.

The Department of Agriculture has grown into an educational institution with a faculty of two thousand specialists making research into all the sciences of production. The Congress appropriates, directly and indirectly, six millions of dollars annually to carry on this work. It reaches every state and territory in the Union and the islands of the sea lately come under our flag. Cooperation is had with the state experiment stations, and with many other institutions and individuals. The world is carefully searched for new varieties of grains, fruits, grasses, vegetables, trees, and shrubs, suitable to various localities in our country; and marked benefit to our producers has resulted.

The activities of our age in lines of research have reached the tillers of the soil and inspired them with ambition to know more of the principles that govern the forces of nature with which they have to deal. Nearly half of the people of this country devote their energies to growing things from the soil. Until a recent date little has been done to prepare these millions for their life work. In most lines of human activity college-trained men are the leaders. The farmer had no opportunity for special training until the Congress made provision for it forty years ago. During these years progress has been made and teachers have been prepared. Over five thousand students are in attendance at our state agricultural colleges. The federal government expends ten millions of dollars annually toward this education and for research in Washington and in the several states and territories. The Department of Agriculture has given facilities for postgraduate work to five hundred young men during the last seven years, preparing them for advanced lines of work in the department and in the state institutions. . . .

It is the cardinal principle of the forest-reserve policy of this administration that the reserves are for use. Whatever interferes with the use of their resources is to be avoided by every possible means. But these resources must be used in such a way as to make them permanent.

The forest policy of the government is just now a subject of vivid public interest throughout the West and to the people of the United States in general. The forest reserves themselves are of extreme value to the present as well as to the future welfare of all the western public-land states. They powerfully affect the use and disposal of the public lands. They are of special importance because they preserve the water supply and the supply of timber for domestic purposes, and so promote settlement under the reclamation act. Indeed, they are essential to the welfare of every one of the great interests of the West.

Forest reserves are created for two principal purposes. The first is to preserve the water supply. This is their most important use. The principal users of the water thus preserved are irrigation ranchers and settlers, cities and towns to whom their municipal water supplies are of the very first importance, users and furnishers of water power, and the users of water for domestic, manufacturing, mining, and other purposes. All these are directly dependent upon the forest reserves.

The second reason for which forest reserves are created is to preserve the timber supply for various classes of wood users. Among the more important of these are settlers under the reclamation act and other acts, for whom a cheap and accessible supply of timber for domestic uses is absolutely necessary; miners and prospectors, who are in serious danger of losing their timber supply by fire or through export by lumber companies when timber lands adjacent to their mines pass into private ownership; lumbermen, transportation companies, builders, and commercial interests in general. . . .

The forest-reserve policy can be successful only when it has the full support of the people of the West. It cannot safely, and should not in any case, be imposed upon them against their will. But neither can we accept the views of those whose only interest in the forest is temporary; who are anxious to reap what they have not sown and then move away, leaving desolation behind them. On the contrary, it is everywhere and always the interest of the permanent settler and the permanent businessman, the man with a stake in the country, which must be considered and which must decide. . . .

I have repeatedly called attention to the confusion which exists in government forest matters because the work is scattered among three independent organizations. The United States is the only one of the great nations in which the forest work of the government is not concentrated under one department, in consonance with the plainest dictates of good administration and common sense. The present arrangement is bad from every point of view. Merely to mention it is to prove that it should be terminated at once. As I have repeatedly recommended, all the forest work of the government should be concentrated in the Department of Agriculture, where the larger part of that work is already done, where practically all of the trained foresters of the government are employed, where chiefly in Washington there is comprehensive first-hand knowledge of the problems of the reserves acquired on the ground, where all problems relating to growth from the soil are already gathered, and where all the sciences auxiliary to forestry are at hand for prompt and effective cooperation. . . .

The creation of a forest service in the Department of Agriculture will have for its important results:

First. A better handling of all forest work, because it will be under a single head, and because the vast and indispensable experience of the department in all matters pertaining to the forest reserves, to forestry in general, and to other forms of production from the soil, will be easily and rapidly accessible.

Second. The reserves themselves, being handled from the point of view of the man in the field, instead of the man in the office, will be more easily and more widely useful to the people of the West than has been the case hitherto.

Third. Within a comparatively short time the reserves will become self-supporting. This is important because continually and rapidly increasing appropriations will be necessary for the proper care of this exceedingly important interest of the nation, and they can and should be offset by returns from the national forests. Under similar circumstances the forest possessions of other great nations form an important source of revenue to their governments.

Every administrative officer concerned is convinced of the necessity for the proposed consolidation of forest work in the Department of Agriculture, and I myself have urged it more than once in former messages. Again I commend it to the early and favorable consideration of the Congress. The interests of the nation at large and of the West in particular have suffered greatly because of the delay. . . .

In connection with the work of the forest reserves I desire again to urge upon the Congress the importance of authorizing the president to set aside certain portions of these reserves or other public lands as game refuges for the preservation of the bison, the wapiti, and other large beasts once so abundant in our woods and mountains and on our great plains, and now tending toward extinction. Every support should be given to the authorities of the Yellowstone Park in their successful efforts at preserving the large creatures therein; and at very little expense portions of the public domain in other regions which are wholly unsuited to agricultural settlement could be similarly utilized. We owe it to future generations to keep alive the noble and beautiful creatures which by their presence add such distinctive character to the American wilderness. The limits of the Yellowstone Park should be extended southward. The Canyon of the Colorado should be made a national park; and the national park system should include the Yosemite and as many as possible of the groves of giant trees in California. . . .

The progress of the Indians toward civilization, though not rapid, is perhaps all that could be hoped for in view of the circumstances. Within the past year many tribes have shown, in a degree greater than ever before, an appreciation of the necessity of work. This changed attitude is in part due to the policy recently pursued of reducing the amount of subsistence to the Indians, and thus forcing them, through sheer necessity, to work for a livelihood. The policy, though severe, is a useful one, but it is to be exercised only with judgment and with a full understanding of the conditions which exist in each community for which it is intended. On or near the Indian reservations there is usually very little demand for labor, and if the Indians are to earn their living and when work cannot be furnished from outside (which is always preferable), then it must be furnished by the government. Practical instruction of this kind would in a few years result in the forming of habits of regular industry, which would render the Indian a producer, and would effect a great reduction in the cost of his maintenance.

It is commonly declared that the slow advance of the Indians is due to the unsatisfactory character of the men appointed to take immediate charge of them, and to some extent this is true. While the standard of the employees in the Indian Service shows great improvement over that of bygone years, and while actual corruption or flagrant dishonesty is now the rare exception, it is, nevertheless, the fact that the salaries paid Indian agents are not large enough to attract the best men to that field of work. To achieve satisfactory results the official in charge of an Indian tribe should possess the high qualifications which are required in the manager of a large business, but only in exceptional cases is it possible to secure men of such a type for these positions. Much better service, however, might be obtained from those now holding the places were it practicable to get out of them the best that is in them, and this should be done by bringing them constantly into closer touch with their superior officers. . . .

The distance which separates the agents—the workers in the field—from the Indian Office in Washington is a chief obstacle to Indian progress. Whatever shall more closely unite these two branches of the Indian Service, and shall enable them to cooperate more heartily and more effectively, will be for the increased efficiency of the work and the betterment of the race for whose improvement the Indian Bureau was established. The appointment of a field assistant to the commissioner of Indian Affairs would be certain to ensure this good end. . . .

In dealing with the questions of immigration and naturalization it is indispensable to keep certain facts ever before the minds of those who share in enacting the laws. First and foremost, let us remember that the question of being a good

American has nothing whatever to do with a man's birthplace any more than it has to do with his creed. In every generation from the time this government was founded men of foreign birth have stood in the very foremost rank of good citizenship, and that not merely in one, but in every field of American activity; while to try to draw a distinction between the man whose parents came to this country and the man whose ancestors came to it several generations back is a mere absurdity. Good Americanism is a matter of heart, of conscience, of lofty aspiration, of sound common sense, but not of birthplace or of creed. . . . No fellow citizen of ours is entitled to any peculiar regard because of the way in which he worships his Maker, or because of the birthplace of himself or his parents, nor should he be in any way discriminated against therefor. Each must stand on his worth as a man and each is entitled to be judged solely thereby.

There is no danger of having too many immigrants of the right kind. It makes no difference from what country they come. If they are sound in body and in mind, and, above all, if they are of good character, so that we can rest assured that their children and grandchildren will be worthy fellow citizens of our children and grandchildren, then we should welcome them with cordial hospitality.

But the citizenship of this country should not be debased. It is vital that we should keep high the standard of well-being among our wage-workers, and therefore we should not admit masses of men whose standards of living and whose personal customs and habits are such that they tend to lower the level of the American wage-worker; and above all we should not admit any man of an unworthy type, any man concerning whom we can say that he will himself be a bad citizen, or that his children and grandchildren will detract from instead of adding to the sum of the good citizenship of the country. Similarly we should take the greatest care about naturalization. Fraudulent naturalization, the naturalization of improper persons, is a curse to our government; and it is the affair of every honest voter, wherever born, to see that no fraudulent voting is allowed, that no fraud in connection with naturalization is permitted.

In the past year the cases of false, fraudulent, and improper naturalization of aliens coming to the attention of the executive branches of the government have increased to an alarming degree. Extensive sales of forged certificates of naturalization have been discovered, as well as many cases of naturalization secured by perjury and fraud; and in addition, instances have accumulated showing that many courts issue certificates of naturalization carelessly and upon insufficient evidence. . . .

There should be a comprehensive revision of the naturalization laws. The courts having power to naturalize should be definitely named by national authority; the testimony upon which naturalization may be conferred should be definitely prescribed; publication of impending naturalization applications should be required in advance of their hearing in court; the form and wording of all certificates issued should be uniform throughout the country, and the courts should be required to make returns to the secretary of state at stated periods of all naturalizations conferred.

Not only are the laws relating to naturalization now defective, but those relating to citizenship of the United States ought also to be made the subject of scientific inquiry with a view to probable further legislation. By what acts expatriation may be assumed to have been accomplished, how long an American citizen may reside abroad and receive the protection of our passport, whether any degree of protection should be extended to one who has made the declaration of intention to become a citizen of the United States, but has not secured naturalization, are questions of serious import, involving personal rights and often producing friction between this government and foreign governments. Yet upon these questions our laws are silent. I recommend that an examination be made into the subjects of citizenship, expatriation, and protection of Americans abroad, with a view to appropriate legislation.

The power of the government to protect the integrity of the elections of its own officials is inherent and has been recognized and affirmed by repeated declarations of the Supreme Court. There is no enemy of free government more dangerous and none so insidious as the corruption of the electorate. No one defends or excuses corruption, and it would seem to follow that none would oppose vigorous measures to eradicate it. I recommend the enactment of a law directed against bribery and corruption in federal elections. The details of such a law may be safely left to the wise discretion of the Congress, but it should go as far as under the Constitution it is possible to go, and should include severe penalties against him who gives or receives a bribe intended to influence his act or opinion as an elector; and provisions for the publication not only of the expenditures for nominations and elections of all candidates, but also of all contributions received and expenditures made by political committees. . . .

Alaska, like all our territorial acquisitions, has proved resourceful beyond the expectations of those who made the purchase. It has become the home of many hardy, industrious, and thrifty American citizens. Towns of a permanent character have been built. The extent of its wealth in minerals, timber, fisheries, and agriculture, while great, is probably not comprehended yet in any just measure by our people. We do know, however, that from a very small beginning its products have grown until they are a steady and material contribution to the wealth of the nation. Owing to the immensity of Alaska and its location in the far north, it is a difficult matter to provide many things essential to its growth and to the happiness and comfort of its people by private enterprise alone. It should, therefore, receive reasonable aid from the government. The government has already done excellent work for Alaska in laying cables and building telegraph lines. This work has been done in the most economical and efficient way by the Signal Corps of the army. . . .

Alaska should have a delegate in the Congress. Where possible, the Congress should aid in the construction of needed wagon roads. Additional lighthouses should be provided. In my judgment, it is especially important to aid in such manner as seems just and feasible in the construction of a trunk line of railway to connect the Gulf of Alaska with the Yukon River through American territory. This would be most beneficial to the development of the resources of the territory, and to the comfort and welfare of its people.

Salmon hatcheries should be established in many different streams, so as to secure the preservation of this valuable food fish. Salmon fisheries and canneries should be prohibited on certain of the rivers where the mass of those Indians dwell who live almost exclusively on fish.

The Alaskan natives are kindly, intelligent, anxious to learn, and willing to work. Those who have come under the influence of civilization, even for a limited period, have proved their capability of becoming self-supporting, self-respecting citizens, and ask only for the just enforcement of law and intelligent instruction and supervision. Others, living in more remote regions, primitive, simple hunters and fisher folk, who know only the life of the woods and the waters, are daily being confronted with twentieth-century civilization with all of its complexities. Their country is being overrun by strangers, the game slaughtered and driven away, the streams depleted of fish, and hitherto unknown and fatal diseases brought to them, all of which combine to produce a state of abject poverty and want which must result in their extinction. Action in their interest is demanded by every consideration of justice and humanity.

The needs of these people are:

The abolition of the present fee system, whereby the native is degraded, imposed upon, and taught the injustice of law.

The establishment of hospitals at central points, so that contagious diseases that are brought to them continually by incoming whites may be localized and not allowed to become epidemic, to spread death and destitution over great areas.

The development of the educational system in the form of

practical training in such industries as will assure the Indians self-support under the changed conditions in which they will have to live.

The duties of the office of the governor should be extended to include the supervision of Indian affairs, with necessary assistants in different districts. He should be provided with the means and the power to protect and advise the native people, to furnish medical treatment in time of epidemics, and to extend material relief in periods of famine and extreme destitution. . . .

The steady aim of this nation, as of all enlightened nations, should be to strive to bring ever nearer the day when there shall prevail throughout the world the peace of justice. There are kinds of peace which are highly undesirable, which are in the long run as destructive as any war. Tyrants and oppressors have many times made a wilderness and called it peace. Many times peoples who were slothful or timid or shortsighted, who have been enervated by ease or by luxury, or misled by false teachings, have shrunk in unmanly fashion from doing duty that was stern and that needed self-sacrifice, and have sought to hide from their own minds their shortcomings, their ignoble motives, by calling them love of peace. The peace of tyrannous terror, the peace of craven weakness, the peace of injustice, all these should be shunned as we shun unrighteous war. The goal to set before us as a nation, the goal which should be set before all mankind, is the attainment of the peace of justice, of the peace which comes when each nation is not merely safeguarded in its own rights, but scrupulously recognizes and performs its duty toward others. Generally peace tells for righteousness; but if there is conflict between the two, then our fealty is due first to the cause of righteousness. Unrighteous wars are common, and unrighteous peace is rare; but both should be shunned. The right of freedom and the responsibility for the exercise of that right cannot be divorced. . . .

If these self-evident truths are kept before us, and only if they are so kept before us, we shall have a clear idea of what our foreign policy in its larger aspects should be. It is our duty to remember that a nation has no more right to do injustice to another nation, strong or weak, than an individual has to do injustice to another individual; that the same moral law applies in one case as in the other. But we must also remember that it is as much the duty of the nation to guard its own rights and its own interests as it is the duty of the individual so to do. . . . There is as yet no judicial way of enforcing a right in international law. When one nation wrongs another, or wrongs many others, there is no tribunal before which the wrongdoer can be brought. Either it is necessary supinely to acquiesce in the wrong, and thus put a premium upon brutality and aggression, or else it is necessary for the aggrieved nation valiantly to stand up for its rights. Until some method is devised by which there shall be a degree of international control over offending nations, it would be a wicked thing for the most civilized powers, for those with most sense of international obligations and with keenest and most generous appreciation of the difference between right and wrong, to disarm. If the great civilized nations of the present day should completely disarm, the result would mean an immediate recrudescence of barbarism in one form or another. Under any circumstances a sufficient armament would have to be kept up to serve the purposes of international police; and until international cohesion and the sense of international duties and rights are far more advanced than at present, a nation desirous both of securing respect for itself and of doing good to others must have a force adequate for the work which it feels is allotted to it as its part of the general world duty. Therefore it follows that a self-respecting, just, and far-seeing nation should on the one hand endeavor by every means to aid in the development of the various movements which tend to provide substitutes for war, which tend to render nations in their actions toward one another, and indeed toward their own peoples, more responsive to the general sentiment of humane and civilized mankind; and on the other hand it should keep prepared, while scrupulously avoiding wrongdoing itself, to repel any wrong, and in exceptional cases to take action which in a more advanced stage of international relations would come under the head of the exercise of the international police. A great free people owes it to itself and to all mankind not to sink into helplessness before the powers of evil.

We are in every way endeavoring to help on, with cordial good-will, every movement which will tend to bring us into more friendly relations with the rest of mankind. In pursuance of this policy I shall shortly lay before the Senate treaties of arbitration with all powers which are willing to enter into these treaties with us. It is not possible at this period of the world's development to agree to arbitrate all matters, but there are many matters of possible difference between us and other nations which can be thus arbitrated. Furthermore, at the request of the Interparliamentary Union, an eminent body composed of practical statesmen from all countries, I have asked the Powers to join with this government in a second Hague conference, at which it is hoped that the work already so happily begun at The Hague may be carried some steps further toward completion. This carries out the desire expressed by the first Hague conference itself.

It is not true that the United States feels any land hunger or entertains any projects as regards the other nations of the Western Hemisphere save such as are for their welfare. All that this country desires is to see the neighboring countries stable, orderly, and prosperous. Any country whose people conduct themselves well can count upon our hearty friendship. If a nation shows that it knows how to act with reasonable efficiency and decency in social and political matters, if it keeps order and pays its obligations, it need fear no interference from the United States. Chronic wrongdoing, or an impotence which results in a general loosening of the ties of civilized society, may in America, as elsewhere, ultimately require intervention by some civilized nation, and in the Western Hemisphere the adherence of the United States to the Monroe Doctrine may force the United States, however reluctantly, in flagrant cases of such wrongdoing or impotence, to the exercise of an international police power. If every country washed by the Caribbean Sea would show the progress in stable and just civilization which with the aid of the Platt Amendment Cuba has shown since our troops left the island, and which so many of the republics in both Americas are constantly and brilliantly showing, all question of interference by this nation with their affairs would be at an end. . . .

In asserting the Monroe Doctrine, in taking such steps as we have taken in regard to Cuba, Venezuela, and Panama, and in endeavoring to circumscribe the theater of war in the Far East, and to secure the open door in China, we have acted in our own interest as well as in the interest of humanity at large. There are, however, cases in which, while our own interests are not greatly involved, strong appeal is made to our sympathies. Ordinarily it is very much wiser and more useful for us to concern ourselves with striving for our own moral and material betterment here at home than to concern ourselves with trying to better the condition of things in other nations. We have plenty of sins of our own to war against, and under ordinary circumstances we can do more for the general uplifting of humanity by striving with heart and soul to put a stop to civic corruption, to brutal lawlessness and violent race prejudices here at home than by passing resolutions about wrongdoing elsewhere. Nevertheless there are occasional crimes committed on so vast a scale and of such peculiar horror as to make us doubt whether it is not our manifest duty to endeavor at least to show our disapproval of the deed and our sympathy with those who have suffered by it. The cases must be extreme in which such a course is justifiable. There must be no effort made to remove the mote from our brother's eye if we refuse to remove the beam from our own. But in extreme cases action may be justifiable and proper. What form the action shall take must depend upon the circumstances of the case; that is, upon the degree of the atrocity and upon our power to remedy it. The cases in which we could interfere by force of arms as we interfered to put a stop to intolerable conditions in Cuba are necessarily very few. Yet it is not to be expected that a people like ours, which in spite of certain very obvious shortcomings, nevertheless as a whole shows by its consistent practice its belief in the principles of civil and religious liberty and of orderly freedom, a people among whom even the worst crime, like the crime of lynching, is never more than sporadic, so that individuals and not classes are molested in their fundamental rights—it is inevitable that such a nation should desire eagerly to give expression to its horror on an occasion like that of the massacre of the Jews in Kishineff, or when it witnesses such systematic and long-extended cruelty and oppression as the cruelty and oppression of which the Armenians have been the victims, and which have won for them the indignant pity of the civilized world.

Even where it is not possible to secure in other nations the observance of the principles which we accept as axiomatic, it is necessary for us firmly to insist upon the rights of our own citizens without regard to their creed or race; without regard to whether they were born here or born abroad. It has proved very difficult to secure from Russia the right for our Jewish fellow citizens to receive passports and travel through Russian territory. Such conduct is not only unjust and irritating toward us, but it is difficult to see its wisdom from Russia's standpoint. No conceivable good is accomplished by it. If an American Jew or an American Christian misbehaves himself in Russia he can at once be driven out; but the ordinary American Jew, like the ordinary American Christian, would behave just about as he behaves here, that is, behave as any good citizen ought to behave; and where this is the case it is a wrong against which we are entitled to protest to refuse him his passport without regard to his conduct and character, merely on racial and religious grounds. In Turkey our difficulties arise less from the way in which our citizens are sometimes treated than from the indignation inevitably excited in seeing such fearful misrule as has been witnessed both in Armenia and Macedonia.

The strong arm of the government in enforcing respect for its just rights in international matters is the Navy of the United States. I most earnestly recommend that there be no halt in the work of upbuilding the American navy. There is no more patriotic duty before us as a people than to keep the navy adequate to the needs of this country's position. We have undertaken to build the Isthmian Canal. We have undertaken to secure for ourselves our just share in the trade of the Orient. We have undertaken to protect our citizens from improper treatment in foreign lands. We continue steadily to insist on the application of the Monroe Doctrine to the Western Hemisphere. Unless our attitude in these and all similar matters is to be a mere boastful sham we cannot afford to abandon our naval program. Our voice is now potent for peace, and is so potent because we are not afraid of war. But our protestations upon behalf of peace would neither receive nor deserve the slightest attention if we were impotent to make them good.

The war which now unfortunately rages in the Far East has emphasized in striking fashion the new possibilities of naval warfare. The lessons taught are both strategic and tactical, and are political as well as military. The experiences of the war have shown in conclusive fashion that while seagoing and sea-keeping torpedo-destroyers are indispensable, and fast lightly armed and armored cruisers very useful, yet that the main reliance, the main standby, in any navy worthy the name must be the great battleships, heavily armored and heavily gunned. Not a Russian or Japanese battleship has been sunk by a torpedo-boat, or by gunfire, while among the less protected ships, cruiser after cruiser has been destroyed whenever the hostile squadrons have gotten within range of one another's weapons. There will always be a large field of usefulness for cruisers, especially of the more formidable type. We need to increase the number of torpedo-boat destroyers, paying less heed to their having a knot or two extra speed than to their capacity to keep the seas for weeks and, if necessary, for months at a time. It is wise to build submarine torpedo-boats, as under certain circumstances they might be very useful. But most of all we need to continue building our fleet of battleships, or ships so powerfully armed that they can inflict the maximum of damage upon our opponents, and so well protected that they can suffer a severe hammering in return without fatal impairment of their ability to fight and maneuver. Of course ample means must be provided for enabling the personnel of the navy to be brought to the highest point of efficiency. Our great fighting ships and torpedo-boats must be ceaselessly trained and maneuvered in squadrons. The officers and men can only learn their trade thoroughly by ceaseless practice on the high seas. In the event of war it would be far better to have no ships at all than to have ships of a poor and ineffective type, or ships which, however good, were yet manned by untrained and unskillful crews. The best officers and men in a poor ship could do nothing against fairly good opponents; and, on the other hand, a modern warship is useless unless the officers and men aboard her have become adepts in their duties. The marksmanship in our navy has improved in an extraordinary degree during the last three years, and on the whole the types of our battleships are improving; but much remains to be done. Sooner or later we shall have to provide for some method by which there will be promotions for merit as well as for seniority, or else retirement of all those who after a certain age have not advanced beyond a certain grade; while no effort must be spared to make the service attractive to the enlisted men in order that they may be kept as long as possible in it. Reservation public schools should be provided wherever there are navy yards.

Within the last three years the United States has set an example in disarmament where disarmament was proper. By law our army is fixed at a maximum of one hundred thousand and a minimum of sixty thousand men. When there was insurrection in the Philippines we kept the army at the maximum. Peace came in the Philippines, and now our army has been reduced to the minimum at which it is possible to keep it with due regard to its efficiency. The guns now mounted require twenty-eight thousand men, if the coast fortifications are to be adequately manned. Relatively to the nation, it is not now so large as the police force of New York or Chicago, relatively to the population of either city. We need more officers; there are not enough to perform the regular army work. It is very important that the officers of the army should be accustomed to handle their men in masses, as it is also important that the National Guard of the several states should be accustomed to actual field maneuvering, especially in connection with the regulars. For this reason we are to be congratulated upon the success of the field maneuvers at Manassas last fall, maneuvers in which a larger number of regulars and National Guard took part than was ever before assembled together in time of peace. No other civilized nation has, relatively to its population, such a diminutive army as ours; and while the army is so small we are not to be excused if we fail to keep it at a very high grade of proficiency. It must be incessantly practiced; the standard for the enlisted men should be kept very high, while at the same time the service should be made as attractive as possible; and the standard for the officers should be kept even higher—which, as regards the upper ranks, can best be done by introducing some system of selection and rejection into the promotions. We should be able, in the event of some sudden emergency, to put into the field one first-class army corps, which should be, as a whole, at least the equal of any body of troops of like number belonging to any other nation. . . .

In the Philippine Islands there has been during the past year a continuation of the steady progress which has obtained ever since our troops definitely got the upper hand of the insurgents. The Philippine people, or, to speak more accurately, the many tribes, and even races, sundered from one another more or less sharply, who go to make up the people of the Philippine Islands, contain many elements of good, and some elements which we have a right to hope stand for progress. At present they are utterly incapable of existing in independence at all or of building up a civilization of their own. I firmly believe that we can help them to rise higher and higher in the scale of civilization and of capacity for self-government, and I most earnestly hope that in the end they will be able to stand, if not entirely alone, yet in some such relation to the United States as Cuba now stands. This end is not yet in sight, and it may be indefinitely postponed if our people are foolish enough to turn the attention of the Filipinos away from the problems of achieving moral and material prosperity, of working for a stable, orderly, and just government, and toward foolish and dangerous intrigues for a complete independence for which they are as yet totally unfit.

On the other hand, our people must keep steadily before their minds the fact that the justification for our stay in the Philippines must ultimately rest chiefly upon the good we are able to do in the islands. I do not overlook the fact that in the development of our interests in the Pacific Ocean and along its coasts, the Philippines have played and will play an important part, and that our interests have been served in more than one way by the possession of the islands. But our chief reason for continuing to hold them must be that we ought in good faith to try to do our share of the world's work, and this particular piece of work has been imposed upon us by the results of the war with Spain. . . . Within two years we shall be trying the experiment of an elective lower house in the Philippine legislature. It may be that the Filipinos will misuse this legislature, and they certainly will misuse it if they are misled by foolish persons here at home into starting an agitation for their own independence or into any factious or improper action. In such case they will do themselves no good, and will stop for the time being all further effort to advance them and give them a greater share in their own government. But if they act with wisdom and self-restraint, if they show that they are capable of electing a legislature which in its turn is capable of taking a sane and efficient part in the actual work of government, they can rest assured that a full and increasing measure of recognition will be given them. . . .

Meanwhile our own people should remember that there is need for the highest standard of conduct among the Americans sent to the Philippine Islands, not only among the public servants, but among the private individuals who go to them. It is because I feel this so deeply that in the administration of these islands I have positively refused to permit any discrimination whatsoever for political reasons, and have insisted that in choosing the public servants consideration should be paid solely to the worth of the men chosen and to the needs of the islands. . . . Unfortunately hitherto those of our people here at home who have specially claimed to be the champions of the Filipinos have in reality been their worst enemies. This will continue to be the case as long as they strive to make the Filipinos independent, and stop all industrial development of the islands by crying out against the laws which would bring it on the ground that capitalists must not "exploit" the islands. Such proceedings are not only unwise, but are most harmful to the Filipinos, who do not need independence at all, but who do need good laws, good public servants, and the industrial development that can only come if the investment of American and foreign capital in the islands is favored in all legitimate ways.

Every measure taken concerning the islands should be taken primarily with a view to their advantage. We should certainly give them lower tariff rates on their exports to the United States; if this is not done it will be a wrong to extend our shipping laws to them. I earnestly hope for the immediate enactment into law of the legislation now pending to encourage American capital to seek investment in the islands in railroads, in factories, in plantations, and in lumbering and mining.

Inaugural Address

March 4, 1905

My Fellow Citizens: No people on earth have more cause to be thankful than ours, and this is said reverently, in no spirit of boastfulness in our own strength, but with gratitude to the Giver of Good, who has blessed us with the conditions which have enabled us to achieve so large a measure of well-being and of happiness. To us as a people it has been granted to lay the foundations of our national life in a new continent. We are the heirs of the ages, and yet we have had to pay few of the penalties which in old countries are exacted by the dead hand of a bygone civilization. We have not been obliged to fight for our existence against any alien race; and yet our life has called for the vigor and effort without which the manlier and hardier virtues wither away. Under such conditions it would be our own fault if we failed; and the success which we have had in the past, the success which we confidently believe the future will bring, should cause in us no feeling of vainglory, but rather a deep and abiding realization of all which life has offered us; a full acknowledgment of the responsibility which is ours; and a fixed determination to show that under a free government a mighty people can thrive best, alike as regards the things of the body and the things of the soul.

Much has been given to us, and much will rightfully be expected from us. We have duties to others and duties to ourselves; and we can shirk neither. We have become a great nation, forced by the fact of its greatness into relations with the other nations of the earth; and we must behave as beseems a people with such responsibilities. Toward all other nations, large and small, our attitude must be one of cordial and sincere friendship. We must show not only in our words but in our deeds that we are earnestly desirous of securing their goodwill by acting toward them in a spirit of just and generous recognition of all their rights. But justice and generosity in a nation, as in an individual, count most when shown not by the weak but by the strong. While ever careful to refrain from wronging others, we must be no less insistent that we are not wronged ourselves. We wish peace; but we wish the peace of justice, the peace of righteousness. We wish it because we think it is right and not because we are afraid. No weak nation that acts manfully and justly should ever have cause to fear us, and no strong power should ever be able to single us out as a subject for insolent aggression.

Our relations with the other powers of the world are important; but still more important are our relations among ourselves. Such growth in wealth, in population, and in power as this nation has seen during the century and a quarter of its national life is inevitably accompanied by a like growth in the problems which are ever before every nation that rises to greatness. Power invariably means both responsibility and danger. Our forefathers faced certain perils which we have outgrown. We now face other perils the very existence of which it was impossible that they should foresee. Modern life is both complex and intense, and the tremendous changes wrought by the extraordinary industrial development of the last half century are felt in every fiber of our social and political being. Never before have men tried so vast and formidable an experiment as that of administering the affairs of a continent under the forms of a democratic republic. The conditions which have told for our marvelous material well-being, which have developed to a very high degree our energy, self-reliance, and individual initiative, have also brought the care and anxiety inseparable from the accumulation of great wealth in industrial centers. Upon the success of our experiment much depends; not only as regards our own welfare, but as regards the welfare of mankind. If we fail, the cause of free self-government throughout the world will rock to its foundations; and therefore our responsibility is heavy, to ourselves, to the world as it is today, and to the generations yet unborn.

There is no good reason why we should fear the future, but there is every reason why we should face it seriously, neither hiding from ourselves the gravity of the problems before us nor fearing to approach these problems with the unbending, un-flinching purpose to solve them aright.

Yet, after all, though the problems are new, though the tasks set before us differ from the tasks set before our fathers who founded and preserved this Republic, the spirit in which these tasks must be undertaken and these problems faced, if our duty is to be well done, remains essentially unchanged. We know that self-government is difficult. We know that no people needs such high traits of character as that people which seeks to govern its affairs aright through the freely expressed will of the freemen who compose it. But we have faith that we shall not prove false to the memories of the men of the mighty past. They did their work; they left us the splendid heritage we now enjoy. We in our turn have an assured confidence that we shall be able to leave this heritage unwasted and enlarged to our children and our children's children. To do so we must show, not merely in great crises, but in the everyday affairs of life, the qualities of practical intelligence, of courage, of hardihood and endurance, and above all the power of devotion to a lofty ideal, which made great the men who founded this Republic in the days of Washington, which made great the men who preserved this Republic in the days of Abraham Lincoln.

Speech at the
Office Building of the
House of Representatives

April 14, 1906

The Man with the Muck-Rake*

Over a century ago Washington laid the cornerstone of the Capitol in what was then little more than a tract of wooded wilderness here beside the Potomac. We now find it necessary to provide by great additional buildings for the business of the government. This growth in the need for the housing of the government is but a proof and example of the way in which the nation has grown and the sphere of action of the national government has grown. We now administer the affairs of a nation in which the extraordinary growth of population has been outstripped by the growth of wealth and the growth in complex interests. The material problems that face us today are not such as they were in Washington's time, but the underlying facts of human nature are the same now as they were then. Under altered external form we war with the same tendencies toward evil that were evident in Washington's time, and are helped by the same tendencies for good. It is about some of these that I wish to say a word today.

In Bunyan's *Pilgrim's Progress* you may recall the description of the Man with the Muck-Rake, the man who could look no way but downward, with the muck-rake in his hand; who was offered a celestial crown for his muck-rake, but who would neither look up nor regard the crown he was offered, but continued to rake to himself the filth of the floor.

*Published in the *Outlook,* April 21, 1906, and *Putnam's,* October 1906.

186

In *Pilgrim's Progress* the Man with the Muck-Rake is set forth as the example of him whose vision is fixed on carnal instead of on spiritual things. Yet he also typifies the man who in this life consistently refuses to see aught that is lofty, and fixes his eyes with solemn intentness only on that which is vile and debasing. Now, it is very necessary that we should not flinch from seeing what is vile and debasing. There is filth on the floor, and it must be scraped up with the muck-rake; and there are times and places where this service is the most needed of all the services that can be performed. But the man who never does anything else, who never thinks or speaks or writes, save of his feats with the muck-rake, speedily becomes, not a help to society, not an incitement to good, but one of the most potent forces for evil.

There are, in the body politic, economic and social, many and grave evils, and there is urgent necessity for the sternest war upon them. There should be relentless exposure of and attack upon every evil man whether politician or businessman, every evil practice, whether in politics, in business, or in social life. I hail as a benefactor every writer or speaker, every man who, on the platform, or in book, magazine, or newspaper, with merciless severity makes such attack, provided always that he in his turn remembers that the attack is of use only if it is absolutely truthful. The liar is no whit better than the thief, and if his mendacity takes the form of slander, he may be worse than most thieves. It puts a premium upon knavery untruthfully to attack an honest man, or even with hysterical exaggeration to assail a bad man with untruth. An epidemic of indiscriminate assault upon character does not good, but very great harm. The soul of every scoundrel is gladdened whenever an honest man is assailed, or even when a scoundrel is untruthfully assailed.

Now, it is easy to twist out of shape what I have just said, easy to affect to misunderstand it, and, if it is slurred over in repetition, not difficult really to misunderstand it. Some persons are sincerely incapable of understanding that to denounce mudslinging does not mean the indorsement of whitewashing; and both the interested individuals who need whitewashing, and those others who practice mudslinging, like to encourage such confusion of ideas. One of the chief counts against those who make indiscriminate assault upon men in business or men in public life is that they invite a reaction which is sure to tell powerfully in favor of the unscrupulous scoundrel who really ought to be attacked, who ought to be exposed, who ought, if possible, to be put in the penitentiary. If Aristides is praised overmuch as just, people get tired of hearing it; and overcensure of the unjust finally and from similar reasons results in their favor.

Any excess is almost sure to invite a reaction; and, unfortunately, the reaction, instead of taking the form of punishment of those guilty of the excess, is very apt to take the form either of punishment of the unoffending or of giving immunity, and even strength, to offenders. The effort to make financial or political profit out of the destruction of character can only result in public calamity. Gross and reckless assaults on character, whether on the stump or in newspaper, magazine, or book, create a morbid and vicious public sentiment, and at the same time act as a profound deterrent to able men of normal sensitiveness and tend to prevent them from entering the public service at any price. As an instance in point, I may mention that one serious difficulty encountered in getting the right type of men to dig the Panama Canal is the certainty that they will be exposed, both without, and, I am sorry to say, sometimes within, Congress, to utterly reckless assaults on their character and capacity.

At the risk of repetition let me say again that my plea is not for immunity to, but for the most unsparing exposure of, the politician who betrays his trust, of the big-businessman who makes or spends his fortune in illegitimate or corrupt ways. There should be a resolute effort to hunt every such man out of the position he has disgraced. Expose the crime, and hunt down the criminal; but remember that even in the case of crime, if it is attacked in sensational, lurid, and untruthful fashion, the attack may do more damage to the public mind than the crime itself. It is because I feel that there should be no rest in the endless war against the forces of evil that I ask that the war be conducted with sanity as well as with resolution. The men with the muck-rakes are often indispensable to the well-being of society; but only if they know when to stop raking the muck, and to look upward to the celestial crown above them, to the crown of worthy endeavor. There are beautiful things above and round about them; and if they gradually grow to feel that the whole world is nothing but muck, their power of usefulness is gone. If the whole picture is painted black there remains no hue whereby to single out the rascals for distinction from their fellows. Such painting finally induces a kind of moral color-blindness; and people affected by it come to the conclusion that no man is really black, and no man really white, but they are all gray. In other words, they neither believe in the truth of the attack, nor in the honesty of the man who is attacked; they grow as suspicious of the accusation as of the offense; it becomes wellnigh hopeless to stir them either to wrath against wrong-doing or to enthusiasm for what is right; and such a mental attitude in the public gives hope to every knave, and is the despair of honest men.

To assail the great and admitted evils of our political and industrial life with such crude and sweeping generalizations as to include decent men in the general condemnation means the searing of the public conscience. There results a general attitude either of cynical belief in and indifference to public corruption or else of a distrustful inability to discriminate between the good and the bad. Either attitude is fraught with untold damage to the country as a whole. The fool who has not sense to discriminate between what is good and what is bad is wellnigh as dangerous as the man who does discriminate and yet chooses the bad. There is nothing more distressing to every good patriot, to every good American, than the hard, scoffing spirit which treats the allegation of dishonesty in a public man as a cause for laughter. Such laughter is worse than the crackling of thorns under a pot, for it denotes not merely the vacant mind but the heart in which high emotions have been choked before they could grow to fruition.

There is any amount of good in the world, and there never was a time when loftier and more disinterested work for the betterment of mankind was being done than now. The forces that tend for evil are great and terrible, but the forces of truth and love and courage and honesty and generosity and sympathy are also stronger than ever before. It is a foolish and timid, no less than a wicked, thing to blink the fact that the forces of evil are strong, but it is even worse to fail to take into account the strength of the forces that tell for good. Hysterical sensationalism is the very poorest weapon wherewith to fight for lasting righteousness. The men who with stern sobriety and truth assail the many evils of our time, whether in the public press, or in magazines, or in books, are the leaders and allies of all engaged in the work for social and political betterment. But if they give good reason for distrust of what they say, if they chill the ardor of those who demand truth as a primary virtue, they thereby betray the good cause, and play into the hands of the very men against whom they are nominally at war.

In his *Ecclesiastical Polity,* that fine old Elizabethan divine, Bishop Hooker, wrote: "He that goeth about to persuade a multitude that they are not so well governed as they ought to be shall never want attentive and favorable hearers; because they know the manifold defects whereunto every kind of regimen is subject, but the secret lets and difficulties, which in public proceedings are innumerable and inevitable, they have not ordinarily the judgment to consider."

This truth should be kept constantly in mind by every free people desiring to preserve the sanity and poise indispensable to the permanent success of self-government. Yet, on the other hand, it is vital not to permit this spirit of sanity and self-command to degenerate into mere mental stagnation. Bad though a state of hysterical excitement is, and evil though the results are which come from the violent oscillations such excitement invariably produces, yet a sodden acquiescence in evil is even worse. At this moment we are passing through a period of great unrest—social, political, and industrial unrest. It is of the utmost importance for our future that this should prove to be not the unrest of mere rebelliousness against life, of mere dissatisfaction with the inevitable inequality of conditions, but the unrest of a resolute and eager ambition to secure the betterment of the individual and the nation. So far as this movement of agitation throughout the country takes the form of a fierce discontent with evil, of a determination to punish the authors of evil, whether in industry or politics, the feeling is to be heartily welcomed as a sign of healthy life.

If, on the other hand, it turns into a mere crusade of appetite against appetite, of a contest between the brutal greed of the "have-nots" and the brutal greed of the "haves," then it has no significance for good, but only for evil. If it seeks to establish a line of cleavage, not along the line which divides good men from bad, but along that other line, running at right angles thereto, which divides those who are well off from those who are less well off, then it will be fraught with immeasurable harm to the body politic.

We can no more and no less afford to condone evil in the man of capital than evil in the man of no capital. The wealthy man who exults because there is a failure of justice in the effort to bring some trust magnate to an account for his misdeeds is as bad as, and no worse than, the so-called labor leader who clamorously strives to excite a foul class feeling on behalf of some other labor leader who is implicated in murder. One attitude is as bad as the other, and no worse; in each case the accused is entitled to exact justice; and in neither case is there need of action by others which can be construed into an expression of sympathy for crime.

It is a prime necessity that if the present unrest is to result in permanent good the emotion shall be translated into action, and that the action shall be marked by honesty, sanity, and self-restraint. There is mighty little good in a mere spasm of reform. The reform that counts is that which comes through steady, continuous growth; violent emotionalism leads to exhaustion.

It is important to this people to grapple with the problems connected with the amassing of enormous fortunes, and the use of those fortunes, both corporate and individual, in business. We should discriminate in the sharpest way between fortunes well-won and fortunes ill-won; between those gained as an incident to performing great services to the community as a whole, and those gained in evil fashion by keeping just within the limits of mere law-honesty. Of course no amount of charity in spending such fortunes in any way compensates for misconduct in making them. As a matter of personal conviction, and without pretending to discuss the details or formulate the system, I feel that we shall ultimately have to consider the adoption of some such scheme as that of a progressive tax on all fortunes, beyond a certain amount, either given in life or devised or bequeathed upon death to any individual—a tax so framed as to put it out of the power of the owner of one of these enormous fortunes to hand on more than a certain amount to any one individual; the tax, of course, to be imposed by the national and not the state government. Such taxation should, of course, be aimed merely at the inheritance or transmission in their entirety of those fortunes swollen beyond all healthy limits.

Again, the national government must in some form exercise supervision over corporations engaged in interstate business—and all large corporations are engaged in interstate business—whether by license or otherwise, so as to permit us to deal with the far-reaching evils of overcapitalization. This year we are making a beginning in the direction of serious effort to settle some of these economic problems by the railway-rate legislation. Such legislation, if so framed, as I am sure it will be, as to secure definite and tangible results, will amount to something of itself; and it will amount to a great deal more insofar as it is taken as a first step in the direction of a policy of superintendence and control over corporate wealth engaged in interstate commerce, this superintendence and control not to be exercised in a spirit of malevolence toward the men who have created the wealth, but with the firm purpose both to do justice to them and to see that they in their turn do justice to the public at large.

The first requisite in the public servants who are to deal in this shape with corporations, whether as legislators or as executives, is honesty. This honesty can be no respecter of persons. There can be no such thing as unilateral honesty. The danger is not really from corrupt corporations; it springs from the corruption itself, whether exercised for or against corporations.

The eighth commandment reads, "Thou shalt not steal." It does not read, "Thou shalt not steal from the rich man." It does not read, "Thou shalt not steal from the poor man." It reads simply and plainly, "Thou shalt not steal." No good whatever will come from that warped and mock morality which denounces the misdeeds of men of wealth and forgets the misdeeds practiced at their expense; which denounces bribery, but blinds itself to blackmail; which foams with rage if a corporation secures favors by improper methods, and merely leers with hideous mirth if the corporation is itself wronged. The only public servant who can be trusted honestly to protect the rights of the public against the misdeed of a corporation is that public man who will just as surely protect the corporation itself from wrongful aggression. If a public man is willing to yield to popular clamor and do wrong to the men of wealth or to rich corporations, it may be set down as certain that if the opportunity comes he will secretly and furtively do wrong to the public in the interest of a corporation.

But, in addition to honesty, we need sanity. No honesty will make a public man useful if that man is timid or foolish, if he is a hot-headed zealot or an impracticable visionary. As we strive for reform we find that it is not at all merely the case of a long uphill pull. On the contrary, there is almost as much of breeching work as of collar work; to depend only on traces means that there will soon be a runaway and an upset. The men of wealth who today are trying to prevent the regulation and control of their business in the interest of the public by the proper government authorities will not succeed, in my judgment, in checking the progress of the movement. But if they did succeed they would find that they had sown the wind and would surely reap the whirlwind, for they would ultimately provoke the violent excesses which accompany a reform coming by convulsion instead of by steady and natural growth.

On the other hand, the wild preachers of unrest and discontent, the wild agitators against the entire existing order, the men who act crookedly, whether because of sinister design or from mere puzzleheadedness, the men who preach destruction without proposing any substitute for what they intend to destroy, or who propose a substitute which would be far worse than the existing evils—all these men are the most dangerous opponents of real reform. If they get their way they will lead the people into a deeper pit than any into which they could fall under the present system. If they fail to get their way they will still do incalculable harm by provoking the kind of reaction which, in its revolt against the senseless evil of their teaching, would enthrone more securely than ever the very evils which their misguided followers believe they are attacking.

More important than aught else is the development of the broadest sympathy of man for man. The welfare of the wageworker, the welfare of the tiller of the soil, upon these depend the welfare of the entire country; their good is not to be sought in pulling down others; but their good must be the prime object of all our statesmanship.

Materially we must strive to secure a broader economic opportunity for all men, so that each shall have a better chance to show the stuff of which he is made. Spiritually and ethically we must strive to bring about clean living and right thinking. We appreciate that the things of the body are important; but we appreciate also that the things of the soul are immeasurably more important. The foundation stone of national life is, and ever must be, the high individual character of the average citizen.

Sixth Annual Message to Congress

December 3, 1906

To the Senate and House of Representatives: As a nation we still continue to enjoy a literally unprecedented prosperity; and it is probable that only reckless speculation and disregard of legitimate business methods on the part of the business world can materially mar this prosperity.

No Congress in our time has done more good work of importance than the present Congress. There were several matters left unfinished at your last session, however, which I most earnestly hope you will complete before your adjournment.

I again recommend a law prohibiting all corporations from contributing to the campaign expenses of any party. Such a bill has already passed one house of Congress. Let individuals contribute as they desire; but let us prohibit in effective fashion all corporations from making contributions for any political purpose, directly or indirectly.

Another bill which has just passed one house of the Congress and which it is urgently necessary should be enacted into law is that conferring upon the government the right of appeal in criminal cases on questions of law. . . . I cannot too strongly urge the passage of the bill in question. A failure to pass it will result in seriously hampering the government in its effort to obtain justice, especially against wealthy individuals or corporations who do wrong; and may also prevent the government from obtaining justice for wage-workers who are not themselves able effectively to contest a case where the judgment of an inferior court has been against them. I have specifically in view a recent decision by a district judge leaving railway employees without remedy for violation of a certain so-called labor statute. It seems an absurdity to permit a single district judge, against what may be the judgment of the immense majority of his colleagues on the bench, to declare a law solemnly enacted by the Congress to be "unconstitutional," and then to deny to the government the right to have the Supreme Court definitely decide the question. . . .

In connection with the delays of the law, I call your attention and the attention of the nation to the prevalence of crime among us, and above all to the epidemic of lynching and mob violence that springs up, now in one part of our country, now in another. Each section, North, South, East, or West, has its own faults; no section can with wisdom spend its time jeering at the faults of another section; it should be busy trying to amend its own shortcomings. To deal with the crime of corruption it is necessary to have an awakened public conscience, and to supplement this by whatever legislation will add speed and certainty in the execution of the law. When we deal with lynching even more is necessary. A great many white men are lynched, but the crime is peculiarly frequent in respect to black men. . . .

Governor Candler of Georgia stated on one occasion some years ago: "I can say of a verity that I have, within the last month, saved the lives of half a dozen innocent Negroes who were pursued by the mob, and brought them to trial in a court of law in which they were acquitted." As Bishop Galloway of Mississippi has finely said: "When the rule of a mob obtains, that which distinguishes a high civilization is surrendered. The mob which lynches a Negro charged with rape will in a little while lynch a white man suspected of crime. Every Christian patriot in America needs to lift up his voice in loud and eternal protest against the mob spirit that is threatening the integrity of this Republic." . . .

Moreover, where any crime committed by a member of one race against a member of another race is avenged in such fashion that it seems as if not the individual criminal, but the whole race, is attacked, the result is to exasperate to the highest degree race feeling. There is but one safe rule in dealing with black men as with white men: it is the same rule that must be applied in dealing with rich men and poor men; that is, to treat each man, whatever his color, his creed, or his social position, with even-handed justice on his real worth as a man. . . . Reward or punish the individual on his merits as an individual. Evil will surely come in the end to both races if we substitute for this just rule the habit of treating all the members of the race, good and bad, alike. . . .

The members of the white race . . . should understand that every lynching represents by just so much a loosening of the bands of civilization; that the spirit of lynching inevitably throws into prominence in the community all the foul and evil creatures who dwell therein. No man can take part in the torture of a human being without having his own moral nature permanently lowered. Every lynching means just so much moral deterioration in all the children who have any knowledge of it, and therefore just so much additional trouble for the next generation of Americans.

Let justice be both sure and swift; but let it be justice under the law, and not the wild and crooked savagery of a mob.

There is another matter which has a direct bearing upon this matter of lynching and of the brutal crime which sometimes calls it forth and at other times merely furnishes the excuse for its existence. It is out of the question for our people as a whole permanently to rise by treading down any of their own number. Even those who themselves for the moment profit by such maltreatment of their fellows will in the long run also suffer. No more shortsighted policy can be imagined than, in the fancied interest of one class, to prevent the education of another class. The free public school, the chance for each boy or girl to get a good elementary education, lies at the foundation of our whole political situation. In every community the poorest citizens, those who need the schools most, would be deprived of them if they only received school facilities proportioned to the taxes they paid. This is as true of one portion of our country as of another. It is as true for the Negro as for the white man. The white man, if he is wise, will decline to allow the Negroes in a mass to grow to manhood and womanhood without education. Unquestionably education such as is obtained in our public schools does not do everything toward making a man a good citizen; but it does much. . . .

In dealing with both labor and capital, with the questions affecting both corporations and trades unions, there is one matter more important to remember than aught else, and that is the infinite harm done by preachers of mere discontent. These are the men who seek to excite a violent class hatred against all men of wealth. They seek to turn wise and proper movements for the better control of corporations and for doing away with the abuses connected with wealth into a campaign of hysterical excitement and falsehood in which the aim is to inflame to madness the brutal passions of mankind. The sinister demagogues and foolish visionaries who are always eager to undertake such a campaign of destruction sometimes seek to associate themselves with those working for a genuine reform in governmental and social methods, and sometimes masquerade as such reformers. In reality they are the worst enemies of the cause they profess to advocate, just as the purveyors of sensational slander in newspaper or magazine are the worst enemies of all men who are engaged in an honest effort to better what is bad in our social and governmental conditions. To preach hatred of the rich man as such, to carry on a campaign of slander and invective against him, to seek to mislead and inflame to madness honest men whose lives are hard and who have not the kind of mental training which will permit them to appreciate the danger in the doctrines preached—all this is to commit a crime against the body politic and to be false to every worthy principle and tradition of American national life. Moreover, while such preaching and such agitation may give a livelihood and a certain notoriety to some of those who take part in it, and may result in the temporary political success of others, in the long run every such movement will either fail or else will provoke a violent reaction, which will itself result not merely in undoing the mischief wrought by the demagogue and the agitator, but also in undoing the good that the honest reformer, the true upholder of popular rights, has painfully and laboriously achieved. . . . The one hope for success for our people lies in a resolute and fearless, but sane and cool-headed, advance along the path marked out last year by this very Congress. There must be a stern refusal to be misled into following either that base creature who appeals and panders to the lowest instincts and passions in order to arouse one set of Americans against their fellows, or that other creature, equally base but no baser, who in a spirit of greed, or to accumulate or add to an already huge fortune, seeks to exploit his fellow Americans with callous disregard to their welfare of soul and body. . . .

In the end the honest man, whether rich or poor, who earns his own living and tries to deal justly by his fellows, has as much to fear from the insincere and unworthy demagogue, promising much and performing nothing, or else performing nothing but evil, who would set on the mob to plunder the rich, as from the crafty corruptionist, who, for his own ends, would permit the common people to be exploited by the very wealthy. If we ever let this government fall into the hands of men of either of these two classes, we shall show ourselves false to America's past. Moreover, the demagogue and the corruptionist often work hand in hand. There are at this moment wealthy reactionaries of such obtuse morality that they regard the public servant who prosecutes them when they violate the law, or who seeks to make them bear their proper share of the public burdens, as being even more objectionable than the violent agitator who hounds on the mob to plunder the rich. There is nothing to choose between such a reactionary and such an agitator; fundamentally they are alike in their selfish disregard of the rights of others; and it is natural that they should join in opposition to any movement of which the aim is fearlessly to do exact and even justice to all.

I call your attention to the need of passing the bill limiting the number of hours of employment of railroad employees. The measure is a very moderate one, and I can conceive of no serious objection to it. Indeed, so far as it is in our power, it should be our aim steadily to reduce the number of hours of labor, with as a goal the general introduction of an eight-hour day. . . . Until recently the eight-hour law on our federal statute books has been very scantily observed. Now, however, largely through the instrumentality of the Bureau of Labor, it is being rigidly enforced, and I shall speedily be able to say whether or not there is need of further legislation in reference thereto; for our purpose is to see it obeyed in spirit no less than in letter. Half-holidays during summer should be established for government employees; it is as desirable for wage-workers who toil with their hands as for salaried officials whose labor is mental that there should be a reasonable amount of holiday.

Among the excellent laws which the Congress passed at the last session was an employers'-liability law. It was a marked step in advance to get the recognition of employers' liability on the statute books; but the law did not go far enough. In spite of all precautions exercised by employers there are unavoidable accidents and even deaths involved in nearly every line of business connected with the mechanic arts. This inevitable sacrifice of life may be reduced to a minimum, but it cannot be completely eliminated. It is a great social injustice to compel the employee, or rather the family of the killed or disabled victim, to bear the entire burden of such an inevitable sacrifice. In other words, society shirks its duty by laying the whole cost on the victim, whereas the injury comes from what may be called the legitimate risks of the trade. Compensation for accidents or deaths due in any line of industry to the actual conditions under which that industry is carried on, should be paid by that portion of the community for the benefit of which the industry is carried on— that is, by those who profit by the industry. If the entire trade risk is placed upon the employer he will promptly and properly add it to the legitimate cost of production and assess it proportionately upon the consumers of his commodity. It is therefore clear to my mind that the law should place this entire "risk of a trade" upon the employer. Neither the federal law, nor, as far as I am informed, the state laws dealing with the question of employers' liability are sufficiently thoroughgoing. The federal law should of course include employees in navy yards, arsenals, and the like. . . .

The present Congress has taken long strides in the direction of securing proper supervision and control by the national government over corporations engaged in interstate business—and the enormous majority of corporations of any size are engaged in interstate business. The passage of the railway-rate bill, and only to a less degree the passage of the pure-food bill, and the provision for increasing and rendering more effective national control over the beef-packing industry, mark an important advance in the proper direction. In the short session it will perhaps be difficult to do much further along this line; and it may be best to wait until the laws have been in operation for a number of months before endeavoring to increase their scope, because only operation will show with exactness their merits and their shortcomings and thus give opportunity to define what further remedial legislation is needed. Yet in my judgment it will in the end be advisable in connection with the packing-house inspection law to provide for putting a date on the label and for charging the cost of inspection to the packers. All these laws have already justified their enactment. The Interstate Commerce Law, for instance, has rather amusingly falsified the predictions, both of those who asserted that it would ruin the railroads and of those who asserted that it did not go far enough and would accomplish nothing. During the last five months the railroads have shown increased earnings and some of them unusual dividends;

while during the same period the mere taking effect of the law has produced an unprecedented, a hitherto unheard-of, number of voluntary reductions in freights and fares by the railroads. Since the founding of the commission there has never been a time of equal length in which anything like so many reduced tariffs have been put into effect. . . .

It cannot too often be repeated that experience has conclusively shown the impossibility of securing by the actions of nearly half a hundred different state legislatures anything but ineffective chaos in the way of dealing with the great corporations which do not operate exclusively within the limits of any one state. In some method, whether by a national license law or in other fashion, we must exercise, and that at an early date, a far more complete control than at present over these great corporations—a control that will, among other things, prevent the evils of excessive overcapitalization, and that will compel the disclosure by each big corporation of its stockholders and of its properties and business, whether owned directly or through subsidiary or affiliated corporations. This will tend to put a stop to the securing of inordinate profits by favored individuals at the expense whether of the general public, the stockholders, or the wage-workers. Our effort should be not so much to prevent consolidation as such, but so to supervise and control it as to see that it results in no harm to the people. The reactionary or ultraconservative apologists for the misuse of wealth assail the effort to secure such control as a step toward socialism. As a matter of fact, it is these reactionaries and ultraconservatives who are themselves most potent in increasing socialistic feeling. One of the most efficient methods of averting the consequences of a dangerous agitation, which is 80 percent wrong, is to remedy the 20 percent of evil as to which the agitation is well founded. The best way to avert the very undesirable move for the governmental ownership of railways is to secure by the government on behalf of the people as a whole such adequate control and regulation of the great interstate common carriers as will do away with the evils which give rise to the agitation against them. So the proper antidote to the dangerous and wicked agitation against the men of wealth as such is to secure by proper legislation and executive action the abolition of the grave abuses which actually do obtain in connection with the business use of wealth under our present system—or rather no system—of failure to exercise any adequate control at all. Some persons speak as if the exercise of such governmental control would do away with the freedom of individual initiative and dwarf individual effort. This is not a fact. It would be a veritable calamity to fail to put a premium upon individual initiative, individual capacity and effort; upon the energy, character, and foresight which it is so important to encourage in the individual. But as a matter of fact the deadening and degrading effect of pure socialism, and especially of its extreme form communism, and the destruction of individual character which they would bring about, are in part achieved by the wholly unregulated competition which results in a single individual or corporation rising at the expense of all others until his or its rise effectually checks all competition and reduces former competitors to a position of utter inferiority and subordination.

In enacting and enforcing such legislation as this Congress already has to its credit, we are working on a coherent plan, with the steady endeavor to secure the needed reform by the joint action of the moderate men, the plain men who do not wish anything hysterical or dangerous, but who do intend to deal in resolute common-sense fashion with the real and great evils of the present system. The reactionaries and the violent extremists show symptoms of joining hands against us. Both assert, for instance, that if logical, we should go to government ownership of railroads and the like; the reactionaries, because on such an issue they think the people would stand with them, while the extremists care rather to preach discontent and agitation than to achieve solid results. As a matter of fact, our position is as remote from that of the Bourbon reactionary as from that of the impracticable or sinister visionary. We hold that the government should not conduct the business of the nation, but that it should exercise such supervision as will ensure its being conducted in the interest of the nation. Our aim is, so far as may be, to secure, for all decent, hard-working men, equality of opportunity and equality of burden. . . .

The question of taxation is difficult in any country, but it is especially difficult in ours with its federal system of government. Some taxes should on every ground be levied in a small district for use in that district. Thus the taxation of real estate is peculiarly one for the immediate locality in which the real estate is found. Again, there is no more legitimate tax for any state than a tax on the franchises conferred by that state upon street railroads and similar corporations which operate wholly within the state boundaries, sometimes in one and sometimes in several municipalities or other minor divisions of the state. But there are many kinds of taxes which can only be levied by the general government so as to produce the best results, because, among other reasons, the attempt to impose them in one particular state too often results merely in driving the corporation or individual affected to some other locality or other state. The national government has long derived its chief revenue from a tariff on imports and from an internal or excise tax. In addition to these there is every reason why, when next our system of taxation is revised, the national government should impose a graduated inheritance tax, and, if possible, a graduated income tax. The man of great wealth owes a peculiar obligation to the state, because he derives special advantages from the mere existence of government. Not only should he recognize this obligation in the way he leads his daily life and in the way he earns and spends his money, but it should also be recognized by the way in which he pays for the protection the state gives him. On the one hand, it is desirable that he should assume his full and proper share of the burden of taxation; on the other hand, it is quite as necessary that in this kind of taxation, where the men who vote the tax pay but little of it, there should be clear recognition of the danger of inaugurating any such system save in a spirit of entire justice and moderation. Whenever we, as a people, undertake to remodel our taxation system along the lines suggested, we must make it clear beyond peradventure that our aim is to distribute the burden of supporting the government more equitably than at present; that we intend to treat rich man and poor man on a basis of absolute equality, and that we regard it as equally fatal to true democracy to do or permit injustice to the one as to do or permit injustice to the other.

I am well aware that such a subject as this needs long and careful study in order that the people may become familiar with what is proposed to be done, may clearly see the necessity of proceeding with wisdom and self-restraint, and may make up their minds just how far they are willing to go in the matter; while only trained legislators can work out the project in necessary detail. But I feel that in the near future our national legislators should enact a law providing for a graduated inheritance tax by which a steadily increasing rate of duty should be put upon all moneys or other valuables coming by gift, bequest, or devise to any individual or corporation. It may be well to make the tax heavy in proportion as the individual benefited is remote of kin. In any event, in my judgment the pro rata of the tax should increase very heavily with the increase of the amount left to any one individual after a certain point has been reached. It is most desirable to encourage thrift and ambition, and a potent source of thrift and ambition is the desire on the part of the breadwinner to leave his children well off. This object can be attained by making the tax very small on moderate amounts of property left; because the prime object should be to put a constantly increasing burden on the inheritance of those swollen fortunes which it is certainly of no benefit to this country to perpetuate. . . .

In its incidents, and apart from the main purpose of raising revenue, an income tax stands on an entirely different footing from an inheritance tax; because it involves no question of the perpetuation of fortunes swollen to an unhealthy size. The question is in its essence a question of the proper adjustment of burdens to benefits. As the law now stands it is undoubtedly difficult to devise a national income tax which shall be constitutional. But whether it is absolutely impossible is another question; and if possible it is most certainly desirable. The first purely income tax law was passed by the Congress in 1861, but the most important law dealing with the subject was that of 1894. This the court held to be unconstitutional.

The question is undoubtedly very intricate, delicate, and troublesome. The decision of the court was only reached by one majority. It is the law of the land, and of course is accepted as such and loyally obeyed by all good citizens. Nevertheless, the hesitation evidently felt by the court as a whole in coming to a conclusion, when considered together with the previous decisions on the subject, may perhaps indicate the possibility of devising a constitutional income tax law which shall substantially accomplish the results aimed at. The difficulty of amending the Constitution is so great that only real necessity can justify a resort thereto. Every effort should be made in dealing with this subject, as with the subject of the proper control by the national government over the use of corporate wealth in interstate business, to devise legislation which without such action shall attain the desired end; but if this fails, there will ultimately be no alternative to a constitutional amendment. . . .

It is a mere truism to say that no growth of great cities, no growth of wealth, no industrial development can atone for any falling off in the character and standing of the farming population. During the last few decades this fact has been recognized with ever-increasing clearness. There is no longer any failure to realize that farming, at least in certain branches, must become a technical and scientific profession. This means that there must be open to farmers the chance for technical and scientific training, not theoretical merely but of the most severely practical type. The farmer represents a peculiarly high type of American citizenship, and he must have the same chance to rise and develop as other American citizens have. . . .

Several factors must cooperate in the improvement of the farmer's condition. He must have the chance to be educated in the widest possible sense—in the sense which keeps ever in view the intimate relationship between the theory of education and the facts of life. In all education we should widen our aims. It is a good thing to produce a certain number of trained scholars and students; but the education superintended by the state must seek rather to produce a hundred good citizens than merely one scholar, and it must be turned now and then from the class book to the study of the great book of nature itself. This is especially true of the farmer, as has been pointed out again and again by all observers most competent to pass practical judgment on the problems of our country life. . . .

The Department of Agriculture has broken new ground in many directions, and year by year it finds how it can improve its methods and develop fresh usefulness. Its constant effort is to give the governmental assistance in the most effective way; that is, through associations of farmers rather than to or through individual farmers. It is also striving to coordinate its work with the agricultural departments of the several states, and so far as its own work is educational, to coordinate it with the work of other educational authorities. Agricultural education is necessarily based upon general education, but our agricultural educational institutions are wisely specializing themselves, making their courses relate to the actual teaching of the agricultural and kindred sciences to young country people or young city people who wish to live in the country. . . .

I am well aware of how difficult it is to pass a constitutional amendment. Nevertheless in my judgment the whole question of marriage and divorce should be relegated to the authority of the national Congress. At present the wide differences in the laws of the different states on this subject result in scandals and abuses; and surely there is nothing so vitally essential to the welfare of the nation, nothing around which the nation should so bend itself to throw every safeguard, as the home life of the average citizen. The change would be good from every standpoint. In particular it would be good because it would confer on the Congress the power at once to deal radically and efficiently with polygamy; and this should be done whether or not marriage and divorce are dealt with. It is neither safe nor proper to leave the question of polygamy to be dealt with by the several states. Power to deal with it should be conferred on the national government.

When home ties are loosened; when men and women cease to regard a worthy family life, with all its duties fully performed, and all its responsibilities lived up to, as the life best worth living; then evil days for the commonwealth are at hand. There are regions in our land, and classes of our population, where the birth rate has sunk below the death rate. Surely it should need no demonstration to show that willful sterility is, from the standpoint of the nation, from the standpoint of the human race, the one sin for which the penalty is national death, race death; a sin for which there is no atonement; a sin which is the more dreadful exactly in proportion as the men and women guilty thereof are in other respects, in character, and bodily and mental powers, those whom for the sake of the state it would be well to see the fathers and mothers of many healthy children, well brought up in homes made happy by their presence. No man, no woman, can shirk the primary duties of life, whether for love of ease and pleasure, or for any other cause, and retain his or her self-respect. . . .

It is a mistake, and it betrays a spirit of foolish cynicism, to maintain that all international governmental action is, and must ever be, based upon mere selfishness, and that to advance ethical reasons for such action is always a sign of hypocrisy. This is no more necessarily true of the action of governments than of the action of individuals. It is a sure sign of a base nature always to ascribe base motives for the actions of others. Unquestionably no nation can afford to disregard proper considerations of self-interest, any more than a private individual can so do. But it is equally true that the average private individual in any really decent community does many actions with reference to other men in which he is guided, not by self-interest, but by public spirit, by regard for the rights of others, by a disinterested purpose to do good to others, and to raise the tone of the community as a whole. Similarly, a really great nation must often act, and as a matter of fact often does act, toward other nations in a spirit not in the least of mere self-interest, but paying heed chiefly to ethical reasons; and as the centuries go by this disinterestedness in international action, this tendency of the individuals comprising a nation to require that nation to act with justice toward its neighbors steadily grows and strengthens. It is neither wise nor right for a nation to disregard its own needs, and it is foolish—and may be wicked—to think that other nations will disregard theirs. But it is wicked for a nation only to regard its own interest, and foolish to believe that such is the sole motive that actuates any other nation. It should be our steady aim to raise the ethical standard of national action just as we strive to raise the ethical standard of individual action.

Not only must we treat all nations fairly, but we must treat with justice and goodwill all immigrants who come here under the law. Whether they are Catholic or Protestant, Jew or Gentile; whether they come from England or Germany, Russia, Japan, or Italy, matters nothing. All we have a right to question is the man's conduct. If he is honest and upright in his dealings with his neighbor and with the state, then he is entitled to respect and good treatment. Especially do we need to remember our duty to the stranger within our gates. It is the sure mark of a low civilization, a low morality, to abuse or discriminate against or in any way humiliate such stranger who has come here lawfully and who is conducting himself properly. To remember this is incumbent on every American citizen, and it is of course peculiarly incumbent on every government official, whether of the nation or of the several states.

I am prompted to say this by the attitude of hostility here and there assumed toward the Japanese in this country. This hostility is sporadic and is limited to a very few places. Nevertheless, it is most discreditable to us as a people, and it may be fraught with the gravest consequences to the nation. The friendship between the United States and Japan has been continuous since the time, over half a century ago, when Commodore Perry, by his expedition to Japan, first opened the islands to western civilization. Since then the growth of Japan has been literally astounding. There is not only nothing to parallel it, but nothing to approach it in the history of civilized mankind. Japan has a glorious and ancient past. Her civilization is older than that of the nations of northern Europe—the nations from whom the people of the United States have chiefly sprung. But fifty years ago Japan's development was still that of the Middle Ages. During that fifty years the progress of the country in every walk in life has been a marvel to mankind, and she now stands as one of the greatest of civilized nations; great in the arts of war and in the arts of peace; great in military, in industrial, in artistic development and achievement. . . . The admirable management of the Japanese Red Cross during the late war, the efficiency and humanity of the Japanese officials, nurses, and doctors, won the respectful admiration of all acquainted with the facts. Through the Red Cross the Japanese people sent over a hundred thousand dollars to the sufferers of San Francisco, and the gift was accepted with gratitude by our people. The courtesy of the Japanese, nationally and individually, has become proverbial. To no other country has there been such an increasing number of visitors from this land as to Japan. In return, Japanese have come here in great numbers. They are welcome, socially and intellectually, in all our colleges and institutions of higher learning, in all our professional and social bodies. The Japanese have won in a single generation the right to stand abreast of the foremost and most enlightened peoples of Europe and America; they have won on their own merits and by their own exertions the right to treatment on a basis of full and frank equality. The overwhelming mass of our people cherish a lively regard and respect for the people of Japan, and in almost every quarter of the Union the stranger from Japan is treated as he deserves; that is, he is treated as the stranger from any part of civilized Europe is and deserves to be treated. But here and there a most unworthy feeling has manifested itself toward the Japanese—the feeling that has been shown in shutting them out from the common schools in San Francisco, and in mutterings against them in one or two other places, because of their efficiency as workers. To shut them out from the public schools is a wicked absurdity, when there are no first-class colleges in the land, including the universities and colleges of California, which do not gladly welcome Japanese students and on which Japanese students do not reflect credit. . . .

It is only a very small body of our citizens that act badly. Where the federal government has power it will deal summarily with any such. Where the several states have power I earnestly ask that they also deal wisely and promptly with such conduct, or else this small body of wrongdoers may bring shame upon the great mass of their innocent and right-thinking fellows—that is, upon our nation as a whole. Good manners should be an international no less than an individual attribute. I ask fair treatment for the Japanese as I would ask fair treatment for Germans or Englishmen, Frenchmen, Russians, or Italians. I ask it as due to humanity and civilization. I ask it as due to ourselves because we must act uprightly toward all men.

I recommend to the Congress that an act be passed specifically providing for the naturalization of Japanese who come here intending to become American citizens. One of the great embarrassments attending the performance of our international obligations is the fact that the Statutes of the United States are entirely inadequate. They fail to give to the national government sufficiently ample power, through United States courts and by the use of the army and navy, to protect aliens in the rights secured to them under solemn treaties which are the law of the land. I therefore earnestly recommend that the criminal and civil statutes of the United States be so amended and added to as to enable the president, acting for the United States government, which is responsible in our international relations, to enforce the rights of aliens under treaties. . . . The mob of a single city may at any time perform acts of lawless violence against some class of foreigners which would plunge us into war. That city by itself would be powerless to make defense against the foreign power thus assaulted, and if independent of this government it would never venture to perform or permit the performance of the acts complained of. The entire power and the whole duty to protect the offending city or the offending community lies in the hands of the United States government. It is unthinkable that we should continue a policy under which a given locality may be allowed to commit a crime against a friendly nation, and the United States government limited, not to preventing the commission of the crime, but, in the last resort, to defending the people who have committed it against the consequences of their own wrongdoing.

Last August an insurrection broke out in Cuba which it speedily grew evident that the existing Cuban government was powerless to quell. This government was repeatedly asked by the then Cuban government to intervene, and finally was notified by the president of Cuba that he intended to resign; that his decision was irrevocable; that none of the other constitutional officers would consent to carry on the government, and that he was powerless to maintain order. It was evident that chaos was impending, and there was every probability that if steps were not immediately taken by this government to try to restore order, the representatives of various European nations in the island would apply to their respective governments for armed intervention in order to protect the lives and property of their citizens. Thanks to the preparedness of our navy, I was able immediately to send enough ships to Cuba to prevent the situation from becoming hopeless; and I furthermore dispatched to Cuba the secretary of war and the assistant secretary of state, in order that they might grapple with the situation on the ground. All efforts to secure an agreement between the contending factions, by which they should themselves come to an amicable understanding and settle upon some modus vivendi—some provisional government of their own—failed. Finally the president of the republic resigned. The quorum of Congress assembled failed by deliberate purpose of its members, so that there was no power to act on his resignation, and the government came to a halt. In accordance with the so-called Platt Amendment, which was embodied in the constitution of Cuba, I thereupon proclaimed a provisional government for the island, the secretary of war acting as provisional governor until he could be replaced by Mr. Magoon, the late minister to Panama and governor of the Canal Zone on the Isthmus; troops were sent to support them and to relieve the navy, the expedition being handled with most satisfactory speed and efficiency. The insurgent chiefs immediately agreed that their troops should lay down their arms and disband; and the agreement was carried out. The provisional government has left the personnel of the old government and the old laws, so far as might be, unchanged, and will thus administer the island for a few months until tranquillity can be restored, a new election properly held, and a new government inaugurated. Peace has come in the island; and the harvesting of the sugar-cane crop, the great crop of the island, is about to proceed.

When the election has been held and the new government inaugurated in peaceful and orderly fashion the provisional government will come to an end. I take this opportunity of expressing upon behalf of the American people, with all possible solemnity, our most earnest hope that the people of Cuba will realize the imperative need of preserving justice and keeping order in the island. The United States wishes nothing of Cuba except that it shall prosper morally and materially, and wishes nothing of the Cubans save that they shall be able to preserve order among themselves and therefore to preserve their independence. If the elections become a farce, and if the insurrectionary habit becomes confirmed in the island, it is absolutely out of the question that the island should continue independent; and the United States, which has assumed the sponsorship before the civilized world for Cuba's career as a nation, would again have to intervene and to see that the government was managed in such orderly fashion as to secure the safety of life and property. The path to be trodden by those who exercise self-government is always hard, and we should have every charity and patience with the Cubans as they tread this difficult path. I have the utmost sympathy with, and regard for, them; but I most earnestly adjure them solemnly to weigh their responsibilities and to see that when their new government is started it shall run smoothly, and with freedom from flagrant denial of right on the one hand, and from insurrectionary disturbances on the other.

The Second International Conference of American Republics, held in Mexico in the years 1901–1902, provided for the holding of the third conference within five years, and committed the fixing of the time and place and the arrangements for the conference to the governing board of the Bureau of American Republics, composed of the representatives of all the American nations in Washington. That board discharged the duty imposed upon it with marked fidelity and painstaking care, and upon the courteous invitation of the United States of Brazil the conference was held at Rio de Janeiro, continuing from the twenty-third of July to the twenty-ninth of August last. Many subjects of common interest to all the American nations were discussed by the conference, and the conclusions reached, embodied in a series of resolutions and proposed conventions, will be laid before you upon the coming in of the final report of the American delegates. They contain many matters of importance relating to the extension of trade, the increase of communication, the smoothing away of barriers to free intercourse, and the promotion of a better knowledge and good understanding between the different countries represented. The meetings of the conference were harmonious and the conclusions were reached with substantial unanimity. . . .

Incidentally to the meeting of the conference, the secretary of state visited the city of Rio de Janeiro and was cordially received by the conference, of which he was made an honorary president. The announcement of his intention to make this visit was followed by most courteous and urgent invitations from nearly all the countries of South America to visit them as the guest of their governments. . . . He carried with him a message of peace and friendship, and of strong desire for good understanding and mutual helpfulness; and he was everywhere received in the spirit of his message. The members of government, the press, the learned professions, the man of business, and the great masses of the people united everywhere in emphatic response to his friendly expressions and in doing honor to the country and cause which he represented.

In many parts of South America there has been much misunderstanding of the attitude and purposes of the United States toward the other American republics. An idea had become prevalent that our assertion of the Monroe Doctrine implied, or carried with it, an assumption of superiority, and of a right to exercise some kind of protectorate over the countries to whose territory that doctrine applies. Nothing could be farther from the truth. Yet that impression continued to be a serious barrier to good understanding, to friendly intercourse, to the introduction of American capital and the extension of American trade. The impression was so widespread that apparently it could not be reached by any ordinary means.

It was part of Secretary Root's mission to dispel this unfounded impression, and there is just cause to believe that he has succeeded. . . .

The destruction of the Pribilof Islands fur seals by pelagic sealing still continues. The herd which, according to the surveys made in 1874 by direction of the Congress, numbered 4,700,000, and which, according to the survey of both American and Canadian commissioners in 1891, amounted to 1,000,000, has now been reduced to about 180,000. This result has been brought about by Canadian and some other sealing vessels killing the female seals while in the water during their annual pilgrimage to and from the south, or in search of food. As a rule the female seal when killed is pregnant, and also has an unweaned pup on land, so that, for each skin taken by pelagic sealing, as a rule, three lives are destroyed—the mother, the unborn offspring, and the nursing pup, which is left to starve to death. No damage whatever is done to the herd by the carefully regulated killing on land; the custom of pelagic sealing is solely responsible for all of the present evil, and is alike indefensible from the economic standpoint and from the standpoint of humanity.

In 1896 over 16,000 young seals were found dead from starvation on the Pribilof Islands. In 1897 it was estimated that since pelagic sealing began upward of 400,000 adult female seals had been killed at sea, and over 300,000 young seals had died of starvation as the result. The revolting barbarity of such a practice, as well as the wasteful destruction which it involves, needs no demonstration and is its own condemnation. The Bering Sea Tribunal, which sat in Paris in 1893, and which decided against the claims of the United States to exclusive jurisdiction in the waters of Bering Sea and to a property right in the fur seals when outside of the three-mile limit, determined also upon certain regulations which the tribunal considered sufficient for the proper protection and preservation of the fur seal in, or habitually resorting to, the Bering Sea. The tribunal by its regulations established a close season, from the first of May to the thirty-first of July, and excluded all killing in the waters within sixty miles around the Pribilof Islands. They also provided that the regulations which they had determined upon, with a view to the protection and preservation of the seals, should be submitted every five years to new examination, so as to enable both interested governments to consider whether, in the light of past experience, there was occasion for any modification thereof.

The regulations have proved plainly inadequate to accomplish the object of protection and preservation of the fur seals, and for a long time this government has been trying in vain to secure from Great Britain such revision and modification of the regulations as were contemplated and provided for by the award of the tribunal of Paris.

The process of destruction has been accelerated during recent years by the appearance of a number of Japanese vessels engaged in pelagic sealing. As these vessels have not been bound even by the inadequate limitations prescribed by the tribunal of Paris, they have paid no attention either to the close season or to the sixty-mile limit imposed upon the Canadians, and have prosecuted their work up to the very islands themselves. On July 16 and 17, the crews from several Japanese vessels made raids upon the island of St. Paul, and before they were beaten off by the very meager and insufficiently armed guard, they succeeded in killing several hundred seals and carrying off the skins of most of them. Nearly all the seals killed were females, and the work was done with frightful barbarity. Many of the seals appear to have been skinned alive, and many were found half skinned and still alive. The raids were repelled only by the use of firearms, and five of the raiders were killed, two were wounded, and twelve captured, including the two wounded. Those captured have since been tried and sentenced to imprisonment. An attack of this kind had been wholly unlooked for, but such provision of vessels, arms, and ammunition will now be made that its repetition will not be found profitable.

Suitable representations regarding the incident have been made to the government of Japan, and we are assured that all practicable measures will be taken by that country to prevent any recurrence of the outrage. On our part, the guard on the island will be increased, and better equipped and organized, and a better revenue-cutter patrol service about the islands will be established; next season a United States war vessel will also be sent there.

We have not relaxed our efforts to secure an agreement with Great Britain for adequate protection of the seal herd, and negotiations with Japan for the same purpose are in progress.

The laws for the protection of the seals within the jurisdiction of the United States need revision and amendment. Only the islands of St. Paul and St. George are now, in terms, included in the government reservation, and the other islands are also to be included. The landing of aliens as well as citizens upon the islands, without a permit from the Department of Commerce and Labor, for any purpose except in case of stress of weather or for water, should be prohibited under adequate penalties. The approach of vessels for the excepted purposes should be regulated. The authority of the government agents on the islands should be enlarged, and the chief agent should have the powers of a committing magistrate. The entrance of a vessel into the territorial waters surrounding the islands with intent to take seals should be made a criminal offense and cause of forfeiture. Authority for seizures in such cases should be given, and the presence on any such vessel of seals or sealskins, or the paraphernalia for taking them, should be made prima facie evidence of such intent. I recommend what legislation is needed to accomplish these ends; and I commend to your attention the report of Mr. Sims, of the Department of Commerce and Labor, on this subject. . . .

It must ever be kept in mind that war is not merely justifiable, but imperative, upon honorable men, upon an honorable nation, where peace can only be obtained by the sacrifice of conscientious conviction or of national welfare. Peace is normally a great good, and normally it coincides with righteousness; but it is righteousness and not peace which should bind the conscience of a nation as it should bind the conscience of an individual; and neither a nation nor an individual can surrender conscience to another's keeping. Neither can a nation, which is an entity, and which does not die as individuals die, refrain from taking thought for the interest of the generations that are to come, no less than for the interest of the generation of today; and no public men have a right, whether from short-sightedness, from selfish indifference, or from sentimentality, to sacrifice national interests which are vital in character. A just war is in the long run far better for a nation's soul than the most prosperous peace obtained by acquiescence in wrong or injustice. Moreover, though it is criminal for a nation not to prepare for war, so that it may escape the dreadful consequences of being defeated in war, yet it must always be remembered that even to be defeated in war may be far better than not to have fought at all. As has been well and finely said, a beaten nation is not necessarily a disgraced nation; but the nation or man is disgraced if the obligation to defend right is shirked.

We should as a nation do everything in our power for the cause of honorable peace. It is morally as indefensible for a nation to commit a wrong upon another nation, strong or weak, as for an individual thus to wrong his fellows. We should do all in our power to hasten the day when there shall be peace among the nations—a peace based upon justice and not upon cowardly submission to wrong. We can accomplish a good deal in this direction, but we cannot accomplish everything, and the penalty of attempting to do too much would almost inevitably be to do worse than nothing; for it must be remembered that fantastic extremists are not in reality leaders of the causes which they espouse, but are ordinarily those who do most to hamper the real leaders of the cause and to damage the cause itself. As yet there is no likelihood of establishing any kind of international power, of whatever sort, which can effectively check wrong-doing, and in these circumstances it would be both a foolish and an evil thing for a great and free nation to deprive itself of the power to protect its own rights and even in exceptional cases to stand up for the rights of others. Nothing would more promote iniquity, nothing would further defer the reign upon earth of peace and righteousness, than for the free and enlightened peoples which, though with much stumbling and many shortcomings, nevertheless strive toward justice, deliberately to render themselves powerless while leaving every despotism and barbarism armed and able to work their wicked will. The chance for the settlement of disputes peacefully, by arbitration, now depends mainly upon the possession by the nations that mean to do right of sufficient armed strength to make their purpose effective.

The United States Navy is the surest guarantor of peace which this country possesses. It is earnestly to be wished that we would profit by the teachings of history in this matter. A strong and wise people will study its own failures no less than its triumphs, for there is wisdom to be learned from the study of both, of the mistake as well as of the success. For this purpose nothing could be more instructive than a rational study of the War of 1812, as it is told, for instance, by Captain Mahan. There was only one way in which that war could have been avoided. If during the preceding twelve years a navy relatively as strong as that which this country now has had been built up, and an army provided relatively as good as that which the country now has, there never would have been the slightest necessity of fighting the war; and if the necessity had arisen the war would under such circumstances have ended with our speedy and overwhelming triumph. But our people during those twelve years refused to make any preparations whatever, regarding either the army or the navy. They saved a million or two of dollars by so doing; and in mere money paid a hundredfold for each million they thus saved during the three years of war which followed—a war which brought untold suffering upon our people, which at one time threatened the gravest national disaster, and which, in spite of the necessity of waging it, resulted merely in what was in effect a drawn battle, while the balance of defeat and triumph was almost even.

I do not ask that we continue to increase our navy. I ask merely that it be maintained at its present strength; and this can be done only if we replace the obsolete and outworn ships by new and good ones, the equals of any afloat in any navy. To stop building ships for one year means that for that year the navy goes back instead of forward. The old battleship *Texas,* for instance, would now be of little service in a standup fight with a powerful adversary. The old double-turret monitors have out-worn their usefulness, while it was a waste of money to build the modern single-turret monitors. All these ships should be re-placed by others; and this can be done by a well-settled program of providing for the building each year of at least one first-class battleship equal in size and speed to any that any nation is at the same time building; the armament presumably to consist of as large a number as possible of very heavy guns of one caliber, together with smaller guns to repel torpedo attack; while there should be heavy armor, turbine engines, and, in short, every modern device. Of course, from time to time, cruisers, colliers, torpedo-boat destroyers or torpedo boats, will have to be built also. All this, be it remembered, would not increase our navy, but would merely keep it at its present strength. Equally of course, the ships will be absolutely useless if the men aboard them are not so trained that they can get the best possible service out of the formidable but delicate and complicated mechanisms intrusted to their care. The marksmanship of our men has so improved during the last five years that I deem it within bounds to say that the navy is more than twice as efficient, ship for ship, as half a decade ago. The navy can only attain proper efficiency if enough officers and men are provided, and if these officers and men are given the chance (and required to take advantage of it) to stay continually at sea and to exercise the fleets singly and above all in squadron, the exercise to be of every kind and to include unceasing practice at the guns, conducted under condi-tions that will test marksmanship in time of war.

In both the army and the navy there is urgent need that everything possible should be done to maintain the highest stan-dard for the personnel, alike as regards the officers and the enlisted men. I do not believe that in any service there is a finer body of enlisted men and of junior officers than we have in both the army and the navy, including the Marine Corps. All possible encouragement to the enlisted men should be given, in pay and otherwise, and everything practicable done to render the service attractive to men of the right type. They should be held to the strictest discharge of their duty, and in them a spirit should be encouraged which demands not the mere performance of duty, but the performance of far more than duty, if it conduces to the honor and the interest of the American nation; and in return the amplest consideration should be theirs. . . .

MESSAGE TO CONGRESS ON CONDITIONS AT THE PANAMA CANAL SITE

December 17, 1906

To the Senate and House of Representatives: In the month of November I visited the Isthmus of Panama, going over the Canal Zone with considerable care; and also visited the cities of Panama and Colon, which are not in the Zone or under the United States flag, but as to which the United States government, through its agents, exercises control for certain sanitary purposes.

The USS *Louisiana,* on which I was, anchored off Colon about half-past two on Wednesday afternoon, November 14. I came aboard her, after my stay on shore, at about half-past nine on Saturday evening, November 17. On Wednesday afternoon and evening I received the president of Panama and his suite, and saw members of the Canal Commission, and various other gentlemen, perfecting the arrangements for my visit, so that every hour that I was ashore could be employed to advantage. I was three days ashore—not a sufficient length of time to allow of an exhaustive investigation of the minutiae of the work of any single department, still less to pass judgment on the engineering problems, but enough to enable me to get a clear idea of the salient features of the great work and of the progress that has been made as regards the sanitation of the Zone, Colon, and Panama, the caring for and houseing of the employees, and the actual digging of the canal. The Zone is a narrow strip of land, and it can be inspected much as one can inspect fifty or sixty miles of a great railroad, at the point where it runs through mountains or overcomes other natural obstacles.

I chose the month of November for my visit partly because it is the rainiest month of the year, the month in which the work goes forward at the greatest disadvantage, and one of the two months which the medical department of the French Canal Company found most unhealthy.

Immediately after anchoring on the afternoon of Wednesday there was a violent storm of wind and rain. From that time we did not again see the sun until Saturday morning, the rain continuing almost steadily, but varying from a fine drizzle to a torrential downpour, . . . and for the six days ending noon, November 16, 10.24 inches fell. The Chagres rose in flood to a greater height than it had attained during the last fifteen years, tearing out the track in one place. It would have been impossible to see the work going on under more unfavorable weather conditions. . . .

On Thursday morning we landed at about half-past seven, and went slowly over the line of the Panama Railway, ending with an expedition in a tug at the Pacific entrance of the canal out to the islands where the dredging for the canal will cease. . . . I was driven through Panama, and in a public square was formally received and welcomed by the president and other members of the government; and in the evening I attended a dinner given by the president, and a reception, which was also a government function. I also drove through the streets of Panama for the purpose of observing what had been done. We slept at the Hotel Tivoli, at Ancon, which is on a hill directly outside of the city of Panama, but in the Zone.

On Friday morning we left the hotel at seven o'clock, and spent the entire day going through the Culebra cut—the spot in which most work will have to be done in any event. We watched the different steam shovels working; we saw the drilling and blasting; we saw many of the dirt trains (of the two different types used), both carrying the earth away from the steam shovels and depositing it on the dumps—some of the dumps being run out in the jungle merely to get rid of the earth, while in other cases they are being used for double-tracking the railway, and in preparing to build the great dams. I visited many of the different villages, inspecting thoroughly many different buildings—the local receiving hospitals, the houses in which the . . . workmen live, . . . as well as the commissary stores, the bathhouses, the water-closets. . . . During the day I talked with scores of different men—superintendents and heads of departments, divisions, and bureaus; steam-shovel men, machinists, conductors, engineers, clerks, wives of the American employees, health officers, . . . laborers. . . . I saw the lieutenants, the chief executive and administrative officers, under the engineering and sanitary departments. I also saw and had long talks with two deputations —one of machinists and one representing the railway men of the dirt trains—listening to what they had to say as to rate of pay and various other matters, and going over, as much in detail as possible, all the different questions they brought up. As to some matters I was able to meet their wishes; as to others, I felt that what they requested could not be done consistently with my duty to the United States government as a whole; as to yet others I reserved judgment.

On Saturday morning we started at eight o'clock from the hotel. We went through the Culebra cut, stopping off to see the marines, and also to investigate certain towns; one, of white employees, as to which in certain respects complaint had been made to me; and another town where I wanted to see certain houses of the colored employees. We went over the site of the proposed Gatun Dam, having on the first day inspected the sites of the proposed La Boca and Sosa dams. We went out on a little toy railway to the reservoir, which had been built to supply the people of Colon with water for their houses. There we took lunch at the engineers' mess. We then went through the stores and shops of Cristobal, inspecting carefully the houses of both the white and colored employees, married and unmarried, together with the other buildings. . . .

Each day from twelve to eighteen hours were spent in going over and inspecting all there was to be seen, and in examining various employees. Throughout my trip I was accompanied by the surgeon general of the navy, Dr. Rixey; by the chairman of the Isthmian Canal Commission, Mr. Shonts; by Chief Engineer Stevens; by Dr. Gorgas, the chief sanitary officer of the commission; by Mr. Bishop, the secretary of the commission; by Mr. Ripley, the principal assistant engineer; by Mr. Jackson Smith, who has had practical charge of collecting and handling the laboring force; by Mr. Bierd, general manager of the railway; and by Mr. Rogers, the general counsel of the commission; and many other officials joined us from time to time.

At the outset I wish to pay a tribute to the amount of work done by the French Canal Company under very difficult circumstances. Many of the buildings they put up were excellent and are still in use, though, naturally, the houses are now getting out of repair and are being used as dwelling only until other houses can be built, and much of the work they did in the Culebra cut, and some of the work they did in digging has been of direct and real benefit. This country has never made a better investment than the forty million dollars which it paid to the French company for work and betterments, including especially the Panama Railroad. . . .

The wisdom of the canal management has been shown in nothing more clearly than in the way in which the foundations of the work have been laid. To have yielded to the natural impatience of ill-informed outsiders and begun all kinds of experiments in work prior to a thorough sanitation of the Isthmus, and to a fairly satisfactory working out of the problem of getting and keeping a sufficient labor supply, would have been disastrous. The various preliminary measures had to be taken first; and these could not be taken so as to allow us to begin the real work of construction prior to January 1 of the present year. It then became necessary to have the type of the canal decided, and the only delay has been the necessary delay until the twenty-ninth day of June, the date when the Congress definitely and wisely settled that we should have an eighty-five-foot-level canal. Immediately after that the work began in hard earnest, and has been continued with increasing vigor ever since; and it will continue so to progress in the future. When the contracts are let the conditions will be such as to ensure a constantly increasing amount of performance.

The first great problem to be solved, upon the solution of which the success of the rest of the work depended, was the problem of sanitation. This was from the outset under the direction of Dr. W. C. Gorgas, who is to be made a full member of the commission, if the law as to the composition of the commission remains unchanged. It must be remembered that his work was not mere sanitation as the term is understood in our ordinary municipal work. Throughout the Zone and in the two cities of Panama and Colon, in addition to the sanitation work proper, he has had to do all the work that the Marine Hospital Service does as regards the nation, that the health department officers do in the various states and cities, and that Colonel Waring did in New York when he cleaned its streets. The results have been astounding. The Isthmus had been a byword for deadly unhealthfulness. Now, after two years of our occupation, the conditions as regards sickness and the death rate compare favorably with reasonably healthy localities in the United States. Especial care has been devoted to minimizing the risk due to the presence of those species of mosquitoes which have been found to propogate malarial and yellow fevers. In all the settlements, the little temporary towns or cities composed of the white and black employees, which grow up here and there in the tropical jungle as the needs of the work dictate, the utmost care is exercised to keep the conditions healthy. Everywhere are to be seen the drainage ditches which in removing the water have removed the breeding places of the mosquitoes, while the whole jungle is cut away for a considerable space around the habitations, thus destroying the places in which the mosquitoes take shelter.

These drainage ditches and clearings are in evidence in every settlement, and, together with the invariable presence of mosquito screens around the piazzas, and of mosquito doors to the houses, not to speak of the careful fumigation that has gone on in all infected houses, doubtless explain the extraordinary absence of mosquitoes. As a matter of fact, but a single mosquito, and this not of the dangerous species, was seen by any member of our party during my three days on the Isthmus. Equal care is taken by the inspectors of the Health Department to secure cleanliness in the houses and proper hygienic conditions of every kind. . . .

I inspected the large hospitals at Ancon and Colon, which are excellent examples of what tropical hospitals should be. I also inspected the receiving hospitals in various settlements. I went through a number of the wards in which the colored men are treated, a number of those in which the white men are treated —Americans and Spaniards. Both white men and black men are treated exactly alike, and their treatment is as good as that which could be obtained in our first-class hospitals at home. . . . Not only are the men carefully cared for whenever they apply for care, but so far as practicable a watch is kept to see that if they need it they are sent to the hospitals, whether they desire to go or not. . . .

Just at present the health showing on the Isthmus is remarkably good—so much better than in most sections of the United States that I do not believe that it can possibly continue at quite its present average. Thus, early in the present year a band of several hundred Spaniards were brought to the Isthmus as laborers, and additions to their number have been made from time to time; yet since their arrival in February last but one of those Spaniards thus brought over to work on the canal has died of disease, and he of typhoid fever. Two others were killed, one in a railroad accident, and one by a dynamite explosion. There has been for the last six months a wellnigh steady decline in the death rate for the population of the Zone, this being largely due to the decrease in deaths from pneumonia, which has been the most fatal disease on the Isthmus. In October there were ninety-nine deaths of every kind among the employees of the Isthmus. There were then on the rolls 5,500 whites, seven-eighths of them being Americans. Of these whites but two died of disease, and as it happened neither man was an American. Of the 6,000 white Americans, including some 1,200 women and children, not a single death has occurred in the past three months, whereas in an average city in the United States the number of deaths for a similar number of people in that time would have been about thirty from disease. This very remarkable showing cannot of course permanently obtain, but it certainly goes to prove that if good care is taken the Isthmus is not a particularly unhealthy place. In October, of the 19,000 Negroes on the roll, eighty-six died from disease; pneumonia being the most destructive disease, and malarial fever coming second. . . .

In Panama and Colon the death rate has also been greatly reduced, this being directly due to the vigorous work of the special brigade of employees who have been inspecting houses where the stegomyia mosquito is to be found, and destroying its larvae and breeding places, and doing similar work in exterminating the malarial mosquitoes—in short, in performing all kinds of hygienic labor. A little over a year ago all kinds of mosquitoes, including the two fatal species, were numerous about the Culebra cut. In this cut during last October every room of every house was carefully examined, and only two mosquitoes, neither of them of the two fatal species, were found. Unfaltering energy in inspection and in disinfecting, and in the work of draining and of clearing brush, are responsible for the change. . . .

The sanitation work in the cities of Panama and Colon has been just as important as in the Zone itself, and in many respects much more difficult; because it was necessary to deal with the already existing population, which naturally had scant sympathy with revolutionary changes, the value of which they were for a long time not able to perceive. . . . In Panama 90 percent of the streets that are to be paved at all are already paved with an excellent brick pavement laid in heavy concrete, a few of the streets being still in process of paving. The sewer and water services in the city are of the most modern hygienic type, some of the service having just been completed.

In Colon the conditions are peculiar, and it is as regards Colon that most of the very bitter complaint has been made. Colon is built on a low coral island, covered at more or less shallow depths with vegetable accumulations or mold, which affords sustenance and strength to many varieties of low-lying tropical plants. One-half of the surface of the island is covered with water at high tide, the average height of the land being one and one-half feet above low tide. The slight undulations furnish shallow, natural reservoirs or fresh-water breeding places for every variety of mosquito, and the ground tends to be lowest in the middle. When the town was originally built no attempt was made to fill the low ground, either in the streets or on the building sites, so that the entire surface was practically a quag-mire; when the quagmire became impassable, certain of the streets were crudely improved by filling especially bad mud holes with soft rock or other material. In September 1905, a systematic effort was begun to formulate a general plan for the proper sanitation of the city; in February last temporary relief measures were taken, while in July the prosecution of the work was begun in good earnest. The results are already visible in the sewering, draining, guttering, and paving of the streets. Some four months will be required before the work of sewerage and street improvement will be completed, but the progress already made is very marked. . . .

It was not practicable, with the force at the commission's dis-posal, and in view of the need that the force should be used in the larger town of Panama, to begin this work before early last winter. Water mains were then laid in the town and water was furnished to the people early in March from a temporary reservoir. This reservoir proved to be of insufficient capacity before the end of the dry season, and the shortage was made up by hauling water over the Panama Railroad, so that there was at all times an ample supply of the very best water. Since that time the new reservoir back of Mount Hope has been practically completed. I visited this reservoir. It is a lake over a mile long and half a mile broad. It now carries some five hundred million gallons of first-class water. . . .

One of the most amusing (as well as dishonest) attacks made upon the commission was in connection with this reservoir. The writer in question usually confined himself to vague general mendacity; but in this case he specifically stated that there was no water in the vicinity fit for a reservoir (I drank it and it was excellent), and that this particular reservoir would never hold water anyway. Accompanying this message . . . is a photograph of the reservoir as I myself saw it, and as it has been in existence ever since the article in question was published. With typical American humor, the engineering corps at work at the reservoir have christened a large boat which is now used on the reservoir by the name of the individual who thus denied the possibility of the reservoir's existence.

I rode through the streets of Colon, seeing them at the height of the rainy season, after two days of almost unexampled downpour, when they were at their very worst. Taken as a whole, they were undoubtedly very bad; as bad as Pennsylvania Avenue in Washington before Grant's administration. Front Street is already in thoroughly satisfactory shape however. Some of the side streets are also in good condition. In others the change in the streets is rapidly going on. Through three-fourths of the town it is now possible to walk, even during the period of tremendous rain, in low shoes without wetting one's feet, owing to the rapidity with which the surface water is carried away in the ditches. In the remaining one-fourth of the streets the mud is very deep—about as deep as in the ordinary street of a low-lying prairie river town of the same size in the United States during early spring. All men to whom I spoke were a unit in saying that the conditions of the Colon streets were 100 percent better than a year ago. The most superficial examination of the town shows the progress that has been made and is being made in macadamizing the streets. Complaint was made to me by an entirely reputable man as to the character of some of the material used for repairing certain streets. On investigation the complaint proved well founded, but it also appeared that the use of the material in question had been abandoned, the commission after having tried it in one or two streets finding it not appropriate.

The result of the investigation of this honest complaint was typical of what occurred when I investigated most of the other honest complaints made to me. That is, where the complaints were not made wantonly or maliciously, they almost always proved due to failure to appreciate the fact that time was necessary in the creation and completion of this titanic work in a tropic wilderness. It is impossible to avoid some mistakes in building a giant canal through jungle-covered mountains and swamps, while at the same time sanitating tropical cities, and providing for the feeding and general care of from twenty to thirty thousand workers. The complaints brought to me, either of insufficient provision in caring for some of the laborers, or of failure to finish the pavements of Colon, or of failure to supply water, or of failure to build wooden sidewalks for the use of the laborers in the rainy season, on investigation proved, almost without exception, to be due merely to the utter inability of the commission to do everything at once. . . .

Care and forethought have been exercised by the commission, and nothing has reflected more credit upon them than their refusal either to go ahead too fast or to be deterred by the fear of criticism from not going ahead fast enough. It is curious to note the fact that many of the most severe critics of the commission criticize them for precisely opposite reasons, some complaining bitterly that the work is not in a more advanced condition, while the others complain that it has been rushed with such haste that there has been insufficient preparation for the hygiene and comfort of the employees. As a matter of fact, neither criticism is just. It would have been impossible to go quicker than the commission has gone, for such quickness would have meant insufficient preparation. On the other hand, to refuse to do anything until every possible future contingency had been met would have caused wholly unwarranted delay. The right course to follow was exactly the course which has been followed. . . .

Next in importance to the problem of sanitation, and indeed now of equal importance, is the problem of securing and caring for the mechanics, laborers, and other employees who actually do the work on the canal and the railroad. This great task has been under the control of Mr. Jackson Smith, and on the whole has been well done. At present there are some six thousand white employees and some nineteen thousand colored employees on the Isthmus. I went over the different places where the different kinds of employees were working; I think I saw representatives of every type both at their work and in their homes; and I conversed with probably a couple of hundred of them all told, choosing them at random from every class and including those who came especially to present certain grievances. I found that those who did not come specifically to present grievances almost invariably expressed far greater content and satisfaction with the conditions than did those who called to make complaint.

Nearly five thousand of the white employees had come from the United States. No man can see these young, vigorous men energetically doing their duty without a thrill of pride in them as Americans. They represent on the average a high class. Doubtless to Congress the wages paid them will seem high, but as a matter of fact the only general complaint which I found had any real basis among the complaints made to me upon the Isthmus was that, owing to the peculiar surroundings, the cost of living, and the distance from home, the wages were really not as high as they should be. In fact, almost every man I spoke to felt that he ought to be receiving more money—a view, however, which the average man who stays at home in the United States probably likewise holds as regards himself. I append figures of the wages paid, so that the Congress can judge the matter for itself. . . .

The white Americans are employed, some of them in office work, but the majority in handling the great steam shovels, as engineers and conductors on the dirt trains, as machinists in the great repair shops, as carpenters and timekeepers, superintendents, and foremen of divisions and of gangs, and so on and so on. Many of them have brought down their wives and families; and the children when not in school are running about and behaving precisely as the American small boy and girl behave at home. The bachelors among the employees live sometimes in small separate houses, sometimes in large houses; quarters being furnished free to all the men, married and unmarried. Usually the bachelors sleep two in a room, as they would do in this country. I found a few cases where three were in a room; and I was told of, although I did not see, large rooms in which four were sleeping; for it is not possible in what is really a vast system of construction camps always to provide in advance as ample house-room as the commission intend later to give. In one case, where the house was an old French house with a leak in the roof, I did not think the accommodations were good. But in every other case among the scores of houses I entered at random, the accommodations were good; every room was neat and clean, usually having books, magazines, and small ornaments; and in short just such a room as a self-respecting craftsman would be glad to live in at home. The quarters for the married people were even better. Doubtless there must be here and there a married couple who, with or without reason, are not contented with their house on the Isthmus; but I never happened to strike such a couple. . . . The houses themselves were excellent—bathroom, sitting room, piazza, and bedrooms being all that could be desired. . . .

The housewives purchase their supplies directly, or through their husbands, from the commissary stores of the commission. All to whom I spoke agreed that the supplies were excellent, and all but two stated that there was no complaint to be made; these two complained that the prices were excessive as compared to the prices in the states. On investigation I did not feel that this complaint was well founded. The married men ate at home. The unmarried men sometimes ate at private boardinghouses, or private messes, but more often, judging by the answers of those whom I questioned, at the government canteens or hotels where the meal costs thirty cents to each employee. This thirty-cent meal struck me as being as good a meal as we get in the United States at the ordinary hotel in which a fifty-cent meal is provided. Three-fourths of the men whom I questioned stated that the meals furnished at these government hotels were good, the remaining one-fourth that they were not good. I myself took dinner at the La Boca government hotel, no warning whatever having been given of my coming. There were two rooms, as generally in these hotels. In one the employees were allowed to dine without their coats, while in the other they had to put them on. The thirty-cent meal included soup, native beef (which was good), mashed potatoes, peas, beets, chili con carne, plum pudding, tea, coffee—each man having as much of each dish as he desired. On the table there was a bottle of liquid quinine tonic which two-thirds of the guests, as I was informed, used every day. There were neat tablecloths and napkins. The men, who were taking the meal at or about the same time, included railroad men, machinists, shipwrights, and members of the office force. The rooms were clean, comfortable, and airy, with mosquito screens around the outer piazza. I was informed by some of those present that this hotel, and also the other similar hotels, were every Saturday night turned into clubhouses where the American officials, the schoolteachers, and various employees, appeared, bringing their wives, there being dancing and singing. There was a piano in the room, which I was informed was used for the music on these occasions. My meal was excellent, and two newspaper correspondents who had been on the Isthmus several days informed me that it was precisely like the meals they had been getting elsewhere at other government hotels. One of the employees was a cousin of one of the Secret Service men who was with me, and he stated that the meals had always been good, but that after a time he grew tired of them because they seemed so much alike. . . .

The West India laborers are fairly, but only fairly, satisfactory. Some of the men do very well indeed; the better class, who are to be found as foremen, as skilled mechanics, as policemen, are good men; and many of the ordinary day laborers are also good. . . . I questioned many of these Jamaica laborers as to the conditions of their work and what, if any, changes they wished. I received many complaints from them, but as regards most of these complaints they themselves contradicted one another. In all cases where the complaint was as to their treatment by any individual it proved on examination that this individual was himself a West India man of color, either a policeman, a storekeeper, or an assistant storekeeper. Doubtless there must be many complaints against Americans; but those to whom I spoke did not happen to make any such complaint to me. There was no complaint of the housing; I saw but one set of quarters for colored laborers which I thought poor, and this was in an old French house. The barracks for unmarried men are roomy, well ventilated, and clean, with canvas bunks for each man, and a kind of false attic at the top, where the trunks and other belongings of the different men are kept. The clothes are hung on clotheslines, nothing being allowed to be kept on the floor. In each of these big rooms there were tables and lamps, and usually a few books or papers, and in almost every room there was a Bible; the books being the property of the laborers themselves. The cleanliness of the quarters is secured by daily inspection.

The quarters for the married Negro laborers were good. They were neatly kept, and in almost every case the men living in them, whose wives or daughters did the cooking for them, were far better satisfied and of a higher grade than the ordinary bachelor Negroes. Not only were the quarters in which these Negro laborers were living much superior to those in which I am informed they live at home, but they were much superior to the huts to be seen in the jungles of Panama itself, beside the railroad tracks. . . .

The Negroes generally do their own cooking, the bachelors cooking in sheds provided by the government and using their own pots. In the different camps there was a wide variation in the character of these cooking sheds. In some, where the camps were completed, the kitchen or cooking sheds, as well as the bathrooms and water-closets, were all in excellent trim, while there were board sidewalks leading from building to building. In other camps the kitchens or cook sheds had not been floored, and the sidewalks had not been put down, while in one camp the bathhouses were not yet up. In each case, however, every effort was being made to hurry on the construction, and I do not believe that the delays had been greater than were inevitable in such work. The laborers are accustomed to do their own cooking; but there was much complaint, especially among the bachelors, as to the quantity, and some as to the quality, of the food they got from the commissary department, especially as regards yams. On the other hand, the married men and their wives, and the more advanced among the bachelors, almost invariably expressed themselves as entirely satisfied with their treatment at the commissary stores; except that they stated that they generally could not get yams there, and had to purchase them outside. The chief complaint was that the prices were too high. . . .

The main work is now being done in the Culebra cut. It was striking and impressive to see the huge steam shovels in full play, the dumping trains carrying away the rock and earth they dislodged. The implements of French excavating machinery, which often stand a little way from the line of work, though of excellent construction, look like the veriest toys when compared with these new steam shovels, just as the French dumping cars seem like toy cars when compared with the long trains of huge cars, dumped by steam plows, which are now in use. This represents the enormous advance that has been made in machinery during the past quarter of a century. . . . The old French cars had to be entirely discarded. We still have in use a few of the more modern, but not most modern, cars, which hold but twelve yards of earth. They can be employed on certain lines with sharp curves. But the recent cars hold from twenty-five to thirty yards apiece, and instead of the old clumsy methods of unloading them, a steam plow is drawn from end to end of the whole vestibuled train, thus immensely economizing labor. In the rainy season the steam shovels can do but little in dirt, but they work steadily in rock and in the harder ground. There were some twenty-five at work during the time I was on the Isthmus, and their tremendous power and efficiency were most impressive. . . .

It is not only natural but inevitable that a work as gigantic as this which has been undertaken on the Isthmus should arouse every species of hostility and criticism. The conditions are so new and so trying, and the work so vast, that it would be absolutely out of the question that mistakes should not be made. Checks will occur. Unforeseen difficulties will arise. From time to time seemingly well-settled plans will have to be changed. At present twenty-five thousand men are engaged on the task. After a while the number will be doubled. . . . In a place which has been for ages a byword for unhealthfulness, and with so large a congregation of strangers suddenly put down and set to hard work, there will now and then be outbreaks of disease; there will now and then be shortcomings in administration; there will be unlooked-for accidents to delay the excavation of the cut or the building of the dams and locks. Each such incident will be entirely natural, and, even though serious, no one of them will mean more than a little extra delay or trouble. Yet each, when discovered by sensation mongers and retailed to timid folk of little faith, will serve as an excuse for the belief that the whole work is being badly managed. Experiments will continually be tried in housing, in hygiene, in street repairing, in dredging, and in digging earth and rock. Now and then an experiment will be a failure; and among those who hear of it a certain proportion of doubting Thomases will at once believe that the whole work is a failure. Doubtless here and there some minor rascality will be uncovered; but as to this, I have to say that after the most painstaking inquiry I have been unable to find a single reputable person who had so much as heard of any serious accusations affecting the honesty of the commission or of any responsible officer under it. . . .

I have investigated every complaint brought to me for which there seemed to be any shadow of foundation. In two or three cases, all of which I have indicated in the course of this message, I came to the conclusion that there was foundation for the complaint, and that the methods of the commission in the respect complained of could be bettered. In the other instances the complaints proved absolutely baseless, save in two or three instances where they referred to mistakes which the commission had already itself found out and corrected.

So much for honest criticism. There remains an immense amount of as reckless slander as has ever been published. Where the slanderers are of foreign origin I have no concern with them. Where they are Americans, I feel for them the heartiest contempt and indignation; because, in a spirit of wanton dishonesty and malice, they are trying to interfere with, and hamper the execution of, the greatest work of the kind ever attempted, and are seeking to bring to naught the efforts of their countrymen to put to the credit of America one of the giant feats of the ages. The outrageous accusations of these slanderers constitute a gross libel upon a body of public servants who, for trained intelligence, expert ability, high character, and devotion to duty, have never been excelled anywhere. There is not a man among those directing the work on the Isthmus who has obtained his position on any other basis than merit alone, and not one who has used his position in any way for his own personal or pecuniary advantage. . . .

Of the success of the enterprise I am as well convinced as one can be of any enterprise that is human. It is a stupendous work upon which our fellow countrymen are engaged down there on the Isthmus, and while we should hold them to a strict accountability for the way in which they perform it, we should yet recognize, with frank generosity, the epic nature of the task on which they are engaged and its worldwide importance. They are doing something which will redound immeasurably to the credit of America, which will benefit all the world, and which will last for ages to come. Under Mr. Shonts and Mr. Stevens and Dr. Gorgas this work has started with every omen of good fortune. They and their worthy associates, from the highest to the lowest, are entitled to the same credit that we should give to the picked men of a victorious army; for this conquest of peace will, in its great and far-reaching effect, stand as among the very greatest conquests, whether of peace or of war, which have ever been won by any of the peoples of mankind. A badge is to be given to every American citizen who for a specified time has taken part in this work; for participation in it will hereafter be held to reflect honor upon the man participating just as it reflects honor upon a soldier to have belonged to a mighty army in a great war for righteousness. Our fellow countrymen on the Isthmus are working for our interest and for the national renown in the same spirit and with the same efficiency that the men of the army and navy work in time of war. It behooves us in our turn to do all we can to hold up their hands and to aid them in every way to bring their great work to a triumphant conclusion.

SPEECH BEFORE
THE CONFERENCE ON
THE CONSERVATION OF
NATURAL RESOURCES

White House, Washington, D.C., May 13, 1908

Governors of the Several States, and Gentlemen: I welcome you to this conference at the White House. You have come hither at my request so that we may join together to consider the question of the conservation and use of the great fundamental sources of wealth of this nation. So vital is this question that for the first time in our history the chief executive officers of the states separately, and of the state together forming the nation, have met to consider it.

With the governors come men from each state chosen for their special acquaintance with the terms of the problem that is before us. Among them are experts in natural resources and representatives of national organizations concerned in the development and use of these resources; the senators and representatives in Congress; the Supreme Court, the Cabinet, and the Inland Waterways Commission have likewise been invited to the conference, which is therefore national in a peculiar sense.

This conference on the conservation of natural resources is in effect a meeting of the representatives of all the people of the United States called to consider the weightiest problem now before the nation; and the occasion for the meeting lies in the fact that the natural resources of our country are in danger of exhaustion if we permit the old wasteful methods of exploiting them longer to continue.

With the rise of peoples from savagery to civilization, and

with the consequent growth in the extent and variety of the needs of the average man, there comes a steadily increasing growth of the amount demanded by this average man from the actual resources of the country. Yet, rather curiously, at the same time the average man is apt to lose his realization of this dependence upon nature.

Savages, and very primitive peoples generally, concern themselves only with superficial natural resources; with those which they obtain from the actual surface of the ground. As peoples become a little less primitive, their industries, although in a rude manner, are extended to resources below the surface; then, with what we call civilization and the extension of knowledge, more resources come into use, industries are multiplied, and foresight begins to become a necessary and prominent factor in life. Crops are cultivated; animals are domesticated; and metals are mastered.

Every step of the progress of mankind is marked by the discovery and use of natural resources previously unused. Without such progressive knowledge and utilization of natural resources population could not grow, nor industries multiply, nor the hidden wealth of the earth be developed for the benefit of mankind.

From the first beginnings of civilization, on the banks of the Nile and the Euphrates, the industrial progress of the world has gone on slowly, with occasional setbacks, but on the whole steadily, through tens of centuries to the present day. But of late the rapidity of the process has increased at such a rate that more space has been actually covered during the century and a quarter occupied by our national life than during the preceding six thousand years that take us back to the earliest monuments of Egypt, to the earliest cities of the Babylonian plain.

When the founders of this nation met at Independence Hall in Philadelphia the conditions of commerce had not fundamentally changed from what they were when the Phoenician keels first furrowed the lonely waters of the Mediterranean. The differences were those of degree, not of kind, and they were not in all cases even those of degree. Mining was carried on fundamentally as it had been carried on by the pharaohs in the countries adjacent to the Red Sea.

The wares of the merchants of Boston, of Charleston, like the wares of the merchants of Nineveh and Sidon, if they went by water, were carried by boats propelled by sails or oars; if they went by land they were carried in wagons drawn by beasts of draft or in packs on the backs of beasts of burden. The ships that crossed the high seas were better than the ships that had once crossed the Aegean, but they were of the same type, after all—they were wooden ships propelled by sails; and on land, the roads were not as good as the roads of the Roman Empire, while the service of the posts was probably inferior.

In Washington's time anthracite coal was known only as a useless black stone; and the great fields of bituminous coal were undiscovered. As steam was unknown, the use of coal for power production was undreamed of. Water was practically the only source of power, save the labor of men and animals; and this power was used only in the most primitive fashion. But a few small iron deposits had been found in this country, and the use of iron by our countrymen was very small. Wood was practically the only fuel, and what lumber was sawed was consumed locally, while the forests were regarded chiefly as obstructions to settlement and cultivation.

Such was the degree of progress to which civilized mankind had attained when this nation began its career. It is almost impossible for us in this day to realize how little our Revolutionary ancestors knew of the great store of natural resources whose discovery and use have been such vital factors in the growth and greatness of this nation, and how little they required to take from this store in order to satisfy their needs.

Since then our knowledge and use of the resources of the present territory of the United States have increased a hundredfold. Indeed, the growth of this nation by leaps and bounds makes one of the most striking and important chapters in the history of the world. Its growth has been due to the rapid development, and alas! that it should be said, to the rapid destruction of our natural resources. Nature has supplied to us in the United States, and still supplies to us, more kinds of resources in a more lavish degree than has ever been the case at any other time or with any other people. Our position in the world has been attained by the extent and thoroughness of the control we have achieved over nature; but we are more, and not less, dependent upon what she furnishes than at any previous time of history since the days of primitive man.

Yet our fathers, though they knew so little of the resources of the country, exercised a wise forethought in reference thereto. Washington clearly saw that the perpetuity of the states could only be secured by union, and that the only feasible basis of union was an economic one; in other words, that it must be based on the development and use of their natural resources. Accordingly, he helped to outline a scheme of commercial development, and by his influence an interstate waterways commission was appointed by Virginia and Maryland.

It met near where we are now meeting, in Alexandria, adjourned to Mount Vernon, and took up the consideration of interstate commerce by the only means then available, that of water. Further conferences were arranged, first at Annapolis, and then at Philadelphia. It was in Philadelphia that the representatives of all the states met for what was in its original conception merely a waterways conference; but when they had closed their deliberations the outcome was the Constitution which made the states into a nation.

The Constitution of the United States thus grew in large part out of the necessity for united action in the wise use of one of our natural resources. The wise use of all of our natural resources, which are our national resources as well, is the great material question of today. I have asked you to come together now because the enormous consumption of these resources, and the threat of imminent exhaustion of some of them, due to reckless and wasteful use, once more calls for common effort, common action.

Since the days when the Constitution was adopted, steam and electricity have revolutionized the industrial world. Nowhere has the revolution been so great as in our own country. The discovery and utilization of mineral fuels and alloys have given us the lead over all other nations in the production of steel. The discovery and utilization of coal and iron have given us our railways, and have led to such industrial development as has never before been seen. The vast wealth of lumber in our forests, the riches of our soils and mines, the discovery of gold and mineral oils, combined with the efficiency of our transportation, have made the conditions of our life unparalleled in comfort and convenience.

The steadily increasing drain on these natural resources has promoted to an extraordinary degree the complexity of our industrial and social life. Moreover, this unexampled development has had a determining effect upon the character and opinions of our people. The demand for efficiency in the great task has given us vigor, effectiveness, decision, and power, and a capacity for achievement which in its own lines has never yet been matched. So great and so rapid has been our material growth that there has been a tendency to lag behind in spiritual and moral growth; but that is not the subject upon which I speak to you today. Disregarding for the moment the question of moral purpose, it is safe to say that the prosperity of our people depends directly on the energy and intelligence with which our natural resources are used. It is equally clear that these resources are the final basis of national power and perpetuity. Finally, it is ominously evident that these resources are in the course of rapid exhaustion.

This nation began with the belief that its landed possessions were illimitable and capable of supporting all the people who might care to make our country their home; but already the limit of unsettled land is in sight, and indeed but little land fitted for agriculture now remains unoccupied save what can be reclaimed by irrigation and drainage. We began with an unapproached heritage of forests; more than half of the timber is gone. We began with coal fields more extensive than those of any other nation and with iron ores regarded as inexhaustible, and many experts now declare that the end of both iron and coal is in sight.

The mere increase in our consumption of coal during 1907 over 1906 exceeded the total consumption in 1876, the Centennial year. The enormous stores of mineral oil and gas are largely gone. Our natural waterways are not gone, but they have been so injured by neglect, and by the division of responsibility and utter lack of system in dealing with them, that there is less navigation on them now than there was fifty years ago. Finally, we began with soils of unexampled fertility and we have so impoverished them by injudicious use and by failing to check erosion that their crop-producing power is diminishing instead of increasing. In a word, we have thoughtlessly, and to a large degree unnecessarily, diminished the resources upon which not only our prosperity but the prosperity of our children must always depend.

We have become great because of the lavish use of our resources and we have just reason to be proud of our growth. But the time has come to inquire seriously what will happen when our forests are gone, when the coal, the iron, the oil, and the gas are exhausted, when the soils shall have been still further impoverished and washed into the streams, polluting the rivers, denuding the fields, and obstructing navigation. These questions do not relate only to the next century or to the next generation. It is time for us now as a nation to exercise the same reasonable foresight in dealing with our great natural resources that would be shown by any prudent man in conserving and widely using the property which contains the assurance of well-being for himself and his children.

The natural resources I have enumerated can be divided into two sharply distinguished classes accordingly as they are or are not capable of renewal. Mines if used must necessarily be exhausted. The minerals do not and cannot renew themselves. Therefore in dealing with the coal, the oil, the gas, the iron, the metals generally, all that we can do is to try to see that they are wisely used. The exhaustion is certain to come in time.

The second class of resources consists of those which cannot only be used in such manner as to leave them undiminished for our children, but can actually be improved by wise use. The soil, the forests, the waterways come in this category. In dealing with mineral resources, man is able to improve on nature only by putting the resources to a beneficial use which in the end exhausts them; but in dealing with the soil and its products man can improve on nature by compelling the resources to renew and even reconstruct themselves in such manner as to serve increasingly beneficial uses—while the living waters can be so controlled as to multiply their benefits.

Neither the primitive man nor the pioneer was aware of any duty to posterity in dealing with the renewable resources. When the American settler felled the forests, he felt that there was plenty of forest left for the sons who came 'after him. When he exhausted the soil of his farm he felt that his son could go West and take up another. So it was with his immediate successors. When the soil-wash from the farmer's fields choked the neighboring river he thought only of using the railway rather than boats for moving his produce and supplies.

Now all this is changed. On the average the son of the farmer of today must make his living on his father's farm. There is no difficulty in doing this if the father will exercise wisdom. No wise use of a farm exhausts its fertility. So with the forests. We are over the verge of a timber famine in this country, and it is unpardonable for the nation or the states to permit any further cutting of our timber save in accordance with a system which will provide that the next generation shall see the timber increased instead of diminished. Moreover, we can add enormous tracts of the most valuable possible agricultural land to the national domain by irrigation in the arid and semiarid regions and by drainage of great tracts of swamp land in the humid regions. We can enormously increase our transportation facilities by the canalization of our rivers so as to complete a great system of waterways on the Pacific, Atlantic, and Gulf coasts and in the Mississippi valley, from the Great Plains to the Alleghenies and from the northern lakes to the mouth of the mighty Father of Waters. But all these various uses of our natural resources are so closely connected that they should be coordinated and should be treated as part of one coherent plan and not in haphazard and piecemeal fashion.

It is largely because of this that I appointed the Waterways Commission last year and that I have sought to perpetuate its work. I wish to take this opportunity to express in heartiest fashion my acknowledgment to all the members of the commission. At great personal sacrifice of time and effort they have rendered a service to the public for which we cannot be too grateful. Especial credit is due to the initiative, the energy, the devotion to duty, and the farsightedness of Gifford Pinchot, to whom we owe so much of the progress we have already made in handling this matter of the coordination and conservation of natural resources. If it had not been for him this convention neither would nor could have been called.

We are coming to recognize as never before the right of the nation to guard its own future in the essential matter of natural resources. In the past we have admitted the right of the individual to injure the future of the Republic for his own present profit. The time has come for a change. As a people we have the right and the duty, second to none other but the right and duty of obeying the moral law, of requiring and doing justice, to protect ourselves and our children against the wasteful development of our natural resources, whether that waste is caused by the actual destruction of such resources or by making them impossible of development hereafter.

Any right-thinking father earnestly desires and strives to leave his son both an untarnished name and a reasonable equipment for the struggle of life. So this nation as a whole should earnestly desire and strive to leave to the next generation the national honor unstained and the national resources unexhausted. There are signs that both the nation and the states are waking to a realization of this great truth. On March 10, 1908, the Supreme Court of Maine rendered an exceedingly important judicial decision. This opinion was rendered in response to questions as to the right of the legislature to restrict the cutting of trees on private land for the prevention of droughts and floods, the preservation of the natural water supply, and the prevention of the erosion of such lands, and the consequent filling up of rivers, ponds, and lakes. The forests and waterpower of Maine constitute the larger part of her wealth and form the basis of her industrial life, and the question submitted by the Maine Senate to the supreme court and the answer of the supreme court alike bear testimony to the wisdom of the people of Maine, and clearly define a policy of conservation of natural resources, the adoption of which is of vital importance not merely to Maine but to the whole country.

Such a policy will preserve soil, forests, waterpower as a heritage for the children and the children's children of the men and women of this generation; for any enactment that provides for the wise utilization of the forests, whether in public or private ownership, and for the conservation of the water resources of the country, must necessarily be legislation that will promote both private and public welfare; for flood prevention, waterpower development, preservation of the soil, and improvement of navigable rivers are all promoted by such a policy of forest conservation.

The opinion of the Maine supreme bench sets forth unequivocally the principle that the property rights of the individual are subordinate to the rights of the community and especially that the waste of wild timber land derived originally from the state, involving as it would the impoverishment of the state and its people and thereby defeating one great purpose of government, may properly be prevented by state restrictions.

The court says that there are two reasons why the right of the public to control and limit the use of private property is peculiarly applicable to property in land:

First, such property is not the result of productive labor, but is derived solely from the state itself, the original owner; second, the amount of land being incapable of increase, if the owners of large tracts can waste them at will without state restriction, the state and its people may be helplessly impoverished and one great purpose of government defeated. . . . We do not think the proposed legislation would operate to "take" private property within the inhibition of the Constitution. While it might restrict the owner of wild and uncultivated lands in his use of them, might delay his taking some of the product, might delay his anticipated profits and even thereby might cause him some loss of profit, it would nevertheless leave him his lands, their product and increase, untouched, and without diminution of title, estate, or quantity. He would still have large measure of control and large opportunity to realize values. He might suffer delay but not deprivation. . . . The proposed legislation . . . would be within the legislative power and would not operate as a taking of private property for which compensation must be made.

The Court of Errors and Appeals of New Jersey has adopted a similar view, which has recently been sustained by the Supreme Court of the United States. In delivering the opinion of the Court on April 6, 1908, Mr. Justice Holmes said:

The state as quasi-sovereign and representative of the interests of the public has a standing in court to protect the atmosphere, the water, and the forests within its territory, irrespective of the assent or dissent of the private owners of the land most immediately concerned. . . . It appears to us that few public interests are more obvious, indisputable, and independent of particular theory than the interest of the public of a state to maintain the rivers that are wholly within it substantially undiminished, except by such drafts upon them as the guardian of the public welfare may permit for the purpose of turning them to a more perfect use. This public interest is omnipresent wherever there is a state, and grows more pressing as population grows. . . . We are of opinion further that the constitutional power of the state to insist that its natural advantages shall remain unimpaired by its citizens is not dependent upon any nice estimate of the extent of present use or speculation as to future needs. The legal conception of the necessary is apt to be confined to somewhat rudimentary wants, and there are benefits from a great river that might escape a lawyer's view. But the state is not required to submit even to an aesthetic analysis. Any analysis may be inadequate. It finds itself in possession of what all admit to be a great public good, and what it has it may keep and give no one a reason for its will.

These decisions reach the root of the idea of conservation of our resources in the interests of our people. Finally, let us remember that the conservation of our natural resources, though the gravest problem of today, is yet but part of another and greater problem to which this nation is not yet awake, but to which it will awake in time, and with which it must hereafter grapple if it is to live—the problem of national efficiency, the patriotic duty of insuring the safety and continuance of the nation. When the people of the United States consciously undertake to raise themselves as citizens, and the nation and the states in their several spheres, to the highest pitch of excellence in private, state, and national life, and to do this because it is the first of all the duties of true patriotism, then and not till then the future of this nation, in quality and in time, will be assured.

UGANDA AND THE
GREAT NYANZA LAKES

From African Game Trails, *1910*

When we left Nairobi it was with real regret that we said goodbye to the many friends who had been so kind to us: officials, private citizens, almost everyone we had met—including Sir Percy Girouard, the new governor. At Kijabe the men and women from the American mission—and the children too —were down at the station to wish us good luck; and at Nakuru the settlers from the neighborhood gathered on the platform to give us a farewell cheer. The following morning we reached Kisumu on Lake Victoria Nyanza. It is in the Kavirondo country, where the natives, both men and women, as a rule go absolutely naked, although they are peaceable and industrious. In the native market they had brought in baskets, iron spade heads, and food, to sell to the native and Indian traders who had their booths round about; the meat market, under the trees, was especially interesting.

At noon we embarked in a smart little steamer, to cross the lake. Twenty-four hours later we landed at Entebbe, the seat of the English governor of Uganda. Throughout our passage the wind hardly ruffled the smooth surface of the lake. As we steamed away from the eastern shore the mountains behind us and on our right hand rose harsh and barren, yet with a kind of forbidding beauty. Dark clouds hung over the land we had left, and a rainbow stretched across their front. At nightfall, as the red sunset faded, the lonely waters of the vast inland sea stretched, oceanlike, west and south into a shoreless gloom. Then the darkness deepened, the tropic stars blazed overhead, and the light of the half moon drowned in silver the embers of the sunset.

Next morning we steamed along and across the equator; the last time we were to cross it, for thenceforth our course lay northward. We passed by many islands, green with meadow and forest, beautiful in the bright sunshine, but empty with the emptiness of death. A decade previously these islands were thronged with tribes of fisher folk; their villages studded the shores, and their long canoes, planks held together with fiber, furrowed the surface of the lake. Then, from out of the depths of the Congo forest came the dreadful scourge of the sleeping sickness, and smote the doomed peoples who dwelt beside the Victorian Nile, and on the coasts of the Nyanza Lakes and in the lands between. Its agent was a biting fly, brother to the tsetse whose bite is fatal to domestic animals. This fly dwells in forests, beside lakes and rivers; and wherever it dwells, after the sleeping sickness came it was found that man could not live. In this country, between and along the shores of the great lakes, two hundred thousand people died in slow torment, before the hard-taxed wisdom and skill of medical science and governmental administration could work any betterment whatever in the situation. Men still die by thousands, and the disease is slowly spreading into fresh districts. But it has proved possible to keep it within limits in the regions already affected; yet only by absolutely abandoning certain districts, and by clearing all the forest and brush in tracts which serve as barriers to the fly, and which permit passage through the infected belts. . . .

When we landed there was nothing in the hot, laughing, tropical beauty of the land to suggest the grisly horror that brooded so near. In green luxuriance the earth lay under a cloudless sky, yielding her increase to the sun's burning caresses, and men and women were living their lives and doing their work well and gallantly.

At Entebbe we stayed with the acting governor, Mr. Boyle, at Kampalla with the district commissioner, Mr. Knowles; both of them veteran administrators, and the latter also a mighty hunter; and both of them showed us every courtesy, and treated us with all possible kindness. Entebbe is a pretty little town of

English residents, chiefly officials; with well-kept roads, a golf course, tennis courts, and an attractive clubhouse. The whole place is bowered in flowers, on tree, bush, and vine, of every hue —masses of lilac, purple, yellow, blue, and fiery crimson. Kampalla is the native town, where the little King of Uganda, a boy, lives, and his chiefs of state, and where the native council meets; and it is the headquarters of the missions, both Church of England and Roman Catholic.

Kampalla is an interesting place; and so is all Uganda. The first explorers who penetrated thither, half a century ago, found . . . a veritable semicivilization. . . . The people were industrious tillers of the soil, who owned sheep, goats, and some cattle; they wore decent clothing, and hence were styled "womanish" by the savages of the Upper Nile region, who prided themselves on the nakedness of their men as a proof of manliness; they were unusually intelligent and ceremoniously courteous; . . . there were certain excellent governmental customs, of binding observance, which in the aggregate might almost be called an unwritten constitution. Alone among the natives of tropical Africa the people of Uganda have proved very accessible to Christian teaching, so that the creed of Christianity is now dominant among them. For their good fortune, England has established a protectorate over them. Most wisely the English government officials, and as a rule the missionaries, have bent their energies to developing them along their own lines, in government, dress, and ways of life; constantly striving to better them and bring them forward, but not twisting them aside from their natural line of development, nor wrenching them loose from what was good in their past, by attempting the impossible task of turning an entire native population into black Englishmen at one stroke. . . .

We visited the Church of England mission, where we were received by Bishop Tucker, and the two Catholic missions, where we were received by Bishops Hanlon and Streicher; we went through the churches and saw the schools with the pupils actually at work. In all the missions we were received with

American and British flags and listened to the children singing the "Star-Spangled Banner." The Church of England mission has been at work for a quarter of a century; what has been accomplished by Bishop Tucker and those associated with him makes one of the most interesting chapters in all recent missionary history. I saw the high school, where the sons of the chiefs are being trained in large numbers for their future duties, and I was especially struck by the admirable medical mission, and by the handsome cathedral, built by the native Christians themselves without outside assistance in either money or labor. At dinner at Mr. Knowles's, Bishop Tucker gave us exceedingly interesting details of his past experiences in Uganda, and of the progress of the missionary work. . . .

At Bishop Hanlon's mission, where I lunched with the bishop, there was a friend, Mother Paul, an American; before I left America I had promised that I would surely see her, and look into the work which she, and the sisters associated with her, were doing. It was delightful seeing her; she not merely spoke my language but my neighborhood dialect. . . . She had been teaching her pupils to sing some lines of the "Star-Spangled Banner," in English, in my especial honor; and of course had been obliged, in writing it out, to use spelling far more purely phonetic than I had ever dreamed of using. . . .

In addition to scholastic exercises Mother Paul and her associates were training their schoolchildren in all kinds of industrial work, taking especial pains to develop those industries that were natural to them and would be of use when they returned to their own homes. Both at Bishop Hanlon's mission, and at Bishop Streicher's, the mission of the White Fathers— originally a French organization, which has established churches and schools in almost all parts of Africa—the fathers were teaching the native men to cultivate coffee and various fruits and vegetables.

I called on the little king, who is being well trained by his English tutor—few tutors perform more exacting or responsible duties—and whose comfortable house was furnished in

English fashion. I met his native advisers, shrewd, powerful-looking men; and went into the Council Chamber, where I was greeted by the Council, substantial-looking men, well-dressed in the native fashion, and representing all the districts of the kingdom. When we visited the king it was after dark, and we were received by smart-looking black soldiers in ordinary khaki uniform, while accompanying them were other attendants dressed in the old-time native fashion; men with flaming torches, and others with the big Uganda drums which they beat to an accompaniment of wild cries. These drums are characteristic of Uganda; each chief has one, and beats upon it his own peculiar tattoo. The king, and all other people of consequence, white, Indian, or native, went round in rickshaws, one man pulling in the shafts and three others pushing behind. The rickshaw men ran well, and sang all the time, the man in the shafts serving as shanty-man, while the three behind repeated in chorus every second or two a kind of clanging note; and this went on without a break, hour after hour. The natives looked well and were dressed well: the men in long flowing garments of white, the women usually in brown cloth made in the old native style out of the bark of the bark cloth tree. The clothes of the chiefs were tastefully ornamented. All the people, gentle and simple, were very polite and ceremonious both to one another and to strangers. Now and then we met parties of Sikh soldiers, tall, bearded, fine-looking men with turbans; and there were Indian and Swahili and even Arab and Persian traders.

The houses had mud walls and thatched roofs. The gardens were surrounded by braided cane fences. In the gardens and along the streets were many trees; among them bark-cloth trees, from which the bark is stripped every year for cloth; great incense trees, the sweet-scented gum oozing through wounds in the bark; and date palms, in the fronds of which hung the nests of the golden weaver birds, now breeding. White cow herons, tamer than barnyard fowls, accompanied the cattle, perching on their backs, or walking beside them. Beautiful kavirondo cranes came familiarly round the houses. It was all strange and attractive. Birds sang everywhere. The air was heavy with the fragrance of flowers of many colors; the whole place was a riot of lush growing plants. Every day there were terrific thunderstorms. At Kampalla three men had been killed by lightning within six weeks; a year or two before our host, Knowles, had been struck by lightning and knocked senseless, a huge zigzag mark being left across his body, and the links of his gold watch chain being fused; it was many months before he completely recovered.

Knowles arranged a *situtunga* hunt for us. The *situtunga* is closely related to the bushbuck but is bigger, with very long hoofs, and shaggy hair like a waterbuck. It is exclusively a beast of the marshes, making its home in the thick reedbeds, where the water is deep; and it is exceedingly shy, so that very few white men have shot, or even seen, it. Its long hoofs enable it to go over the most treacherous ground, and it swims well; in many of its haunts, in the thick papyrus, the water is waist-deep on a man. Through the papyrus, and the reeds and marsh grass, it makes well-beaten paths. Where it is in any danger of molestation it is never seen abroad in the daytime, venturing from the safe cover of the high reeds only at night; but fifty miles inland, in the marsh grass on the edge of a big papyrus swamp, Kermit caught a glimpse of half a dozen feeding in the open, knee-deep in water, long after sunrise. On the hunt in question a patch of marsh was driven by a hundred natives, while the guns were strung along the likely passes which led to another patch of marsh. A fine *situtunga* buck came to Kermit's post, and he killed it as it bolted away. It had stolen up so quietly through the long marsh grass that he only saw it when it was directly on him. Its stomach contained not grass, but the leaves and twig tips of a shrub which grows in and alongside of the marshes.

The day after this hunt our safari started on its march northwestward to Lake Albert Nyanza. We had taken with us from East Africa our gun-bearers, tent boys, and the men whom the naturalists had trained as skinners. The porters were men of Uganda; the *askaris* were from the constabulary, and widely different races were represented among them, but all had been drilled into soldierly uniformity. The porters were well-clad, well-behaved, fine-looking men, and did their work better than the *shenzis,* the wild Meru of Kikiu tribesmen, whom we had occasionally employed in East Africa; but they were not the equals of the regular East African porters. I think this was largely because of their inferior food, for they ate chiefly yams and plantains; in other words inferior sweet potatoes and bananas. They were quite as fond of singing as the East African porters, and in addition were cheered on the march by drum and fife; several men had fifes, and one carried nothing but one of the big Uganda drums, which he usually bore at the head of the safari, marching in company with the flag-bearer. Every hour or two the men would halt, often beside one of the queer little wickerwork booths in which native hucksters disposed of their wares by the roadside.

Along the road we often met wayfarers; once or twice bullock carts; more often men carrying rolls of hides or long bales of cotton on their heads; or a set of Bahima herdsmen, with clear-cut features, guarding their herds of huge-horned Angola cattle.

All greeted us most courteously, frequently crouching or kneeling, as is their custom when they salute a superior; and we were scrupulous to acknowledge their salutes, and to return their greetings in the native fashion, with words of courtesy and long drawn *e-h-h-s* and *a-a-h-s*. Along the line of march the chiefs had made preparations to receive us. Each afternoon, as we came to the spot where we were to camp for the night, we found a cleared space strewed with straw and surrounded by a plaited reed fence. Within this space cane houses, with thatched roofs of coarse grass, had been erected, some for our stores, one for a kitchen, one, which was always decked with flowers, as a rest-house for ourselves; the later with open sides, the roof upheld by cane pillars, so that it was cool and comfortable, and afforded a welcome shelter, either from the burning sun if the weather was clear, or from the pelting, driving tropical storms if there was rain. The moon was almost full when we left Kampalla, and night after night it lent a half-unearthly beauty to the tropical landscape.

Sometimes in the evenings the mosquitoes bothered us; more often they did not; but in any event we slept well under our nettings. Usually at each camp we found either the head chief of the district, or a subchief, with presents; eggs, chickens, sheep, once or twice a bullock, always pineapples and bananas. The chief was always well dressed in flowing robes, and usually welcomed us with dignity and courtesy (sometimes, however, permitting the courtesy to assume the form of servility); and we would have him in to tea, where he was sure to enjoy the bread and jam. Sometimes he came in a rickshaw, sometimes in a kind of wickerwork palanquin, sometimes on foot. When we left his territory we made him a return gift. . . .

The first day's march from Kampalla led us through *shambas,* the fields of sweet potatoes and plantations of bananas being separated by hedges or by cane fences. Then for two or three days we passed over low hills and through swampy valleys, the whole landscape covered by a sea of elephant grass, the close-growing, coarse blades more than twice the height of a man on horseback. Here and there it was dotted with groves of strange trees; in these groves monkeys of various kinds—some black, some red-tailed, some auburn—chattered as they raced away among the branches; there were brilliant rollers and bee-eaters; little green and yellow parrots, and gray parrots with red tails; and many colored butterflies. Once or twice we saw the handsome, fierce, short-tailed eagle, the bateleur eagle, and scared one from a reedbuck fawn it had killed. Among the common birds there were black drongos, and musical bush shrikes; small black magpies with brown tails; white-headed kites and slate-colored sparrow-hawks; palm swifts, big hornbills; blue and mottled kingfishers, which never went near the water, and had their upper mandibles red and their under ones black; barbets, with swollen, sawtoothed bills, their plumage iridescent purple above and red below; bulbuls, also dark purple above and red below, which whistled and bubbled incessantly as they hopped among the thick bushes, behaving much like our own yellow-breasted chats; and a multitude of other birds, beautiful or fantastic. There were striped squirrels too, reminding us of the big Rocky Mountain chipmunk or Say's chipmunk, but with smaller ears and a longer tail.

Christmas day we passed on the march. There is not much use in trying to celebrate Christmas unless there are small folks to hang up their stockings on Christmas Eve, to rush gleefully in at dawn next morning to open the stockings, and after breakfast to wait in hopping expectancy until their elders throw open the doors of the room in which the big presents are arranged, those for each child on a separate table.

Forty miles from the coast the elephant grass began to disappear. The hills became somewhat higher, there were thorn trees, and stately royal palms of great height, their stems swollen and bulging at the top, near the fronds. Parasitic ferns, with leaves as large as cabbage leaves, grew on the branches of the acacias. One kind of tree sent down from its branches to the ground roots which grew into thick trunks. There were wide, shallow marshes, and although the grass was tall it was no longer above a man's head. Kermit and I usually got two or three hours' hunting each day. We killed singing waterbuck, bushbuck, and bohor reedbuck. . . . I killed a very handsome harnessed bushbuck ram. It was rather bigger than a good-sized white-tail buck, its brilliant red coat beautifully marked with rows of white spots, its twisted black horns sharp and polished. . . .

It was pleasant to stride along the road in the early mornings, followed by the safari, and we saw many a glorious sunrise. But as noon approached it grew very hot, under the glare of the brazen equatorial sun, and we were always glad when we approached our new camp, with its grass-strewn ground, its wickerwork fence, and cool, open rest-house. The local subchief and his elders were usually drawn up to receive me at the gate, bowing, clapping their hands, and uttering their long-drawn *e-h-h-s;* and often banana saplings or branches would be stuck in the ground to form avenues of approach, and the fence and rest-house might be decorated with flowers of many kinds. Sometimes we were met with music, on instruments of one string, of three strings, of ten strings—rudimentary fiddles and harps; and there was a much more complicated instrument, big and cumbrous, made of bars of wood placed on two banana stems, the bars being struck with a hammer, as if they were keys; its tones were deep and good. Along the road we did not see habitations or people; but continually there led away from it, twisting through the tall grass and the bush jungles, native paths, the earth beaten brown and hard by countless bare feet; and these, crossing and recrossing in a network, led to plantation after plantation of bananas and sweet potatoes, and clusters of thatched huts.

In the afternoon, as the sun began to get well beyond the meridian, we usually sallied forth to hunt, under the guidance of some native who had come in to tell us where he had seen game that morning. The jungle was so thick in places and the grass was everywhere so long, that without such guidance there was little successful hunting to be done in only two or three hours. We might come back with a buck, or with two or three guinea-fowl, or with nothing. . . .

Ten days from Kampalla we crossed the little Kafu River, the black, smooth current twisting quickly along between beds of plumed papyrus. Beyond it we entered the native kingdom of Unyoro. It is part of the British protectorate of Uganda, but is separate from the native kingdom of Uganda, though its people in ethnic type and social development seem much the same. We halted for a day at Hoima, a spread-out little native town, pleasantly situated among hills, and surrounded by plantations of cotton, plaintains, yams, millet, and beans. It is the capital of Unyoro, where the king lives, as well as three or four English officials, and Episcopalian and Roman Catholic missionaries. The king, accompanied by his prime minister and by the English commissioner, called on me, and I gave him five o'clock tea; he is a Christian, as are most of his chiefs and headmen, and they are sending their children to the mission schools.

A heron, about the size of our night heron but with a longer neck, and with a curiously crowlike voice, strolled about among the native houses at Hoima; and the kites almost brushed us with their wings as they swooped down for morsels of food. The cheerful, confiding little wagtails crossed the threshold of the rest-house in which we sat. Black and white crows and vultures came around camp; and handsome, dark hawks, with white on their wings and tails, and with long, conspicuous crests, perched upright on the trees. There were many kinds of doves; one pretty little fellow was but six inches long. At night the jackals wailed with shrill woe among the gardens.

From Hoima we entered a country covered with the tall, rank elephant grass. It was traversed by papyrus-bordered streams, and broken by patches of forest. The date-palms grew tall, and among the trees were some with orange-red flowers like trumpet flowers, growing in grapeshaped clusters; and both the flowers and the seed-pods into which they turned stood straight up in rows above the leafy tops of the trees that bore them.

The first evening, as we sat in the cool, open cane rest-house, word was brought us that an elephant was close at hand. We found him after ten minutes' walk; a young bull, with very small tusks, not worth shooting. For three-quarters of an hour we watched him, strolling about and feeding, just on the edge of a wall of high elephant grass. Although we were in plain sight, ninety yards off, and sometimes moved about, he never saw us; for an elephant's eyes are very bad. He was feeding on some thick, luscious grass, in the usual leisurely elephant fashion, plucking a big tuft, waving it nonchalantly about in his trunk, and finally tucking it into his mouth; pausing to rub his side against a tree, or to sway to and fro as he stood; and continually waving his tail and half cocking his ears.

At noon on January 5, 1910, we reached Butiaba, a sandspit

and marsh on the shores of Lake Albert Nyanza. We had marched about 160 miles from Lake Victoria. We camped on the sandy beach by the edge of the beautiful lake, looking across its waters to the mountains that walled in the opposite shore. At midday the whole landscape trembled in the white, glaring heat; as the afternoon waned a wind blew off the lake, and the west kindled in ruddy splendor as the sun went down.

SPEECH AT
OSAWATOMIE, KANSAS

August 31, 1910

THE NEW NATIONALISM*

We come here today to commemorate one of the epoch-making events of the long struggle for the rights of man—the long struggle for the uplift of humanity. Our country—this great Republic—means nothing unless it means the triumph of a real democracy, the triumph of popular government, and, in the long run, of an economic system under which each man shall be guaranteed the opportunity to show the best that there is in him. That is why the history of America is now the central feature of the history of the world; for the world has set its face hopefully toward our democracy; and, O my fellow citizens, each one of you carries on your shoulders not only the burden of doing well for the sake of your own country, but the burden of doing well and of seeing that this nation does well for the sake of mankind.

There have been two great crises in our country's history: first, when it was formed, and then, again, when it was perpetuated; and, in the second of these great crises—in the time of stress and strain which culminated in the Civil War, on the outcome of which depended the justification of what had been done earlier, you men of the Grand Army, you men who fought through the Civil War, not only did you justify your generation, not only did you render life worth living for our generation, but you justified the wisdom of Washington and Washington's colleagues. If this Republic had been founded by them only to be split asunder into fragments when the strain came, then the judgment of the world would have been that Washington's

*Published in *The New Nationalism,* 1910.

264

work was not worth doing. It was you who crowned Washington's work, as you carried to achievement the high purpose of Abraham Lincoln.

Now, with this second period of our history the name of John Brown will be forever associated; and Kansas was the theater upon which the first act of the second of our great national life dramas was played. It was the result of the struggle in Kansas which determined that our country should be in deed as well as in name devoted to both union and freedom; that the great experiment of democratic government on a national scale should succeed and not fail. In name we had the Declaration of Independence in 1776; but we gave the lie by our acts to the words of the Declaration of Independence until 1865; and words count for nothing except insofar as they represent acts. This is true everywhere; but, O my friends, it should be truest of all in political life. A broken promise is bad enough in private life. It is worse in the field of politics. No man is worth his salt in public life who makes on the stump a pledge which he does not keep after election; and, if he makes such a pledge and does not keep it, hunt him out of public life. I care for the great deeds of the past chiefly as spurs to drive us onward in the present. I speak of the men of the past partly that they may be honored by our praise of them, but more that they may serve as examples for the future.

It was a heroic struggle; and, as is inevitable with all such struggles, it had also a dark and terrible side. Very much was done of good, and much also of evil; and, as was inevitable in such a period of revolution, often the same man did both good and evil. For our great good fortune as a nation, we, the people of the United States as a whole, can now afford to forget the evil, or, at least, to remember it without bitterness, and to fix our eyes with pride only on the good that was accomplished. Even in ordinary times there are very few of us who do not see the problems of life as through a glass, darkly; and when the glass is clouded by the murk of furious popular passion, the vision of the best and the bravest is dimmed. Looking back, we are all of us now able to do justice to the valor and the disinterestedness and the love of the right, as to each it was given to see the right, shown both by the men of the North and the men of the South in that contest which was finally decided by the attitude of the West. We can admire the heroic valor, the sincerity, the self-devotion shown alike by the men who wore the blue and the men who wore the gray; and our sadness that such men should have had to fight one another is tempered by the glad knowledge that ever hereafter their descendants shall be found fighting side by side, struggling in peace as well as in war for the uplift of their common country, all alike resolute to raise to the highest pitch of honor and usefulness the nation to which they all belong. As for the veterans of the Grand Army of the Republic, they deserve honor and recognition such as is paid to no other citizens of the Republic; for to them the Republic owes its all; for to them it owes its very existence. It is because of what you and your comrades did in the dark years that we of today walk, each of us, head erect, and proud that we belong, not to one of a dozen little squabbling contemptible commonwealths, but to the mightiest nation upon which the sun shines.

I do not speak of this struggle of the past merely from the historic standpoint. Our interest is primarily in the application today of the lessons taught by the contest of half a century ago. It is of little use for us to pay lip-loyalty to the mighty men of the past unless we sincerely endeavor to apply to the problems of the present precisely the qualities which in other crises enabled the men of that day to meet those crises. It is half melancholy and half amusing to see the way in which well-meaning people gather to do honor to the men who, in company with John Brown, and under the lead of Abraham Lincoln, faced and solved the great problems of the nineteenth century, while, at the same time, these same good people nervously shrink from, or frantically denounce, those who are trying to meet the problems of the twentieth century in the spirit which was accountable for the successful solution of the problems of Lincoln's time.

Of that generation of men to whom we owe so much, the man to whom we owe most is, of course, Lincoln. Part of our debt to him is because he forecast our present struggle and saw the way out. He said: "I hold that while man exists it is his duty to improve not only his own condition, but to assist in ameliorating mankind."

And again: "Labor is prior to, and independent of, capital. Capital is only the fruit of labor, and could never have existed if labor had not first existed. Labor is the superior of capital, and deserves much the higher consideration."

If that remark was original with me, I should be even more strongly denounced as a communist agitator than I shall be anyhow. It is Lincoln's. I am only quoting it; and that is one side; that is the side the capitalist should hear. Now, let the working man hear his side.

"Capital has its rights, which are as worthy of protection as any other rights. . . . Nor should this lead to a war upon the owners of property. Property is the fruit of labor; . . . property is desirable; is a positive good in the world."

And then comes a thoroughly Lincolnlike sentence: "Let not him who is houseless pull down the house of another, but let him work diligently and build one for himself, thus by example assuring that his own shall be safe from violence when built."

It seems to me that, in these words, Lincoln took substantially the attitude that we ought to take; he showed the proper sense of proportion in his relative estimates of capital and labor, of human rights and property rights. Above all, in this speech, as in many others, he taught a lesson in wise kindliness and charity; an indispensable lesson to us of today. But this wise kindliness and charity never weakened his arm or numbed his heart. We cannot afford weakly to blind ourselves to the actual conflict which faces us today. The issue is joined, and we must fight or fail.

In every wise struggle for human betterment one of the main objects, and often the only object, has been to achieve in large measure equality of opportunity. In the struggle for this great end, nations rise from barbarism to civilization, and through it people press forward from one stage of enlightenment to the next. One of the chief factors in progress is the destruction of special privilege. The essence of any struggle for healthy liberty has always been, and must always be, to take from some one man or class of men the right to enjoy power, or wealth, or position, or immunity, which has not been earned by service to his or their fellows. That is what you fought for in the Civil War, and that is what we strive for now.

At many stages in the advance of humanity, this conflict between the men who possess more than they have earned and the men who have earned more than they possess is the central condition of progress. In our day it appears as the struggle of freemen to gain and hold the right of self-government as against the special interests, who twist the methods of free government into machinery for defeating the popular will. At every stage, and under all circumstances, the essence of the struggle is to equalize opportunity, destroy privilege, and give to the life and citizenship of every individual the highest possible value both to himself and to the commonwealth. That is nothing new. All I ask in civil life is what you fought for in the Civil War. I ask that civil life be carried on according to the spirit in which the army was carried on. You never get perfect justice, but the effort in handling the army was to bring to the front the men who could do the job. Nobody grudged promotion to Grant, or Sherman, or Thomas, or Sheridan, because they earned it. The only complaint was when a man got promotion which he did not earn.

Practical equality of opportunity for all citizens, when we achieve it, will have two great results. First, every man will have a fair chance to make of himself all that in him lies; to reach the highest point to which his capacities, unassisted by special privilege of his own and unhampered by the special privilege of others, can carry him, and to get for himself and his family substantially what he has earned. Second, equality of opportunity means that the commonwealth will get from every citizen the highest service of which he is capable. No man who carries the burden of the special privileges of another can give to the commonwealth that service to which it is fairly entitled.

I stand for the square deal. But when I say that I am for the square deal, I mean not merely that I stand for fair play under the present rules of the game, but that I stand for having those rules changed so as to work for a more substantial equality of opportunity and of reward for equally good service. One word of warning, which, I think, is hardly necessary in Kansas. When I say I want a square deal for the poor man, I do not mean that I want a square deal for the man who remains poor because he has not got the energy to work for himself. If a man who has had a chance will not make good, then he has got to quit. And you men of the Grand Army, you want justice for the brave man who fought, and punishment for the coward who shirked his work. Is not that so?

Now, this means that our government, national and state, must be freed from the sinister influence or control of special interests. Exactly as the special interests of cotton and slavery threatened our political integrity before the Civil War, so now the great special business interests too often control and corrupt the men and methods of government for their own profit. We must drive the special interests out of politics. That is one of our tasks today. Every special interest is entitled to justice—full, fair, and complete—and, now, mind you, if there were any attempt by mob violence to plunder and work harm to the special interest, whatever it may be, that I most dislike, and the wealthy man, whomsoever he may be, for whom I have the greatest contempt, I would fight for him, and you would if you were worth your salt. He should have justice. For every special interest is entitled to justice, but not one is entitled to a vote in Congress, to a voice on the bench, or to representation in any public office. The Constitution guarantees protection to property, and we must make that promise good. But it does not give the right of suffrage to any corporation.

The true friend of property, the true conservative, is he who insists that property shall be the servant and not the master of the commonwealth; who insists that the creature of man's making shall be the servant and not the master of the man who made it. The citizens of the United States must effectively control the mighty commercial forces which they have themselves called into being.

There can be no effective control of corporations while their political activity remains. To put an end to it will be neither a short nor an easy task, but it can be done.

We must have complete and effective publicity of corporate affairs, so that the people may know beyond peradventure whether the corporations obey the law and whether their management entitles them to the confidence of the public. It is necessary that laws should be passed to prohibit the use of corporate funds directly or indirectly for political purposes; it is still more necessary that such laws should be thoroughly enforced. Corporate expenditures for political purposes, and especially such expenditures by public-service corporations, have supplied one of the principal sources of corruption in our political affairs.

It has become entirely clear that we must have government supervision of the capitalization; not only of public-service corporations, including, particularly, railways, but of all corporations doing an interstate business. I do not wish to see the nation forced into the ownership of the railways if it can possibly be avoided, and the only alternative is thoroughgoing and effective regulation, which shall be based on a full knowledge of all the facts, including a physical valuation of property. This physical valuation is not needed, or, at least, is very rarely needed, for fixing rates; but it is needed as the basis of honest capitalization.

We have come to recognize that franchise should never be granted except for a limited time, and never without proper provision for compensation to the public. It is my personal belief that the same kind and degree of control and supervision which should be exercised over public-service corporations should be extended also to combinations which control necessaries of life, such as meat, oil, and coal, or which deal in them on an important scale. I have no doubt that the ordinary man who has control of them is much like ourselves. I have no doubt he would like to do well, but I want to have enough supervision to help him realize that desire to do well.

I believe that the officers, and, especially, the directors, of corporations should be held personally responsible when any corporation breaks the law.

Combinations in industry are the result of an imperative economic law which cannot be repealed by political legislation. The effort at prohibiting all combination has substantially failed. The way out lies not in attempting to prevent such combinations but in completely controlling them in the interest of the public welfare. For that purpose the federal Bureau of Corporations is an agency of first importance. Its powers, and, therefore, its efficiency, as well as that of the Interstate Commerce Commission, should be largely increased. We have a right to expect from the Bureau of Corporations and from the Interstate Commerce Commission a very high grade of public service. We should be as sure of the proper conduct of the interstate railways and the proper management of interstate business as we are now sure of the conduct and management of the national banks, and we should have as effective supervision in one case as in the other. The Hepburn Act, and the amendment to the act in the shape in which it finally passed Congress at the last session, represent a long step in advance, and we must go yet further.

There is a widespread belief among our people that, under the methods of making tariffs which have hitherto obtained, the special interests are too influential. Probably this is true of both the big special interests and the little special interests. These methods have put a premium on selfishness, and, naturally, the selfish big interests have gotten more than their smaller, though equally selfish, brothers. The duty of Congress is to provide a method by which the interest of the whole people shall be all that receives consideration. To this end there must be an expert tariff commission, wholly removed from the possibility of political pressure or of improper business influence. Such a commission can find the real difference between cost of production, which is mainly the difference of labor cost here and abroad. As fast as its recommendations are made, I believe in revising one schedule at a time. A general revision of the tariff almost inevitably leads to logrolling and the subordination of the general public interest to local and special interests.

The absence of effective state and, especially, national restraint upon unfair money-getting has tended to create a small class of enormously wealthy and economically powerful men, whose chief object is to hold and increase their power. The prime need is to change the conditions which enable these men to accumulate power which it is not for the general welfare that they should hold or exercise. We grudge no man a fortune which represents his own power and sagacity, when exercised with entire regard to the welfare of his fellows. Again, comrades over there, take the lesson from your own experience. Not only did you not grudge, but you gloried in the promotion of the great generals who gained their promotion by leading the army to victory. So it is with us. We grudge no man a fortune in civil life if it is honorably obtained and well used. It is not even enough that it should have been gained without doing damage to the community. We should permit it to be gained only so long as the gaining represents benefit to the community. This, I know, implies a policy of a far more active governmental interference with social and economic conditions in this country than we have yet had, but I think we have got to face the fact that such an increase in governmental control is now necessary.

No man should receive a dollar unless that dollar has been fairly earned. Every dollar received should represent a dollar's worth of service rendered—not gambling in stocks, but service rendered. The really big fortune, the swollen fortune, by the mere fact of its size acquires qualities which differentiate it in kind as well as in degree from what is possessed by men of relatively small means. Therefore, I believe in a graduated income tax on big fortunes, and in another tax which is far more easily collected and far more effective—a graduated inheritance tax on big fortunes, properly safeguarded against evasion and increasing rapidly in amount with the size of the estate.

The people of the United States suffer from periodical financial panics to a degree substantially unknown among the other nations which approach us in financial strength. There is no reason why we should suffer what they escape. It is of profound importance that our financial system should be promptly investigated, and so thoroughly and effectively revised as to make it certain that hereafter our currency will no longer fail at critical times to meet our needs.

It is hardly necessary for me to repeat that I believe in an efficient army and a navy large enough to secure for us abroad that respect which is the surest guarantee of peace. A word of special warning to my fellow citizens who are as progressive as I hope I am. I want them to keep up their interest in our internal affairs; and I want them also continually to remember Uncle Sam's interests abroad. Justice and fair-dealing among nations rest upon principles identical with those which control justice and fair-dealing among the individuals of which naitons are composed, with the vital exception that each nation must do its own part in international police work. If you get into trouble here, you can call for the police; but if Uncle Sam gets into trouble, he has got to be his own policeman, and I want to see him strong enough to encourage the peaceful aspirations of other peoples in connection with us. I believe in national friendships and heartiest goodwill to all nations; but national friendships, like those between men, must be founded on respect as well as on liking, on forbearance as well as upon trust. I should be heartily ashamed of any American who did not try to make the American government act as justly toward the other nations in international relations as he himself would act toward any individual in private relations. I should be heartily ashamed to see us wrong a weaker power, and I should hang my head forever if we tamely suffered wrong from a stronger power.

Of conservation I shall speak more at length elsewhere.

Conservation means development as much as it does protection. I recognize the right and duty of this generation to develop and use the natural resources of our land; but I do not recognize the right to waste them, or to rob, by wasteful use, the generations that come after us. I ask nothing of the nation except that it so behave as each farmer here behaves with reference to his own children. That farmer is a poor creature who skins the land and leaves it worthless to his children. The farmer is a good farmer who, having enabled the land to support himself and to provide for the education of his children, leaves it to them a little better than he found it himself. I believe the same thing of a nation.

Moreover, I believe that the natural resources must be used for the benefit of all our people, and not monopolized for the benefit of the few, and here again is another case in which I am accused of taking a revolutionary attitude. People forget now that one hundred years ago there were public men of good character who advocated the nation selling its public lands in great quantities, so that the nation could get the most money out of it, and giving it to the men who could cultivate it for their own uses. We took the proper democratic ground that the land should be granted in small sections to the men who were actually to till it and live on it. Now, with the waterpower, with the forests, with the mines, we are brought face to face with the fact that there are many people who will go with us in conserving the resources only if they are to be allowed to exploit them for their benefit. That is one of the fundamental reasons why the special interests should be driven out of politics. Of all the questions which can come before this nation, short of the actual preservation of its existence in a great war, there is none which compares in importance with the great central task of leaving this land even a better land for our descendants than it is for us, and training them into a better race to inhabit the land and pass it on. Conservation is a great moral issue, for it involves the patriotic duty of insuring the safety and continuance of the nation. Let me add that the health and vitality of our people are at least as well worth conserving as their forests, waters, lands, and minerals, and in this great work the national government must bear a most important part.

I have spoken elsewhere also of the great task which lies before the farmers of the country to get for themselves and their wives and children not only the benefits of better farming, but also those of better business methods and better conditions of life on the farm. The burden of this great task will fall, as it should, mainly upon the great organizations of the farmers themselves. I am glad it will, for I believe they are all well able to handle it. In particular, there are strong reasons why the departments of agriculture of the various states, the United States Department of Agriculture, and the agricultural colleges and experiment stations should extend their work to cover all phases of farm life, instead of limiting themselves, as they have far too often limited themselves in the past, solely to the question of the production of crops. And now a special word to the farmer. I want to see him make the farm as fine a farm as it can be made; and let him remember to see that the improvement goes on indoors as well as out; let him remember that the farmer's wife should have her share of thought and attention just as much as the farmer himself.

Nothing is more true than that excess of every kind is followed by reaction; a fact which should be pondered by reformer and reactionary alike. We are face to face with new conceptions of the relations of property to human welfare, chiefly because certain advocates of the rights of property as against the rights of men have been pushing their claims too far. The man who wrongly holds that every human right is secondary to his profit must now give way to the advocate of human welfare, who rightly maintains that every man holds his property subject to the general right of the community to regulate its use to whatever degree the public welfare may require it.

But I think we may go still further. The right to regulate the use of wealth in the public interest is universally admitted. Let us admit also the right to regulate the terms and conditions of labor, which is the chief element of wealth, directly in the interest of the common good. The fundamental thing to do for every man is to give him a chance to reach a place in which he will make the greatest possible contribution to the public welfare. Understand what I say there. Give him a chance, not push him up if he will not be pushed. Help any man who stumbles; if he lies down, it is a poor job to try to carry him; but if he is a worthy man, try your best to see that he gets a chance to show the worth that is in him. No man can be a good citizen unless he has a wage more than sufficient to cover the bare cost of living, and hours of labor short enough so that after his day's work is done he will have time and energy to bear his share in the management of the community, to help in carrying the general load. We keep countless men from being good citizens by the conditions of life with which we surround them. We need comprehensive workmen's-compensation acts, both state and national laws to regulate child labor and work for women, and, especially, we need in our common schools not merely education in book-learning, but also practical training for daily life and work. We need to enforce better sanitary conditions for our workers and to extend the use of safety appliances for our workers in industry and commerce, both within and between the states. Also, friends, in the interest of the working man himself we need to set our faces like flint against mob violence just as against corporate greed; against violence and injustice and lawlessness by wage-workers just as much as against lawless cunning and greed and selfish arrogance of employers. If I could ask but one thing of my fellow countrymen, my request would be that, whenever they go in for reform, they remember the two sides, and that they always exact justice from one side as much as from the other. I have small use for the public servant who can always see and denounce the corruption of the capitalist, but who cannot persuade himself, especially before election, to say a word about lawless mob violence. And I have equally small use for the man, be he a judge on the bench, or editor of a great paper, or wealthy and influential private citizen, who can see clearly enough and denounce the lawlessness of mob violence, but whose eyes are closed so that he is blind when the question is one of corruption in business on a gigantic scale. Also remember what I said about excess in reformer and reactionary alike. If the reactionary man, who thinks of nothing but the rights of property, could have his way, he would bring about a revolution; and one of my chief fears in connection with progress comes because I do not want to see our people, for lack of proper leadership, compelled to follow men whose intentions are excellent, but whose eyes are a little too wild to make it really safe to trust them. Here in Kansas there is one paper which habitually denounces me as the tool of Wall Street, and at the same time frantically repudiates the statement that I am a socialist on the ground that that is an unwarranted slander of the socialists.

National efficiency has many factors. It is a necessary result of the principle of conservation widely applied. In the end it will determine our failure or success as a nation. National efficiency has to do not only with natural resources and with men but it is equally concerned with institutions. The state must be made efficient for the work which concerns only the people of the state; and the nation for that which concerns all the people. There must remain no neutral ground to serve as a refuge for lawbreakers, and especially for lawbreakers of great wealth, who can hire the vulpine legal cunning which will teach them how to avoid both jurisdictions. It is a misfortune when the national legislature fails to do its duty in providing a national remedy, so that the only national activity is the purely negative activity of the judiciary in forbidding the state to exercise power in the premises.

I do not ask for overcentralization; but I do ask that we work in a spirit of broad and far-reaching nationalism when we work for what concerns our people as a whole. We are all Americans. Our common interests are as broad as the continent. I speak to you here in Kansas exactly as I would speak in New York or Georgia, for the most vital problems are those which affect us all alike. The national government belongs to the whole American people, and where the whole American people are interested, that interest can be guarded effectively only by the national government. The betterment which we seek must be accomplished, I believe, mainly through the national government.

The American people are right in demanding that New Nationalism, without which we cannot hope to deal with new problems. The New Nationalism puts the national need before sectional or personal advantage. It is impatient of the utter confusion that results from local legislatures attempting to treat national issues as local issues. It is still more impatient of the impotence which springs from overdivision of governmental powers, the impotence which makes it possible for local selfishness or for legal cunning, hired by wealthy special interests, to bring national activities to a deadlock. This New Nationalism regards the executive power as the steward of the public welfare. It demands of the judiciary that it shall be interested primarily in human welfare rather than in property, just as it demands that the representative body shall represent all the people rather than any one class or section of the people.

I believe in shaping the ends of government to protect property as well as human welfare. Normally, and in the long run, the ends are the same; but whenever the alternative must be faced, I am for men and not for property, as you were in the Civil War. I am far from underestimating the importance of dividends; but I rank dividends below human character. Again, I do not have any sympathy with the reformer who says he does not care for dividends. Of course, economic welfare is necessary, for a man must pull his own weight and be able to support his family. I know well that the reformers must not bring upon the people economic ruin, or the reforms themselves will go down in the ruin. But we must be ready to face temporary disaster, whether or not brought on by those who will war against us to the knife. Those who oppose all reform will do well to remember that ruin in its worst form is inevitable if our national life brings us nothing better than swollen fortunes for the few and the triumph in both politics and business of a sordid and selfish materialism.

If our political institutions were perfect, they would absolutely prevent the political domination of money in any part of our affairs. We need to make our political representatives more quickly and sensitively responsive to the people whose servants they are. More direct action by the people in their own affairs under proper safeguards is vitally necessary. The direct primary is a step in this direction, if it is associated with a corrupt-practices act effective to prevent the advantage of the man willing recklessly and unscrupulously to spend money over his more honest competitor. It is particularly important that all moneys received or expended for campaign purposes should be publicly accounted for, not only after election, but before election as well. Political action must be made simpler, easier, and freer from confusion for every citizen. I believe that the prompt removal of unfaithful or incompetent public servants should be made easy and sure in whatever way experience shall show to be most expedient in any given class of cases.

One of the fundamental necessities in a representative government such as ours is to make certain that the men to whom the people delegate their power shall serve the people by whom they are elected, and not the special interests. I believe that every national officer, elected or appointed, should be forbidden to perform any service or receive any compensation, directly or indirectly, from interstate corporations; and a similar provision could not fail to be useful within the states.

The object of government is the welfare of the people. The material progress and prosperity of a nation are desirable chiefly so far as they lead to the moral and material welfare of all good citizens. Just in proportion as the average man and woman are honest, capable of sound judgment and high ideals, active in public affairs—but, first of all, sound in their home life, and the

father and mother of healthy children whom they bring up well
—just so far, and no farther, we may count our civilization a
success. We must have—I believe we have already—a genuine
and permanent moral awakening, without which no wisdom of
legislation or administration really means anything; and, on the
other hand, we must try to secure the social and economic
legislation without which any improvement due to purely moral
agitation is necessarily evanescent. Let me again illustrate by a
reference to the Grand Army. You could not have won simply
as a disorderly and disorganized mob. You needed generals; you
needed careful administration of the most advanced type; and a
good commissary—the cracker line. You well remember that
success was necessary in many different lines in order to bring
about general success. You had to have the administration at
Washington good, just as you had to have the administration in
the field; and you had to have the work of the generals good.
You could not have triumphed without that administration and
leadership; but it would all have been worthless if the average
soldier had not had the right stuff in him. He had to have the
right stuff in him, or you could not get it out of him. In the last
analysis, therefore, vitally necessary though it was to have the
right kind of organization and the right kind of generalship, it
was even more vitally necessary that the average soldier should
have the fighting edge, the right character. So it is in our civil
life. No matter how honest and decent we are in our private
lives, if we do not have the right kind of law and the right kind
of administration of the law, we cannot go forward as a nation.
That is imperative; but it must be an addition to, and not a
substitution for, the qualities that make us good citizens. In the
last analysis, the most important elements in any man's career
must be the sum of those qualities which, in the aggregate, we
speak of as character. If he has not got it, then no law that the
wit of man can devise, no administration of the law by the
boldest and strongest executive, will avail to help him. We must
have the right kind of character—character that makes a man,
first of all, a good man in the home, a good father, a good

husband—that makes a man a good neighbor. You must have that, and, then, in addition, you must have the kind of law and the kind of administration of the law which will give to those qualities in the private citizen the best possible chance for development. The prime problem of our nation is to get the right type of good citizenship, and, to get it, we must have progress, and our public men must be genuinely progressive.

SPEECH BEFORE
THE NATIONAL CONVENTION
OF THE PROGRESSIVE PARTY

Chicago, Illinois, August 6, 1912

A CONFESSION OF FAITH*

To you, men and women who have come here to this great city of this great state formally to launch a new party, a party of the people of the whole Union, the National Progressive party, I extend my hearty greeting. You are taking a bold and a greatly needed step for the service of our beloved country. The old parties are husks, with no real soul within either, divided on artificial lines, boss-ridden and privilege-controlled, each a jumble of incongruous elements, and neither daring to speak out wisely and fearlessly what should be said on the vital issues of the day. This new movement is a movement of truth, sincerity, and wisdom, a movement which proposes to put at the service of all our people the collective power of the people, through their governmental agencies, alike in the nation and in the several states. We propose boldly to face the real and great questions of the day, and not skillfully to evade them as do the old parties. We propose to raise aloft a standard to which all honest men can repair, and under which all can fight, no matter what their past political differences, if they are content to face the future and no longer to dwell among the dead issues of the past. We propose to put forth a platform which shall not be a platform of the ordinary and insincere kind, but shall be a contract with the people; and, if the people accept this contract by putting us in power, we shall hold ourselves under honorable

*Published in *Progressive Principles*, 1913.

282

obligation to fulfill every promise it contains as loyally as if it were actually enforceable under the penalties of the law.

The prime need today is to face the fact that we are now in the midst of a great economic evolution. There is urgent necessity of applying both common sense and the highest ethical standard to this movement for better economic conditions among the mass of our people if we are to make it one of healthy evolution and not one of revolution. It is, from the standpoint of our country, wicked as well as foolish longer to refuse to face the real issues of the day. Only by so facing them can we go forward; and to do this we must break up the old party organizations and obliterate the old cleavage lines on the dead issues inherited from fifty years ago.

Our fight is a fundamental fight against both of the old corrupt party machines, for both are under the dominion of the plunder league of the professional politicians who are controlled and sustained by the great beneficiaries of privilege and reaction. How close is the alliance between the two machines is shown by the attitude of that portion of those northeastern newspapers, including the majority of the great dailies in all the northeastern cities—Boston, Buffalo, Springfield, Hartford, Philadelphia, and, above all, New York—which are controlled by our representative of the interests which, in popular phrase, are conveniently grouped together as the Wall Street interests. The large majority of these papers supported Judge Parker for the presidency in 1904; almost unanimously they supported Mr. Taft for the Republican nomination this year; the large majority are now supporting Professor Wilson for the election. Some of them still prefer Mr. Taft to Mr. Wilson, but all make either Mr. Taft or Mr. Wilson their first choice; and one of the ludicrous features of the campaign is that those papers supporting Professor Wilson show the most jealous partisanship for Mr. Taft whenever they think his interests are jeopardized by the Progressive movement—that, for instance, any electors will obey the will of the majority of the Republican voters at the primaries, and vote for me instead of obeying the will of the

Messrs. Barnes-Penrose-Guggenheim combination by voting for Mr. Taft. No better proof can be given than this of the fact that the fundamental concern of the privileged interests is to beat the new party. Some of them would rather beat it with Mr. Wilson; others would rather beat it with Mr. Taft; but the difference between Mr. Wilson and Mr. Taft they consider as trivial, as a mere matter of personal preference. Their real fight is for either, as against the Progressives. They represent the allied reactionaries of the country, and they are against the new party because to their unerring vision it is evident that the real danger to privilege comes from the new party, and from the new party alone. The men who presided over the Baltimore and the Chicago conventions, and the great bosses who controlled the two conventions, Mr. Root and Mr. Parker, Mr. Barnes and Mr. Murphy, Mr. Penrose and Mr. Taggart, Mr. Guggenheim and Mr. Sullivan, differ from one another of course on certain points. But these are the differences which one corporation lawyer has with another corporation lawyer when acting for different corporations. They come together at once as against a common enemy when the dominion of both is threatened by the supremacy of the people of the United States, now aroused to the need of a national alignment on the vital economic issues of this generation.

Neither the Republican nor the Democratic platform contains the slightest promise of approaching the great problems of today either with understanding or good faith; and yet never was there greater need in this nation than now of understanding and of action taken in good faith, on the part of the men and the organizations shaping our governmental policy. Moreover, our needs are such that there should be coherent action among those responsible for the conduct of national affairs and those responsible for the conduct of state affairs; because our aim should be the same in both state and nation; that is, to use the government as an efficient agency for the practical betterment of social and economic conditions throughout this land. There are other important things to be done, but this is the most important thing.

It is preposterous to leave such a movement in the hands of men who have broken their promises as have the present heads of the Republican organization (not of the Republican voters, for they in no shape represent the rank and file of the Republican voters). These men by their deeds give the lie to their words. There is no health in them, and they cannot be trusted. . . .

If this country is really to go forward along the path of social and economic justice, there must be a new party of nationwide and nonsectional principles, a party where the titular national chiefs and the real state leaders shall be in genuine accord, a party in whose counsels the people shall be supreme, a party that shall represent in the nation and the several states alike the same cause, the cause of human rights and of governmental efficiency. At present both the old parties are controlled by professional politicians in the interests of the privileged classes, and apparently each has set up as its ideal of business and political development a government by financial despotism tempered by make-believe political assassination. Democrat and Republican alike, they represent government of the needy many by professional politicians in the interests of the rich few. This is class government, and class government of a peculiarly unwholesome kind.

It seems to me, therefore, that the time is ripe, and overripe, for a genuine Progressive movement, nationwide and justice-loving, sprung from and responsible to the people themselves, and sundered by a great gulf from both of the old party organizations, while representing all that is best in the hopes, beliefs, and aspirations of the plain people who make up the immense majority of the rank and file of both the old parties.

The first essential in the Progressive program is the right of the people to rule. But a few months ago our opponents were assuring us with insincere clamor that it was absurd for us to talk about desiring that the people should rule, because, as a matter of fact, the people actually do rule. Since that time the actions of the Chicago convention, and to an only less degree of the Baltimore convention, have shown in striking fashion how little the people do rule under our present conditions.

We should provide by national law for presidential primaries. We should provide for the election of United States senators by popular vote. We should provide for a short ballot; nothing makes it harder for the people to control their public servants than to force them to vote for so many officials that they cannot really keep track of any one of them, so that each becomes indistinguishable in the crowd around him. There must be stringent and efficient corrupt-practices acts, applying to the primaries as well as the elections; and there should be publicity of campaign contributions during the campaign.

We should provide throughout this Union for giving the people in every state the real right to rule themselves, and really and not nominally to control their public servants and their agencies for doing the public business; an incident of this being giving the people the right themselves to do this public business if they find it impossible to get what they desire through the existing agencies. I do not attempt to dogmatize as to the machinery by which this end should be achieved. In each community it must be shaped so as to correspond not merely with the needs but with the customs and ways of thought of that community, and no community has a right to dictate to any other in this matter. But wherever representative government has in actual fact become nonrepresentative there the people should secure to themselves the initiative, the referendum, and the recall, doing it in such fashion as to make it evident that they do not intend to use these instrumentalities wantonly or frequently, but to hold them ready for use in order to correct the misdeeds or failures of the public servants when it has become evident that these misdeeds and failures cannot be corrected in ordinary and normal fashion. . . .

The American people, and not the courts, are to determine their own fundamental policies. The people should have power to deal with the effect of the acts of all their governmental agencies. This must be extended to include the effects of judicial

acts as well as the acts of the executive and legislative representatives of the people. Where the judge merely does justice as
between man and man, not dealing with constitutional questions, then the interest of the public is only to see that he is a
wise and upright judge. Means should be devised for making it
easier than at present to get rid of an incompetent judge; means
should be devised by the bar and the bench acting in conjunction
with the various legislative bodies to make justice far more
expeditious and more certain than at present. The stick-in-the-
bark legalism, the legalism that subordinates equity to tech-
nicalities, should be recognized as a potent enemy of justice. But
this is not the matter of most concern at the moment. Our prime
concern is that in dealing with the fundamental law of the land,
in assuming finally to interpret it, and therefore finally to make
it, the acts of the courts should be subject to and not above the
final control of the people as a whole. . . . The people themselves
must be the ultimate makers of their own Constitution, and
where their agents differ in their interpretations of the Constitution the people themselves should be given the chance, after full
and deliberate judgment, authoritatively to settle what interpre-
tation it is that their representatives shall thereafter adopt as
binding. . . .

We in America have peculiar need thus to make the acts of
the courts subject to the people, because, owing to causes which
I need not now discuss, the courts have here grown to occupy
a position unknown in any other country, a position of superiority over both the legislature and the executive. Just at this time,
when we have begun in this country to move toward social and
industrial betterment and true industrial democracy, this attitude on the part of the courts is of grave portent, because
privilege has entrenched itself in many courts just as it formerly
entrenched itself in many legislative bodies and in many executive offices. . . .

I am well aware that every upholder of privilege, every hired
agent or beneficiary of the special interests, including many
well-meaning parlor reformers, will denounce all this as "social-

ism" or "anarchy"—the same terms they used in the past in denouncing the movements to control the railways and to control public utilities. As a matter of fact, the propositions I make constitute neither anarchy nor socialism, but, on the contrary, a corrective to socialism and an antidote to anarchy. . . .

In the last twenty years an increasing percentage of our people have come to depend on industry for their livelihood, so that today the wage-workers in industry rank in importance side by side with the tillers of the soil. As a people we cannot afford to let any group of citizens or any individual citizen live or labor under conditions which are injurious to the common welfare. Industry, therefore, must submit to such public regulation as will make it a means of life and health, not of death or inefficiency. We must protect the crushable elements at the base of our present industrial structure.

The first charge on the industrial statesmanship of the day is to prevent human waste. The dead weight of orphanage and depleted craftsmanship, of crippled workers and workers suffering from trade diseases, of casual labor, of insecure old age, and of household depletion due to industrial conditions are, like our depleted soils, our gashed mountainsides and flooded river-bottoms, so many strains upon the national structure, draining the reserve strength of all industries and showing beyond all peradventure the public element and public concern in industrial health.

Ultimately we desire to use the government to aid, as far as can safely be done, in helping the industrial tool-users to become in part tool-owners, just as our farmers now are. . . .

The public needs have been well summarized as follows:

1. We hold that the public has a right to complete knowledge of the facts of work.

2. On the basis of these facts and with the recent discoveries of physicians and neurologists, engineers and economists, the public can formulate minimum occupational standards below which, demonstrably, work can be prosecuted only at a human deficit.

3. In the third place, we hold that all industrial conditions which fall below such standards should come within the scope of governmental action and control in the same way that subnormal sanitary conditions are subject to public regulation and for the same reason—because they threaten the general welfare.

To the first end, we hold that the constituted authorities should be empowered to require all employers to file with them for public purposes such wage scales and other data as the public element in industry demands. The movement for honest weights and measures has its counterpart in industry. All tallies, scales, and check systems should be open to public inspection and inspection of committees of the workers concerned. All deaths, injuries, and diseases due to industrial operation should be reported to public authorities.

To the second end, we hold that minimum-wage commissions should be established in the nation and in each state to inquire into wages paid in various industries and to determine the standard which the public ought to sanction as a minimum; and we believe that, as a present installment of what we hope for in the future, there should be at once established in the nation and its several states minimum standards for the wages of women, taking the present Massachusetts law as a basis from which to start and on which to improve.

We pledge the federal government to an investigation of industries along the lines pursued by the Bureau of Mines with the view to establishing standards of sanitation and safety; we call for the standardization of mine and factory inspection by interstate agreement or the establishment of a federal standard. We stand for the passage of legislation in the nation and in all states providing standards of compensation for industrial accidents and death, and for diseases clearly due to the nature of conditions of industry, and we stand for the adoption by law of a fair standard of compensation for casualties resulting fatally which shall clearly fix the minimum compensation in all cases. . . .

We stand for a living wage. Wages are subnormal if they fail to provide a living for those who devote their time and energy to industrial occupations. The monetary equivalent of a living wage varies according to local conditions, but must include enough to secure the elements of a normal standard of living— a standard high enough to make morality possible, to provide for education and recreation, to care for immature members of the family, to maintain the family during periods of sickness, and to permit of reasonable saving for old age.

Hours are excessive if they fail to afford the worker sufficient time to recuperate and return to his work thoroughly refreshed. We hold that the night labor of women and children is abnormal and should be prohibited; we hold that the employment of women over forty-eight hours per week is abnormal and should be prohibited. We hold that the seven-day working week is abnormal, and we hold that one day of rest in seven should be provided by law. We hold that the continuous industries, operating twenty-four hours out of twenty-four, are abnormal, and where, because of public necessity or of technical reasons (such as molten metal), the twenty-four hours must be divided into two shifts of twelve hours or three shifts of eight, they should by law be divided into three of eight.

Safety conditions are abnormal when, through unguarded machinery, poisons, electrical voltage, or otherwise, the workers are subjected to unnecessary hazards of life and limb; and all such occupations should come under governmental regulation and control.

Home life is abnormal when tenement manufacture is carried on in the household. It is a serious menace to health, education, and childhood, and should therefore be entirely prohibited. Temporary construction camps are abnormal homes and should be subjected to governmental sanitary regulation.

The premature employment of children is abnormal and should be prohibited; so also the employment of women in manufacturing, commerce, or other trades where work compels standing constantly; and also any employment of women in such trades for a period of at least eight weeks at time of childbirth. . . .

It is abnormal for any industry to throw back upon the community the human wreckage due to its wear and tear, and the hazards of sickness, accident, invalidism, involuntary unemployment, and old age should be provided for through insurance. This should be made a charge in whole or in part upon the industries, the employer, the employee, and perhaps the people at large to contribute severally in some degree. Wherever such standards are not met by given establishments, by given industries, are unprovided for by a legislature, or are balked by unenlightened courts, the workers are in jeopardy, the progressive employer is penalized, and the community pays a heavy cost in lessened efficiency and in misery. What Germany has done in the way of old-age pensions or insurance should be studied by us, and the system adapted to our uses, with whatever modifications are rendered necessary by our different ways of life and habits of thought.

Working women have the same need to combine for protection that working men have; the ballot is as necessary for one class as for the other; we do not believe that with the two sexes there is identity of function; but we do believe that there should be equality of right; and therefore we favor woman suffrage. Surely, if women could vote, they would strengthen the hands of those who are endeavoring to deal in efficient fashion with evils such as the white-slave traffic; evils which can in part be dealt with nationally, but which in large part can be reached only by determined local action, such as insisting on the widespread publication of the names of the owners, the landlords, of houses used for immoral purposes.

No people are more vitally interested than working men and working women in questions affecting the public health. The pure-food law must be strengthened and efficiently enforced. In the national government one department should be entrusted with all the agencies relating to the public health, from the enforcement of the pure-food law to the administration of quarantine. This department, through its special health service, would cooperate intelligently with the various state and municipal bodies established for the same end. There would be no discrimination against or for any one set of therapeutic methods, against or for any one school of medicine or system of healing; the aim would be merely to secure under one administrative body efficient sanitary regulation in the interest of the people as a whole. . . .

The welfare of the farmer is a basic need of this nation. It is the men from the farm who in the past have taken the lead in every great movement within this nation, whether in time of war or in time of peace. It is well to have our cities prosper, but it is not well if they prosper at the expense of the country. I am glad to say that in many sections of our country there has been an extraordinary revival of recent years in intelligent interest in and work for those who live in the open country. In this movement the lead must be taken by the farmers themselves; but our people as a whole, through their governmental agencies, should back the farmers. Everything possible should be done to better the economic condition of the farmer, and also to increase the social value of the life of the farmer, the farmer's wife, and their children. The burdens of labor and loneliness bear heavily on the women in the country; their welfare should be the especial concern of all of us. Everything possible should be done to make life in the country profitable so as to be attractive from the economic standpoint and also to give an outlet among farming people for those forms of activity which now tend to make life in the cities especially desirable for ambitious men and women. There should be just the same chance to live as full, as well-rounded, and as highly useful lives in the country as in the city. . . .

The present conditions of business cannot be accepted as satisfactory. There are too many who do not prosper enough, and of the few who prosper greatly there are certainly some whose prosperity does not mean well for the country. Rational Progressives, no matter how radical, are well aware that nothing the government can do will make some men prosper, and we heartily approve the prosperity, no matter how great, of any man, if it comes as an incident to rendering service to the community; but we wish to shape conditions so that a greater number of the small men who are decent, industrious, and energetic shall be able to succeed, and so that the big man who is dishonest shall not be allowed to succeed at all.

Our aim is to control business, not to strangle it—and, above all, not to continue a policy of make-believe strangle toward big concerns that do evil, and constant menace toward both big and little concerns that do well.

Our aim is to promote prosperity, and then see to its proper division. We do not believe that any good comes to anyone by a policy which means destruction of prosperity; for in such cases it is not possible to divide it because of the very obvious fact that there is nothing to divide. We wish to control big business so as to secure among other things good wages for the wage-workers and reasonable prices for the consumers. Wherever in any business the prosperity of the businessman is obtained by lowering the wages of his workmen and charging an excessive price to the consumers, we wish to interfere and stop such practices. We will not submit to that kind of prosperity any more than we will submit to prosperity obtained by swindling investors or getting unfair advantages over business rivals. But it is obvious that unless the business is prosperous the wage-workers employed therein will be badly paid and the consumers badly served. . . .

Again and again while I was president, from 1902 to 1908, I pointed out that under the antitrust law alone it was neither possible to put a stop to business abuses nor possible to secure the highest efficiency in the service rendered by business to the general public. The antitrust law must be kept on our statute books, and, as hereafter shown, must be rendered more effective in the cases where it is applied. But to treat the antitrust law as an adequate, or as by itself a wise measure of relief and betterment, is a sign not of progress, but of Toryism and reaction. It has been of benefit so far as it has implied the recognition of a real and great evil, and the at least sporadic application of the principle that all men alike must obey the law. But as a sole remedy, universally applicable, it has in actual practice completely broken down; as now applied it works more mischief than benefit. . . .

We Progressives stand for the rights of the people. When these rights can best be secured by insistence upon states' rights, then we are for states' rights; when they can best be secured by insistence upon national rights, then we are for national rights. Interstate commerce can be effectively controlled only by the nation. The states cannot control it under the Constitution, and to amend the Constitution by giving them control of it would amount to a dissolution of the government. The worst of the big trusts have always endeavored to keep alive the feeling in favor of having the states themselves, and not the nation, attempt to do this work, because they know that in the long run such effort would be ineffective. There is no surer way to prevent all successful effort to deal with the trusts than to insist that they be dealt with by the states rather than by the nation, or to create a conflict between the states and the nation on the subject. The well-meaning ignorant man who advances such a proposition does as much damage as if he were hired by the trusts themselves, for he is playing the game of every big crooked corporation in the country. The only effective way in which to regulate the trusts is through the exercise of the collective power of our people as a whole through the governmental agencies established by the Constitution for this very purpose. Grave injustice is done by the Congress when it fails to give the national government complete power in this matter; and still graver injustice by the federal courts when they endeavor in any way to pare down the right of the people collectively to act in this matter as they deem wise; such conduct does itself tend to cause the creation of a twilight zone in which neither the nation nor the states have power. Fortunately, the federal courts have more and more of recent years tended to adopt the true doctrine, which is that all these matters are to be settled by the people themselves, and that the conscience of the people, and not the preferences of any servants of the people, is to be the standard in deciding what action shall be taken by the people. As Lincoln phrased it: "The [question] of national power and state rights as a principle is no other than the principle of generality and locality. Whatever concerns the whole should be confided to the whole—to the general government; while whatever concerns only the state should be left exclusively to the state."

It is utterly hopeless to attempt to control the trusts merely by the antitrust law, or by any law the same in principle, no matter what the modifications may be in detail. . . .

What is needed is the application to all industrial concerns and all cooperating interests engaged in interstate commerce in which there is either monopoly or control of the market of the principles on which we have gone in regulating transportation concerns engaged in such commerce. The antitrust law should be kept on the statute books and strengthened so as to make it genuinely and thoroughly effective against every big concern tending to monopoly or guilty of antisocial practices. At the same time, a national industrial commission should be created which should have complete power to regulate and control all the great industrial concerns engaged in interstate business— which practically means all of them in this country. This commission should exercise over these industrial concerns like powers to those exercised over the railways by the Interstate Commerce Commission, and over the national banks by the comptroller of the currency, and additional powers if found necessary.

The establishment of such a commission would enable us to punish the individual rather than merely the corporation, just as we now do with banks, where the aim of the government is not to close the bank but to bring to justice personally any bank official who has gone wrong. . . .

Such supervision over the issuance of corporate securities would put a stop to exploitation of the people by dishonest capitalists desiring to declare dividends on watered securities, and would open this kind of industrial property to ownership by the people at large. It should have free access to the books of each corporation and power to find out exactly how it treats its employees, its rivals, and the general public. It should have power to compel the unsparing publicity of all the acts of any corporation which goes wrong. The regulation should be primarily under the administrative branch of the government, and not by lawsuit. It should prohibit and effectually punish monopoly achieved through wrong, and also actual wrongs done by industrial corporations which are not monopolies, such as the artificial raising of prices, the artificial restriction on productivity, the elimination of competition by unfair or predatory practices, and the like; leaving industrial organizations free within the limits of fair and honest dealing to promote through the inherent efficiency of organization the power of the United States as a competitive nation among nations, and the greater abundance at home that will come to our people from that power wisely exercised. . . .

The Progressive proposal is definite. It is practicable. We promise nothing that we cannot carry out. We promise nothing which will jeopardize honest business. We promise adequate control of all big business and the stern suppression of the evils connected with big business, and this promise we can absolutely keep. . . .

I believe in a protective tariff, but I believe in it as a principle, approached from the standpoint of the interests of the whole people, and not as a bundle of preferences to be given to favored individuals. In my opinion, the American people favor the principle of a protective tariff, but they desire such a tariff to be established primarily in the interests of the wage-worker and the consumer. The chief opposition to our tariff at the present moment comes from the general conviction that certain interests have been improperly favored by overprotection. I agree with this view. The commercial and industrial experience of this country has demonstrated the wisdom of the protective policy, but it has also demonstrated that in the application of that policy certain clearly recognized abuses have developed. It is not merely the tariff that should be revised, but the method of tariff-making and of tariff administration. Wherever nowadays an industry is to be protected it should be on the theory that such protection will serve to keep up the wages and the standard of living of the wage-worker in that industry with full regard for the interest of the consumer. To accomplish this the tariff to be levied should as nearly as is scientifically possible approximate the differential between the cost of production at home and abroad. This differential is chiefly, if not wholly, in labor cost. No duty should be permitted to stand as regards any industry unless the workers receive their full share of the benefits of that duty. In other words, there is no warrant for protection unless a legitimate share of the benefits gets into the pay envelope of the wage-worker. . . .

The first step should be the creation of a permanent commission of nonpartisan experts whose business shall be to study scientifically all phases of tariff-making and of tariff effects. This commission should be large enough to cover all the different and widely varying branches of American industry. It should have ample powers to enable it to secure exact and reliable information. It should have authority to examine closely all correlated subjects, such as the effect of any given duty on the consumers of the article on which the duty is levied; that is, it should directly consider the question as to what any duty costs the people in the price of living. It should examine into the wages and conditions of labor and life of the workmen in any industry, so as to insure our refusing protection to any industry unless the showing as regards the share labor receives therefrom is satisfactory. This commission would be wholly different from the present unsatisfactory Tariff Board, which was created under a provision of law which failed to give it the powers indispensable if it was to do the work it should do. . . .

The one and only chance to secure stable and favorable business conditions in this country, while at the same time guaranteeing fair play to farmer, consumer, businessman, and wage-worker, lies in the creation of such a commission as I herein advocate. Only by such a commission and only by such activities of the commission will it be possible for us to get a reasonably quick revision of the tariff schedule by schedule— revision which shall be downward and not upward, and at the same time secure a square deal not merely to the manufacturer, but to the wage-worker and to the general consumer.

There can be no more important question than the high cost of living necessities. The main purpose of the Progressive movement is to place the American people in possession of their birthright, to secure for all the American people unobstructed access to the fountains of measureless prosperity which their Creator offers them. We in this country are blessed with great natural resources, and our men and women have a very high standard of intelligence and of industrial capacity. Surely, such being the case, we cannot permanently support conditions under which each family finds it increasingly difficult to secure the necessaries of life and a fair share of its comforts through the earnings of its members. The cost of living in this country has risen during the last few years out of all proportion to the increase in the rate of most salaries and wages; the same situation confronts alike the majority of wage-workers, small-businessmen, small-professional men, the clerks, the doctors, clergymen.

Now, grave though the problem is there is one way to make it graver, and that is to deal with it insincerely, to advance false remedies, to promise the impossible. Our opponents, Republicans and Democrats alike, propose to deal with it in this way. The Republicans in their platform promise an inquiry into the facts. Most certainly there should be such inquiry. But the way the present administration has failed to keep its promises in the past, and the rank dishonesty of action on the part of the Penrose-Barnes-Guggenheim national convention, makes their every promise worthless. The Democratic platform affects to find the entire cause of the high cost of living in the tariff, and promises to remedy it by free trade, especially free trade in the necessaries of life. In the first place, this attitude ignores the patent fact that the problem is worldwide, that everywhere, in England and France, as in Germany and Japan, it appears with greater or less severity; that in England, for instance, it has become a very severe problem, although neither the tariff nor, save to a small degree, the trusts, can there have any possible effect upon the situation. In the second place, the Democratic platform, if it is sincere, must mean that all duties will be taken off the products of the farmer. Yet most certainly we cannot afford to have the farmer struck down. The welfare of the tiller of the soil is as important as the welfare of the wage-worker himself, and we must sedulously guard both. The farmer, the producer of the necessities of life, can himself live only if he raises these necessities for a profit. On the other hand, the consumer who must have that farmer's product in order to live, must be allowed to purchase it at the lowest cost that can give the farmer his profit, and everything possible must be done to eliminate any middleman whose function does not tend to increase the cheapness of distribution of the product; and, moreover, everything must be done to stop all speculating, all gambling with the breadbasket which has even the slightest deleterious effect upon the producer and consumer. There must be legislation which will bring about a closer business relationship between the farmer and the consumer. . . .

Through the proposed interstate industrial commission we can effectively do away with any arbitrary control by combinations of the necessities of life. Furthermore, the governments of the nation and of the several states must combine in doing everything they can to make the farmer's business profitable, so that he shall get more out of the soil, and enjoy better business facilities for marketing what he thus gets. In this manner his return will be increased while the price to the consumer is diminished. The elimination of the middleman by agricultural exchanges and by the use of improved business methods generally, the development of good roads, the reclamation of arid lands and swamplands, the improvement in the productivity of farms, the encouragement of all agencies which tend to bring people back to the soil and to make country life more interesting as well as more profitable—all these movements will help not only the farmer but the man who consumes the farmer's products.

There is urgent need of nonpartisan expert examination into any tariff schedule which seems to increase the cost of living, and, unless the increase thus caused is more than countervailed by the benefit to the class of the community which actually receives the protection, it must of course mean that that particular duty must be reduced. The system of levying a tariff for the protection and encouragement of American industry so as to secure higher wages and better conditions of life for American laborers must never be perverted so as to operate for the impoverishment of those whom it was intended to benefit. . . .

It is also asserted that the trusts are responsible for the high cost of living. I have no question that, as regards certain trusts, this is true. I also have no question that it will continue to be true just as long as the country confines itself to acting as the Baltimore platform demands that we act. This demand is, in effect, for the states and national government to make the futile attempt to exercise forty-nine sovereign and conflicting authorities in the effort jointly to suppress the trusts, while at the same time the national government refuses to exercise proper control over them. . . . Trusts which increase production—unless they do it wastefully, as in certain forms of mining and lumbering—cannot permanently increase the cost of living; it is the trusts which limit production, or which, without limiting production, take advantage of the lack of governmental control, and eliminate competition by combining to control the market, that cause an increase in the cost of living. There should be established at once, as I have elsewhere said, under the national government an interstate industrial commission, which should exercise full supervision over the big industrial concerns doing an interstate business into which an element of monopoly enters. Where these concerns deal with the necessaries of life the commission should not shrink, if the necessity is proved, of going to the extent of exercising regulatory control over the conditions that create or determine monopoly prices. . . .

We believe that there exists an imperative need for prompt legislation for the improvement of our national currency system. The experience of repeated financial crises in the last forty years has proved that the present method of issuing, through private agencies, notes secured by government bonds is both harmful and unscientific. . . . The issue of currency is fundamentally a governmental function. The system to be adopted should have as its basic principles soundness and elasticity. The currency should flow forth readily at the demand of commercial activity, and retire as promptly when the demand diminishes. It should be automatically sufficient for all of the legitimate needs of business in any section of the country. Only by such means can the country be freed from the danger of recurring panics. The control should be lodged with the government, and should be safeguarded against manipulation by Wall Street or the large interests. It should be made impossible to use the machinery or perquisites of the currency system for any speculative purposes. . . .

There can be no greater issue than that of conservation in this country. Just as we must conserve our men, women, and children, so we must conserve the resources of the land on which they live. We must conserve the soil so that our children shall have a land that is more and not less fertile than that our fathers dwelt in. We must conserve the forests, not by disuse but by use, making them more valuable at the same time that we use them. We must conserve the mines. Moreover, we must insure so far as possible the use of certain types of great natural resources for the benefit of the people as a whole. The public should not alienate its fee in the waterpower which will be of incalculable consequence as a source of power in the immediate future. The nation and the states within their several spheres should by immediate legislation keep the fee of the waterpower, leasing its use only for a reasonable length of time on terms that will secure the interests of the public. Just as the nation has gone into the work of irrigation in the West, so it should go into the work of helping reclaim the swamplands of the South. We should undertake the complete development and control of the Mississippi as a national work, just as we have undertaken the work of building the Panama Canal. . . .

In the West, the forests, the grazing lands, the reserves of every kind, should be so handled as to be in the interests of the actual settler, the actual home-maker. He should be encouraged to use them at once, but in such a way as to preserve and not exhaust them. We do not intend that our natural resources shall be exploited by the few against the interests of the many, nor do we intend to turn them over to any man who will wastefully use them by destruction, and leave to those who come after us a heritage damaged by just so much. The man in whose interests we are working is the small farmer and settler, the man who works with his own hands, who is working not only for himself but for his children, and who wishes to leave to them the fruits of his labor. His permanent welfare is the prime factor for consideration in developing the policy of conservation: for our aim is to preserve our natural resources for the public as a whole, for the average man and the average woman who make up the body of the American people.

Alaska should be developed at once, but in the interest of the actual settler. In Alaska the government has an opportunity of starting in what is almost a fresh field to work out various problems by actual experiment. The government should at once construct, own, and operate the railways in Alaska. The government should keep the fee of all the coal fields and allow them to be operated by lessees with the condition in the lease that nonuse shall operate as a forfeit. Telegraph lines should be operated as the railways are. Moreover, it would be well in

Alaska to try a system of land taxation which will, so far as possible, remove all the burdens from those who actually use the land, whether for building or for agricultural purposes, and will operate against any man who holds the land for speculation, or derives an income from it based, not on his own exertions, but on the increase in value due to activities not his own. . . .

In international affairs this country should behave toward other nations exactly as an honorable private citizen behaves toward other private citizens. We should do no wrong to any nation, weak or strong, and we should submit to no wrong. Above all, we should never in any treaty make any promise which we do not intend in good faith to fulfill. I believe it essential that our small army should be kept at a high pitch of perfection, and in no way can it be so damaged as by permitting it to become the plaything of men in Congress who wish to gratify either spite or favoritism, or to secure to localities advantages to which those localities are not entitled. The navy should be steadily built up; and the process of upbuilding must not be stopped until—and not before—it proves possible to secure by international agreement a general reduction of armaments. The Panama Canal must be fortified. It would have been criminal to build it if we were not prepared to fortify it and to keep our navy at such a pitch of strength as to render it unsafe for any foreign power to attack us and get control of it. We have a perfect right to permit our coastwise traffic . . . to pass through that Canal on any terms we choose, and I personally think that no toll should be charged on such traffic. Moreover, in time of war, where all treaties between warring nations, save those connected with the management of the war, at once lapse, the Canal would, of course, be open to the use of our warships and closed to the warships of the nation with which we were engaged in hostilities. But at all times the Canal should be opened on equal terms to the ships of all nations, including our own, engaged in international commerce. That was the understanding of the treaty when it was adopted, and the United States must always, as a matter of honorable obligation, and with scrupulous nicety, live up to every understanding which she has entered into with any foreign power. . . .

Now, friends, this is my confession of faith. I have made it rather long because I wish you to know what my deepest convictions are on the great questions of today, so that if you choose to make me your standard-bearer in the fight you shall make your choice understanding exactly how I feel—and if, after hearing me, you think you ought to choose someone else, I shall loyally abide by your choice. The convictions to which I have come have not been arrived at as the result of study in the closet or the library, but from the knowledge I have gained through hard experience during the many years in which, under many and varied conditions, I have striven and toiled with men. I believe in a larger use of the governmental power to help remedy industrial wrongs, because it has been borne in on me by actual experience that without the exercise of such power many of the wrongs will go unremedied. I believe in a larger opportunity for the people themselves directly to participate in government and to control their governmental agents, because long experience has taught me that without such control many of their agents will represent them badly. By actual experience in office I have found that, as a rule, I could secure the triumph of the causes in which I most believed, not from the politicians and the men who claim an exceptional right to speak in business and government, but by going over their heads and appealing directly to the people themselves. I am not under the slightest delusion as to any power that during my political career I have at any time possessed. Whatever of power I at any time had, I obtained from the people. I could exercise it only so long as, and to the extent that, the people not merely believed in me, but heartily backed me up. Whatever I did as president I was able to do only because I had the backing of the people. When on any point I did not have that backing, when on any point I differed from the people, it mattered not whether I was right or whether I was wrong; my power vanished. I tried my best to lead the people, to advise them, to tell them what I thought was right; if necessary, I never hesitated to tell them what I thought they ought to hear, even though I thought it would be unpleasant for them to hear it; but I recognized that my task was to try to lead them and not to drive them, to take them into my confidence, to try to show them that I was right, and then loyally and in good faith to accept their decision. I will do anything for the people except what my conscience tells me is wrong, and that I can do for no man and no set of men; I hold that a man cannot serve the people well unless he serves his conscience; but I hold also that where his conscience bids him refuse to do what the people desire, he should not try to continue in office against their will. Our government system should be so shaped that the public servant, when he cannot conscientiously carry out the wishes of the people, shall at their desire leave his office and not misrepresent them in office; and I hold that the public servant can by so doing, better than in any other way, serve both them and his conscience.

Surely there never was a fight better worth making than the one in which we are engaged. It little matters what befalls any one of us who for the time being stands in the forefront of the battle. I hope we shall win, and I believe that if we can wake the people to what the fight really means we shall win. But, win or lose, we shall not falter. Whatever fate may at the moment overtake any of us, the movement itself will not stop. Our cause is based on the eternal principles of righteousness; and even though we who now lead may for the time fail, in the end the cause itself shall triumph. Six weeks ago, here in Chicago, I spoke to the honest representatives of a convention which was not dominated by honest men; a convention wherein sat, alas! a majority of men who, with sneering indifference to every principle of right, so acted as to bring to a shameful end a party which had been founded over a half-century ago by men in whose souls burned the fire of lofty endeavor. Now to you men, who, in your turn, have come together to spend and be spent in the endless crusade against wrong, to you who face the future resolute and confident, to you who strive in a spirit of brotherhood for the betterment of our nation, to you who gird yourselves for this great new fight in the never-ending warfare for the good of humankind, I say in closing what in that speech I said in closing: We stand at Armageddon, and we battle for the Lord.

Speech at Milwaukee, Wisconsin

October 14, 1912

The Leader and the Cause*

Friends, I shall ask you to be as quiet as possible. I don't know whether you fully understand that I have just been shot; but it takes more than that to kill a bull moose. But fortunately I had my manuscript, so you see I was going to make a long speech, and there is a bullet—there is where the bullet went through—and it probably saved me from it going into my heart. The bullet is in me now, so that I cannot make a very long speech, but I will try my best.

And now, friends, I want to take advantage of this incident and say a word of solemn warning to my fellow countrymen. First of all, I want to say this about myself: I have altogether too important things to think of to feel any concern over my own death; and now I cannot speak to you insincerely within five minutes of being shot. I am telling you the literal truth when I say that my concern is for many other things. It is not in the least for my own life. I want you to understand that I am ahead of the game, anyway. No man has had a happier life than I have led; a happier life in every way. I have been able to do certain things that I greatly wished to do, and I am interested in doing other things. I can tell you with absolute truthfulness that I am very much uninterested in whether I am shot or not. It was just as when I was colonel of my regiment. I always felt that a private was to be excused for feeling at times some pangs of anxiety

---

*Published in *Progressive Principles*, 1913. Just before beginning his address, Roosevelt was shot by a would-be assassin. The candidate nevertheless delivered the speech, often including extemporaneous remarks relative to the event.

about his personal safety, but I cannot understand a man fit to be a colonel who can pay any heed to his personal safety when he is occupied as he ought to be occupied with the absorbing desire to do his duty.

I am in this cause with my whole heart and soul. I believe that the Progressive movement is for making life a little easier for all our people; a movement to try to take the burdens off the men and especially the women and children of this country. I am absorbed in the success of that movement.

Friends, I ask you now this evening to accept what I am saying as absolutely true, when I tell you I am not thinking of my own success. I am not thinking of my life or of anything connected with me personally. I am thinking of the movement. I say this by way of introduction, because I want to say something very serious to our people and especially to the newspapers. I don't know anything about who the man was who shot me tonight. He was seized at once by one of the stenographers in my party, Mr. Martin, and I suppose is now in the hands of the police. He shot to kill. He shot—the shot, the bullet went in here—I will show you.

I am going to ask you to be as quiet as possible for I am not able to give the challenge of the bull moose quite as loudly. Now, I do not know who he was or what party he represented. He was a coward. He stood in the darkness in the crowd around the automobile and when they cheered me, and I got up to bow, he stepped forward and shot me in the darkness.

Now, friends, of course, I do not know, as I say, anything about him; but it is a very natural thing that weak and vicious minds should be inflamed to acts of violence by the kind of awful mendacity and abuse that have been heaped upon me for the last three months by the papers in the interest of not only Mr. Debs but of Mr. Wilson and Mr. Taft.

Friends, I will disown and repudiate any man of my party who attacks with such foul slander and abuse any opponent of any other party; and now I wish to say seriously to all the daily newspapers, to the Republican, the Democratic, and the Socialist parties, that they cannot, month in and month out and year in and year out, make the kind of untruthful, of bitter assault that they have made and not expect that brutal, violent natures, or brutal and violent characters—especially when the brutality is accompanied by a not very strong mind—they cannot expect that such natures will be unaffected by it.

Now, friends, I am not speaking for myself at all. I give you my word, I do not care a rap about being shot; not a rap.

I have had a good many experiences in my time and this is one of them. What I care for is my country. I wish I were able to impress upon my people—our people—the duty to feel strongly but to speak the truth of their opponents. I say now, I have never said one word on the stump against any opponent that I cannot defend. I have said nothing that I could not substantiate and nothing that I ought not to have said—nothing that I—nothing that, looking back at, I would not say again.

Now, friends, it ought not to be too much to ask that our opponents—[speaking to someone on the stage]—I am not sick at all. I am all right. I cannot tell you of what infinitesimal importance I regard this incident as compared with the great issues at stake in this campaign, and I ask it not for my sake, not the least in the world, but for the sake of our common country, that they make up their minds to speak only the truth, and not to use the kind of slander and mendacity which if taken seriously must incite weak and violent natures to crimes of violence. Don't you make any mistake. Don't you pity me. I am all right. I am all right and you cannot escape listening to the speech either.

And now, friends, this incident that has just occurred—this effort to assassinate me—emphasizes to a peculiar degree the need of this Progressive movement. Friends, every good citizen ought to do everything in his or her power to prevent the coming of the day when we shall see in this country two recognized creeds fighting one another, when we shall see the creed of the "have-nots" arraigned against the creed of the "haves." When that day comes then such incidents as this tonight will be commonplace in our history. When you make poor men—when you permit the conditions to grow such that the poor man as such will be swayed by his sense of injury against the men who try to hold what they improperly have won, when that day comes, the most awful passions will be let loose and it will be an ill day for our country.

Now, friends, what we who are in this movement are endeavoring to do is to forestall any such movement by making this a movement for justice now—a movement in which we ask all just men of generous hearts to join with the men who feel in their souls that lift upward which bids them refuse to be satisfied themselves while their countrymen and countrywomen suffer from avoidable misery. Now, friends, what we Progressives are trying to do is to enroll rich or poor, whatever their social or industrial position, to stand together for the most elementary rights of good citizenship, those elementary rights which are the foundation of good citizenship in this great Republic of ours. [At this point a renewed effort was made to persuade Mr. Roosevelt to conclude his speech.]

My friends are a little more nervous than I am. Don't you waste any sympathy on me. I have had an A-1 time in life and I am having it now.

I never in my life was in any movement in which I was able to serve with such wholehearted devotion as in this; in which I was able to feel as I do in this that common weal. I have fought for the good of our common country.

And now, friends, I shall have to cut short much of the speech that I meant to give you, but I want to touch on just two or three of the points.

In the first place, speaking to you here in Milwaukee, I wish to say that the Progressive party is making its appeal to all our fellow citizens without any regard to their creed or to their birthplace. We do not regard as essential the way in which a man worships his God or as being affected by where he was born. We regard it as a matter of spirit and purpose. In New York, while I was police commissioner, the two men from whom I got the most assistance were Jacob Riis, who was born in Denmark, and Arthur von Briesen, who was born in Germany—both of them as fine examples of the best and highest American citizenship as you could find in any part of this country.

I have just been introduced by one of your own men here—Henry Cochems. His grandfather, his father, and that father's seven brothers all served in the United States Army, and they entered it four years after they had come to this country from Germany. Two of them left their lives, spent their lives, on the field of battle. I am all right—I am a little sore. Anybody has a right to be sore with a bullet in him. You would find that if I was in battle now I would be leading my men just the same. Just the same way I am going to make this speech.

At one time I promoted five men for gallantry on the field of battle. Afterward in making some inquiries about them I found it happened that two of them were Protestants, two Catholics, and one a Jew. One Protestant came from Germany and one was born in Ireland. I did not promote them because of their religion. It just happened that way. If all five of them had been Jews I would have promoted them, or if all five had been Protestants I would have promoted them; or if they had been Catholics. In that regiment I had a man born in Italy who distinguished himself by gallantry; there was a young fellow, a son of Polish parents, and another who came here when he was a child from Bohemia, who likewise distinguished themselves; and friends, I assure you that I was incapable of considering any question whatever, but the worth of each individual as a fighting man. If he was a good fighting man, then I saw that Uncle Sam got the benefit from it. That is all.

I make the same appeal in our citizenship. I ask in our civic life that we in the same way pay heed only to the man's quality of citizenship, to repudiate as the worst enemy that we can have whoever tries to get us to discriminate for or against any man because of his creed or his birthplace.

Now, friends, in the same way I want our people to stand

by one another without regard to differences or class or occupation. I have always stood by the labor unions. I am going to
make one omission tonight. I have prepared my speech because
Mr. Wilson had seen fit to attack me by showing up his record
in comparison with mine. But I am not going to do that tonight.
I am going to simply speak of what I myself have done and of
what I think ought to be done in this country of ours.

It is essential that there should be organizations of labor.
This is an era of organization. Capital organizes and therefore
labor must organize. My appeal for organized labor is twofold;
to the outsider and the capitalist I make my appeal to treat the
laborer fairly, to recognize the fact that he must organize, that
there must be such organization, that the laboring man must
organize for his own protection, and that it is the duty of the rest
of us to help him and not hinder him in organizing. That is
one-half of the appeal that I make.

Now, the other half is to the labor man himself. My appeal
to him is to remember that as he wants justice, so he must do
justice. I want every labor man, every labor leader, every organized union man to take the lead in denouncing crime or violence. I want them to take the lead in denouncing disorder and
in denouncing the inciting of riot; that in this country we shall
proceed under the protection of our laws and with all respect to
the laws, and I want the labor men to feel in their turn that
exactly as justice must be done them so they must do justice.
That they must bear their duty as citizens, their duty to this
great country of ours, and that they must not rest content unless
they do that duty to the fullest degree.

I know these doctors, when they get hold of me, will never
let me go back, and there are just a few things more that I want
to say to you.

And here I have got to make one comparison between Mr.
Wilson and myself, simply because he has invited it and I cannot
shrink from it. Mr. Wilson has seen fit to attack me, to say that
I did not do much against the trusts when I was president. I have
got two answers to make to that. In the first place what I did,

and then I want to compare what I did while I was president with what Mr. Wilson did not do while he was governor.

When I took office the antitrust law was practically a dead letter and the Interstate Commerce Law in as poor a condition. I had to revive both laws. I did. I enforced both. It will be easy enough to do now what I did then, but the reason that it is easy now is because I did it when it was hard.

Nobody was doing anything. I found speedily that the Interstate Commerce Law by being made more perfect could be made a most useful instrument for helping solve some of our industrial problems. So with the antitrust law. I speedily found that almost the only positive good achieved by such a successful lawsuit as the Northern Securities suit, for instance, was in establishing the principle that the government was supreme over the big corporation, but that by itself that law did not accomplish any of the things that we ought to have accomplished; and so I began to fight for the amendment of the law along the lines of the Interstate Commerce Law, and now we propose, we Progressives, to establish an interstate commission having the same power over industrial concerns that the Interstate Commerce Commission has over railroads, so that whenever there is in the future a decision rendered in such important matters as the recent suits against the Standard Oil, the Sugar—no, not that—Tobacco—Tobacco Trust—we will have a commission which will see that the decree of the court is really made effective; that it is not made a merely nominal decree.

Our opponents have said that we intend to legalize monopoly. Nonsense. They have legalized monopoly. At this moment the Standard Oil and Tobacco Trust monopolies are legalized; they are being carried on under the decree of the Supreme Court. Our proposal is really to break up monopoly. Our proposal is to lay down certain requirements, and then require the commerce commission—the industrial commission—to see that the trusts live up to those requirements. Our opponents have spoken as if we were going to let the commission declare what the requirements should be. Not at all. We are going to put the requirements in the law and then see that the commission requires them to obey that law.

And now, friends, as Mr. Wilson has invited the comparison, I only want to say this: Mr. Wilson has said that the states are the proper authorities to deal with the trusts. Well, about 80 percent of the trusts are organized in New Jersey. The Standard Oil, the Tobacco, the Sugar, the Beef, all those trusts are organized in New Jersey and the laws of New Jersey say that their charters can at any time be amended or repealed if they misbehave themselves and give the government ample power to act about those laws, and Mr. Wilson has been governor a year and nine months and he has not opened his lips. The chapter describing what Mr. Wilson has done about the trusts in New Jersey would read precisely like a chapter describing the snakes in Ireland, which ran: "There are no snakes in Ireland." Mr. Wilson has done precisely and exactly nothing about the trusts.

I tell you, and I told you at the beginning, I do not say anything on the stump that I do not believe. I do not say anything I do not know. Let any of Mr. Wilson's friends on Tuesday point out one thing or let Mr. Wilson point out one thing he has done about the trusts as governor of New Jersey.

And now, friends, there is one thing I want to say especially to you people here in Wisconsin. All that I have said so far is what I would say in any part of this Union. I have a peculiar right to ask that in this great contest you men and women of Wisconsin shall stand with us. You have taken the lead in progressive movements here in Wisconsin. You have taught the rest of us to look to you for inspiration and leadership. Now, friends, you have made that movement here locally. You will be doing a dreadful injustice to yourselves; you will be doing a dreadful injustice to the rest of us throughout this Union, if you fail to stand with us now that we are making this national movement. What I am about to say now I want you to understand. If I speak of Mr. Wilson I speak with no mind of bitterness. I merely want to discuss the difference of policy between the Progressive and the Democratic party and to ask you to think for yourselves which party you will follow. I will say that, friends, because the Republican party is beaten. Nobody needs to have any idea that anything can be done with the Republican party.

When the Republican party—not the Republican party— when the bosses in the control of the Republican party, the Barneses and Penroses, last June stole the nomination and wrecked the Republican party for good and all—I want to point out to you nominally they stole that nomination from me, but really it was from you. They did not like me, and the longer they live the less cause they will have to like me. But while they do not like me, they dread you. You are the people that they dread. They dread the people themselves, and those bosses and the big special interests behind them made up their mind that they would rather see the Republican party wrecked than see it come under the control of the people themselves. So I am not dealing with the Republican party. There are only two ways you can vote this year. You can be progressive or reactionary. Whether you vote Republican or Democratic it does not make any difference, you are voting reactionary.

Now, the Democratic party in its platform and through the utterances of Mr. Wilson has distinctly committed itself to the old flintlock, muzzle-loaded doctrine of states' rights, and I have said distinctly that we are for the people's rights. We are for the rights of the people. If they can be obtained best through the national government, then we are for national rights. We are for the people's rights however it is necessary to secure them.

Mr. Wilson has made a long essay against Senator Beveridge's bill to abolish child labor. It is the same kind of an argument that would be made against our bill to prohibit women from working more than eight hours a day in industry. It is the same kind of argument that would have to be made; if it is true, it would apply equally against our proposal to insist that in continuous industries there shall be by law one day's rest in seven and a three-shift eight-hour day. You have labor laws here in Wisconsin, and any chamber of commerce will tell you that because of that fact there are industries that will not come into Wisconsin. They prefer to stay outside where they can work children of tender years, where they can work women fourteen and sixteen hours a day, where, if it is a continuous industry, they can work men twelve hours a day and seven days a week.

Now, friends, I know that you of Wisconsin would never repeal those laws even if they are to your commercial hurt, just as I am trying to get New York to adopt such laws even though it will be to New York's commercial hurt. But if possible I want to arrange it so that we can have justice without commercial hurt, and you can only get that if you have justice enforced nationally. You won't be burdened in Wisconsin with industries not coming to the state if the same good laws are extended all over the other states. Do you see what I mean? The states all compete in a common market; and it is not justice to the employers of a state that has enforced just and proper laws to have them exposed to the competition of another state where no such laws are enforced. Now, the Democratic platform, and their speakers, declare that we shall not have such laws. Mr. Wilson has distinctly declared that you shall not have a national law to prohibit the labor of children, to prohibit child labor. He has distinctly declared that we shall not have a law to establish a minimum wage for women.

I ask you to look at our declaration and hear and read our platform about social and industrial justice and then, friends, vote for the Progressive ticket without regard to me, without regard to my personality, for only by voting for that platform can you be true to the cause of progress throughout this Union.

THE PEACE OF RIGHTEOUSNESS

Syndicated Newspaper Article, November 8, 1914,
and from America and the World War, *1915*

> Come, Peace! Not like a mourner bowed
>   For honor lost and dear ones wasted,
> But proud, to meet a people proud,
>   With eyes that tell o' triumph tasted!
> Come, with han' gripping on the hilt,
>   An' step that proves ye Victory's daughter!
> Longin' for you, our sperits wilt
>   Like shipwrecked men's on raf's for water.
>
> Come, while our country feels the lift
>   Of a great instinct shouting "Forwards!"
> An' knows that freedom ain't a gift
>   Thet tarries long in han's of cowards!
> Come, sech ez mothers prayed for, when
>   They kissed their cross with lips that quivered,
> An' bring fair wages for brave men,
>   A nation saved, a race delivered!

These are the noble lines of a noble poet, written in the sternest days of the great Civil War, when the writer, Lowell, was one among the millions of men who mourned the death in battle of kinsfolk dear to him. No man ever lived who hated an unjust war more than Lowell or who loved with more passionate fervor the peace of righteousness. Yet, like the other great poets of his day and country, like Holmes, who sent his own son to the war, like gentle Longfellow and the Quaker Whittier, he abhorred unrighteousness and ignoble peace more than war. These men had lofty souls. They possessed the fighting edge, without which no man is really great; for in the

317

really great man there must be both the heart of gold and the temper of steel.

In 1864 there were in the North some hundreds of thousands of men who praised peace as the supreme end, as a good more important than all other goods, and who denounced war as the worst of all evils. These men one and all assailed and denounced Abraham Lincoln, and all voted against him for president. Moreover, at that time there were many individuals in England and France who said it was the duty of those two nations to mediate between the North and the South, so as to stop the terrible loss of life and destruction of property which attended our Civil War; and they asserted that any Americans who in such event refused to accept their mediation and to stop the war would thereby show themselves the enemies of peace. Nevertheless, Abraham Lincoln and the men back of him by their attitude prevented all such effort at mediation, declaring that they would regard it as an unfriendly act to the United States. Looking back from a distance of fifty years, we can now see clearly that Abraham Lincoln and his supporters were right. Such mediation would have been a hostile act, not only to the United States but to humanity. The men who clamored for unrighteous peace fifty years ago this fall were the enemies of mankind.

These facts should be pondered by the well-meaning men who always clamor for peace without regard to whether peace brings justice or injustice. Very many of the men and women who are at times misled into demanding peace, as if it were itself an end instead of being a means of righteousness, are men of good intelligence and sound heart who only need seriously to consider the facts, and who can then be trusted to think aright and act aright. There is, however, an element of a certain numerical importance among our people, including the members of the ultrapacifist group, who by their teachings do some real, although limited, mischief. They are a feeble folk, these ultrapacifists, morally and physically; but in a country where voice and vote are alike free, they may, if their teachings are not disregarded, create a condition of things where the crop they have sowed in folly and weakness will be reaped with blood and bitter tears by the brave men and high-hearted women of the nation.

The folly preached by some of these individuals is somewhat startling, and if it were translated from words into deeds it would constitute a crime against the nation. One professed teacher of morality made the plea in so many words that we ought to follow the example of China and deprive ourselves of all power to repel foreign attack. Surely this writer must have possessed the exceedingly small amount of information necessary in order to know that nearly half of China was under foreign dominion and that while he was writing the Germans and Japanese were battling on Chinese territory and domineering as conquerors over the Chinese in that territory. Think of the abject soul of a man capable of holding up to the admiration of free-born American citizens such a condition of serfage under alien rule!

Nor is the folly confined only to the male sex. A number of women teachers in Chicago are credited with having proposed, in view of the war, hereafter to prohibit in the teaching of history any reference to war and battles. Intellectually, of course, such persons show themselves unfit to be retained as teachers a single day, and indeed unfit to be pupils in any school more advanced than a kindergarten. But it is not their intellectual, it is also their moral shortcomings which are striking. The suppression of the truth is, of course, as grave an offense against morals as is the suggestion of the false or even the lie direct; and these teachers actually propose to teach untruths to their pupils.

True teachers of history must tell the facts of history; and if they do not tell the facts both about the wars that were righteous and the wars that were unrighteous, and about the causes that led to these wars and to success or defeat in them, they show themselves morally unfit to train the minds of boys and girls. If in addition to telling the facts they draw the lessons that should be drawn from the facts, they will give their pupils a horror of all wars that are entered into wantonly or with levity or in a spirit of mere brutal aggression or save under dire necessity. But they will also teach that among the noblest deeds of mankind are those that have been done in great wars for liberty, in wars of self-defense, in wars for the relief of oppressed peoples, in wars for putting an end to wrongdoing in the dark places of the globe.

Any teachers, in school or college, who occupied the position that these foolish, foolish teachers have sought to take, would be forever estopped from so much as mentioning Washington and Lincoln; because their lives are forever associated with great wars for righteousness. These teachers would be forever estopped from so much as mentioning the shining names of Marathon and Salamis. They would seek to blind their pupils' eyes to the glory held in the deeds and deaths of Joan of Arc, of Andreas Hofer, of Alfred the Great, of Arnold von Winkelried, of Kosciusko and Rákóczy. They would be obliged to warn their pupils against ever reading Schiller's "William Tell" or the poetry of Koerner. Such men are deaf to the lament running: "Oh, why, Patrick Sarsfield, did we let your ships sail/Across the dark waters from green Innisfail?"

To them Holmes's ballad of Bunker Hill and Whittier's "Laus Deo," MacMaster's "Ode to the Old Continentals" and O'Hara's "Bivouac of the Dead" are meaningless. Their cold and timid hearts are not stirred by the surge of the tremendous "Battle Hymn of the Republic." On them lessons of careers like those of Timoleon and John Hampden are lost; in their eyes the lofty self-abnegation of Robert Lee and Stonewall Jackson was folly; their dull senses do not thrill to the deathless deaths of the men who died at Thermopylae and at the Alamo—the fight of those grim Texans of which it was truthfully said that Thermopylae had its messengers of death but the Alamo had none.

It has actually been proposed by some of these shivering apostles of the gospel of national abjectness that, in view of the destruction that has fallen on certain peaceful powers of Europe, we should abandon all efforts at self-defense, should stop building battleships, and cease to take any measures to defend ourselves if attacked. It is difficult seriously to consider such a proposition. It is precisely and exactly as if the inhabitants of a village in whose neighborhood highway robberies had occurred should propose to meet the crisis by depriving the local policeman of his revolver and club.

There are, however, many high-minded people who do not agree with these extremists, but who nevertheless need to be enlightened as to the actual facts. These good people, who are busy people and not able to devote much time to thoughts about international affairs, are often confused by men whose business it is to know better. For example, a few weeks ago these good people were stirred to a moment's belief that something had been accomplished by the enactment at Washington of a score or two of all-inclusive arbitration treaties; being not unnaturally misled by the fact that those responsible for the passage of the treaties indulged in some not wholly harmless bleating as to the good effects they would produce. As a matter of fact, they *probably* will not produce the smallest effect of any kind or sort. Yet it is *possible* they may have a mischievous effect, inasmuch as under certain circumstances to fulfill them would cause frightful disaster to the United States, while to break them, even although under compulsion and because it was absolutely necessary, would be fruitful of keen humiliation to every right-thinking man who is jealous of our international good name.

If, for example, whatever the outcome of the present war, a great triumphant military despotism declared that it would not recognize the Monroe Doctrine or seized Magdalena Bay, or one of the Dutch West Indies, or the Island of St. Thomas, and fortified it; or if—as would be quite possible—it announced that we had no right to fortify the Isthmus of Panama, and itself landed on adjacent territory to erect similar fortifications; then, under these absurd treaties, we would be obliged, if we happened to have made one of them with one of the countries involved, to go into an interminable discussion of the subject before a joint commission, while the hostile nation proceeded to make its position impregnable. It seems incredible that the

United States government could have made such treaties; but it has just done so, with the warm approval of the professional pacifists.

These treaties were entered into when the administration had before its eyes at that very moment the examples of Belgium and Luxembourg, which showed beyond possibility of doubt, especially when taken in connection with other similar incidents that have occurred during the last couple of decades, that there are various great military empires in the Old World who will pay not one moment's heed to the most solemn and binding treaty, if it is to their interest to break it. If any one of these empires, as the result of the present contest, obtains something approaching to a position of complete predominance in the Old World, it is absolutely certain that it would pay no heed whatever to these treaties, if it desired to better its position in the New World by taking possession of the Dutch or Danish West Indies or of the territory of some weak American state on the mainland of the continent. In such event we would be obliged either instantly ourselves to repudiate the scandalous treaties by which the government at Washington has just sought to tie our hands—and thereby expose ourselves in our turn to the charge of bad faith—or else we should have to abdicate our position as a great power and submit to abject humiliation.

Since these articles of mine were written and published, I am glad to see that James Bryce, a lifelong advocate of peace and the staunchest possible friend of the United States, has taken precisely the position herein taken. He dwells, as I have dwelt, upon the absolute need of protecting small states that behave themselves from absorption in great military empires. He insists, as I have insisted, upon the need of the reduction of armaments, the quenching of the baleful spirit of militarism, and the admission of the peoples everywhere to a fuller share in the control of foreign policy—all to be accomplished by some kind of international league of peace. He adds, however, as the culminating and most important portion of his article: "But no scheme for preventing future wars will have any chance of success unless it rests upon the assurance that the states which enter it will loyally and steadfastly abide by it and that each and all of them will join in coercing by their overwhelming united strength any state which may disregard the obligations it has undertaken."

This is almost exactly what I have said. Indeed, it is almost word for word what I have said—an agreement which is all the more striking because when he wrote it Lord Bryce could not have known what I had written. We must insist on righteousness first and foremost. We must strive for peace always; but we must never hesitate to put righteousness above peace. In order to do this, we must put force back of righteousness, for, as the world now is, national righteousness without force back of it speedily becomes a matter of derision. To the doctrine that might makes right, it is utterly useless to oppose the doctrine of right unbacked by might.

It is not even true that what the pacifists desire is right. The leaders of the pacifists of this country who for five months now have been crying "Peace, peace" have been too timid even to say that they want the peace to be a righteous one. We needlessly dignify such outcries when we speak of them as well-meaning. The weaklings who raise their shrill piping for a peace that shall consecrate successful wrong occupy a position quite as immoral as and infinitely more contemptible than the position of the wrongdoers themselves. The ruthless strength of the great absolutist leaders—Elizabeth of England, Catherine of Russia, Peter the Great, Frederick the Great, Napoleon, Bismarck—is certainly infinitely better for their own nations and is probably better for mankind at large than the loquacious impotence, ultimately trouble-breeding, which has recently marked our own international policy. A policy of blood and iron is sometimes very wicked; but it rarely does as much harm, and never excites as much derision, as a policy of milk and water—and it comes dangerously near flattery to call the foreign policy of the United States under President Wilson and Mr. Bryan merely one of milk and water. Strength at least commands respect; whereas

324 ★ The Essential Theodore Roosevelt

the prattling feebleness that dares not rebuke any concrete wrong, and whose proposals for right are marked by sheer fatuity, is fit only to excite weeping among angels and among men the bitter laughter of scorn.

At this moment any peace which leaves undressed the wrongs of Belgium, and which does not effectively guarantee Belgium and all other small nations that behave themselves, against the repetition of such wrongs would be a well-nigh unmixed evil. As far as we personally are concerned, such a peace would inevitably mean that we should at once and in haste have to begin to arm ourselves or be exposed in our turn to the most frightful risk of disaster. Let our people take thought for the future. What Germany did to Belgium because her need was great and because she possessed the ruthless force with which to meet her need she would, of course, do to us if her need demanded it; and in such event what her representatives now say as to her intentions toward America would trouble her as little as her signature to the neutrality treaties troubled her when she subjugated Belgium. Nor does she stand alone in her views of international morality. More than one of the great powers engaged in this war has shown by her conduct in the past that if it profited her she would without the smallest scruple treat any land in the two Americas as Belgium has been treated. What has recently happened in the Old World should be pondered deeply by the nations of the New World; by Chile, Argentina, and Brazil no less than by the United States. The World War has proved beyond peradventure that the principle underlying the Monroe Doctrine is of vast moment to the welfare of all America, and that neither this nor any other principle can be made effective save as power is put behind it.

Belgium was absolutely innocent of offense. Her cities have been laid waste or held to ransom for gigantic sums of money; her fruitful fields have been trampled into mire; her sons have died on the field of battle; her daughters are broken-hearted fugitives; a million of her people have fled to foreign lands. Entirely disregarding all accusations as to outrages on individuals, it yet remains true that disaster terrible beyond belief has befallen this peaceful nation of six million people who themselves had been guilty of not even the smallest wrongdoing. Louvain and Dinant are smoke-grimed and blood-stained ruins. Brussels has been held to enormous ransom, although it did not even strive to defend itself. Antwerp did strive to defend itself. Because soldiers in the forts attempted to repulse the enemy, hundreds of houses in the undefended city were wrecked with bombs from airships, and throngs of peaceful men, women, and children were driven from their homes by the sharp terror of death. Be it remembered always that not one man in Brussels, not one man in Antwerp, had even the smallest responsibility for the disaster inflicted upon them. Innocence has proved not even the smallest safeguard against such woe and suffering as we in this land can at present hardly imagine.

What befell Antwerp and Brussels will surely some day befall New York or San Francisco, and may happen to many an inland city also, if we do not shake off our supine folly, if we trust for safety to peace treaties unbacked by force. At the beginning of last month, by the appointment of the president, peace services were held in the churches of this land. As far as these services consisted of sermons and prayers of good and wise people who wished peace only if it represented righteousness, who did not desire that peace should come unless it came to consecrate justice and not wrongdoing, good and not evil, the movement represented good. Insofar, however, as the movement was understood to be one for immediate peace without any regard to righteousness or justice, without any regard for righting the wrongs of those who have been crushed by unmerited disaster, then the movement represented mischief, precisely as fifty years ago, in 1864, in our own country a similar movement for peace, to be obtained by acknowledgment of disunion and by the perpetuation of slavery, would have represented mischief. In the present case, however, the mischief was confined purely to those taking part in the movement in an unworthy spirit; for (like the peace parades and newspaper peace petitions) it was a merely subjective phenomenon; it had not the slightest effect of any kind, sort, or description upon any of the combatants abroad and could not possibly have any effect upon them. It is well for our own sakes that we should pray sincerely and humbly for the peace of righteousness; but we must guard ourselves from any illusion as to the news of our having thus prayed producing the least effect upon those engaged in the war.

There is just one way in which to meet the upholders of the doctrine that might makes right. To do so we must prove that right will make might, by backing right with might.

In his second inaugural address Andrew Jackson laid down the rule by which every national American administration ought to guide itself, saying: "The foreign policy adopted by our government is to do justice to all, and to submit to wrong by none."

The statement of the dauntless old fighter of New Orleans is as true now as when he wrote it. We must stand absolutely for righteousness. But to do so is utterly without avail unless we possess the strength and the loftiness of spirit which will back righteousness with deeds and not mere words. We must clear the rubbish from off our souls and admit that everything that has been done in passing peace treaties, arbitration treaties, neutrality treaties, Hague treaties, and the like, with no sanction of force behind them, amounts to literally and absolutely zero, to literally and absolutely nothing, in any time of serious crisis. We must recognize that to enter into foolish treaties which cannot be kept is as wicked as to break treaties which can and ought to be kept. We must labor for an international agreement among the great civilized nations which shall put the full force of all of them back of any one of them, and of any well-behaved weak nation, which is wronged by any other power. Until we have completed this purpose, we must keep ourselves ready, high of heart and undaunted of soul, to back our rights with our strength.

SERVICE AND
SELF-RESPECT

From the Metropolitan, *March 1918, and*
The Great Adventure, *1918*

Unless democracy is based on the principle of service by everybody who claims the enjoyment of any right, it is not true democracy at all. The man who refuses to render, or is ashamed to render, the necessary service is not fit to live in a democracy. And the man who demands from another a service which he himself would esteem it dishonorable or unbecoming to render is to that extent not a true democrat. No man has a right to demand a service which he does not regard as honorable to render; nor has he a right to demand it unless he pays for it in some way, *the payment to include respect for the man who renders it*. Democracy must mean mutuality of service rendered, and of respect for the service rendered.

A leading Russian revolutionist (who is, of course, like every true friend of freedom, an opponent of the Bolsheviki) recently came to this country from Vladivostock. He traversed the Siberian railway. The porter on his train refused to get him hot water or to black his boots; stating with true Bolshevistic logic that democracy meant that nobody must do anything for anyone else and that anyhow his union would turn him out if he rendered such service.

Now, this Bolsheviki porter was foolish with a folly that can only be induced by prolonged and excessive indulgence in Bolshevism or some American analogue. But the root trouble in producing his folly was the fact that under the old system the men whose boots the porter blacked looked down on him for blacking them. Are we entirely free from this attitude in America? Until we are we may as well make up our minds that to just that extent we are providing for the growth of Bolshevism here. No man has a right to ask or accept any service unless under changed conditions he would feel that he could keep his entire self-respect while rendering it. Service which carries with it the slightest implication of social abasement should not be rendered.

For a number of years I lived on a ranch in the old-time cattle country; and I also visited at the house of a backwoods lumberjack friend. In both places we lived under old-style American conditions. We all of us worked, and our social distinctions were essentially based on individual worth. We accepted as a matter of course that the difference in degree of service rendered ought at least roughly to correspond to the difference in reward. Each did most of the purely personal things for himself. But nobody thought of any necessary work as degrading.

I remember that once, when there was a lull in outdoor work, I endeavored to be useful in and around the house. I fed the pigs; and on an idle morning I blacked all the boots. Ordinarily our boots did not need blacking—most of them were not that kind. On this occasion I started, with an enthusiasm that outran my judgment, to black the dress boots of everyone, of both sexes. I coated them with a thick, dull paste; only a few knobs became shiny; and the paste came off freely on what it touched. As a result I temporarily lost not merely the respect but even the affection of all the other inmates of the house. However, I did not lose caste because I had blacked the boots. I lost caste because I had blacked them badly. But I was allowed to continue feeding the pigs. The pigs were not so particular as the humans.

Now, there is no more reason for refusing to bring hot water or black boots or serve a dinner or make up a bed or cook or wash clothes (I have cooked and washed clothes often—but neither wisely nor well) than for refusing to shoe a horse, run a motor, brake a train, sell carpets, manage a bank, or run a farm. A few centuries back men of good lineage felt that they lost caste if they were in trade or finance—in some countries they feel so to this day. In most civilized lands, however, the feeling has disappeared, and it never occurs to anyone to look down on anyone else because he sells things. Just the same feeling should obtain, and as we grow more civilized will obtain, about all other kinds of service. This applies to domestic service. It is as entirely right to employ housemaids, cooks, and gardeners as to employ lawyers, bankers, and businessmen or cashiers, factory hands, and stenographers. But only on condition that we show the same respect to the individuals in one case as in the other cases!

Ultimately I hope that this respect will show itself in the forms of address, in the courtesy titles used, as well as the consideration shown, and the personal liberty expected and accorded. I am not demanding an instant change—I believe in evolution rather than revolution. But I am sure the change is possible and desirable; and even although it would be foolish and undesirable to set up the entirely new standard immediately, I hope we can work toward it. One of the most charming gentlewomen I know, the wife of a man of rare cultivation, ability, and public achievement, lives on the top floor of a tenement-house in a western city. The rooms are comfortably and daintily furnished—with an abundance of books. In this household the maid was introduced to me as Miss So-and-So; and this is the ideal. Of course it cannot be realized until there has been much education *on both sides*. But it should be the ideal. All relations between employer and employee should be based on mutuality of respect and consideration; arrogance met by insolence, or an alternation of arrogance and insolence, offers but a poor substitute.

Mutuality of respect and consideration, service and a reward corresponding as nearly as may be to the service—these make up the ideal of democracy. Such an ideal is as far from the stupid bourbonism of reaction as it is from the vicious lunacy of the Bolsheviki or IWW type. Perhaps the beginning of its realization may come through the introduction of universal military training. Some months ago I went through the national army, or drafted men's, camp at Chillicothe, Ohio. There were some thirty thousand men in the camp—Americans of fine type, who were having the finest kind of education, for these camps are the true universities of American citizenship. An exceptionally efficient and far-seeing army officer, Major-General Glenn, was in command. He kept admirable discipline, he tolerated no slackness, no failure in duty of any kind, and by his initiative and personality he was overcoming all obstacles and making capital soldiers of his men. He showed with especial pride the Red Cross Community House. It is a huge building, very attractive, with a big restaurant, reading rooms, and a dance hall. When off-duty officers and enlisted men come there and bring their friends of both sexes, [there is] absolutely no restriction save, as General Glenn put it, that "every man is to act as a gentleman and every woman as a gentlewoman." (When we have universal service, and every man has served in the ranks, and representatives of every class have commissions, there will be merely the same distinction between sergeants and lieutenants as between captains and colonels.) In the restaurant the major-general and a private from the ranks may—and sometimes do—sit at the same table. All come alike to the dances. All alike enjoy the privileges of the reading rooms. All behave with self-respect. Each respects the others. When they go back to duty each does his allotted task in his allotted position, with eager and zealous efficiency, and with alert, orderly, and instant discipline. Surely this is the military ideal for a democracy—twenty years ago my own regiment realized just this ideal. Surely it also represents substantially the democratic ideal toward which we should strive in civil life. It is as far removed from the brutal and repulsive folly of Bolshevism on the one hand as from the intolerable autocratic tyranny of the Hohenzollern type on the other.

The Great Adventure

From the Metropolitan, *October 1918, and*
The Great Adventure, *1918*

Only those are fit to live who do not fear to die; and none are fit to die who have shrunk from the joy of life and the duty of life. Both life and death are parts of the same Great Adventure. Never yet was worthy adventure worthily carried through by the man who put his personal safety first. Never yet was a country worth living in unless its sons and daughters were of that stern stuff which bade them die for it at need; and never yet was a country worth dying for unless its sons and daughters thought of life not as something concerned only with the selfish evanescence of the individual, but as a link in the great chain of creation and causation, so that each person is seen in his true relations as an essential part of the whole, whose life must be made to serve the larger and continuing life of the whole. Therefore it is that the man who is not willing to die, and the woman who is not willing to send her man to die, in a war for a great cause, are not worthy to live. Therefore it is that the man and woman who in peacetime fear or ignore the primary and vital duties and the high happiness of family life, who dare not beget and bear and rear the life that is to last when they are in their graves, have broken the chain of creation, and have shown that they are unfit for companionship with the souls ready for the Great Adventure.

The wife of a fighting soldier at the front recently wrote as follows to the mother of a gallant boy, who at the front had fought in high air like an eagle, and, like an eagle, fighting had died:

> I write these few lines, not of condolence—for who would dare to pity you?—but of deepest sympathy to you and yours as you stand in the shadow which is the earthly side of those clouds

of glory in which your son's life has just passed. Many will envy you that when the call to sacrifice came you were not found among the paupers to whom no gift of life worth offering had been entrusted. They are the ones to be pitied, not we whose dearest are jeoparding their lives unto the death in the high places of the field. I hope my two sons will live as worthily and die as greatly as yours.

There spoke one dauntless soul to another! America is safe while her daughters are of this kind; for their lovers and their sons cannot fail, as long as beside the hearthstones stand such wives and mothers. And we have many, many such women; and their men are like unto them.

With all my heart I believe in the joy of living; but those who achieve it do not seek it as an end in itself, but as a seized and prized incident of hard work well done and of risk and danger never wantonly courted, but never shirked when duty commands that they be faced. And those who have earned joy, but are rewarded only with sorrow, must learn the stern comfort dear to great souls, the comfort that springs from the knowledge taught in times of iron that the law of worthy living is not fulfilled by pleasure, but by service, and by sacrifice when only thereby can service be rendered.

No nation can be great unless its sons and daughters have in them the quality to rise level to the needs of heroic days. Yet this heroic quality is but the apex of a pyramid of which the broad foundations must solidly rest on the performance of duties so ordinary that to impatient minds they seem commonplace. No army was ever great unless its soldiers possessed the fighting edge. But the finest natural fighting edge is utterly useless unless the soldiers and the junior officers have been through months, and the officers of higher command and the general staff through years, of hard, weary, intensive training. So likewise the citizenship of any country is worthless unless in a crisis it shows the spirit of the two million Americans who in this mighty war have eagerly come forward to serve under the Banner of the Stars, afloat and ashore, and of the other millions who would now be beside them overseas if the chance had been given them; and yet such spirit will in the long run avail nothing unless in the years of peace the average man and average woman of the duty-performing type realize that the highest of all duties, the one essential duty, is the duty of perpetuating the family life, based on the mutual love and respect of the one man and the one woman, and on their purpose to rear the healthy and fine-souled children whose coming into life means that the family and, therefore, the nation shall continue in life and shall not end in a sterile death.

Woe to those who invite a sterile death; a death not for them only, but for the race; the death which is insured by a life of sterile selfishness.

But honor, highest honor, to those who fearlessly face death for a good cause; no life is so honorable or so fruitful as such a death. Unless men are willing to fight and die for great ideals, including love of country, ideals will vanish, and the world will become one huge sty of materialism. And unless the women of ideals bring forth the men who are ready thus to live and die, the world of the future will be filled by the spawn of the unfit. Alone of human beings the good and wise mother stands on a plane of equal honor with the bravest soldier; for she has gladly gone down to the brink of the chasm of darkness to bring back the children in whose hands rests the future of the years. But the mother, and far more the father, who flinch from the vital task earn the scorn visited on the soldier who flinches in battle. And the nation should by action mark its attitude alike toward the fighter in war and toward the child-bearer in peace and war. The vital need of the nation is that its men and women of the future shall be the sons and daughters of the soldiers of the present. Excuse no man from going to war because he is married; but put all unmarried men above a fixed age at the hardest and most dangerous tasks; and provide amply for the children of soldiers, so as to give their wives the assurance of material safety.

In such a matter one can only speak in general terms. At this

334 ★ The Essential Theodore Roosevelt

moment there are hundreds of thousands of gallant men eating out their hearts because the privilege of facing death in battle is denied them. So there are innumerable women and men whose undeserved misfortune it is that they have no children or but one child. These soldiers denied the perilous honor they seek, these men and women heart-hungry for the children of their longing dreams, are as worthy of honor as the men who are warriors in fact, as the women whose children are of flesh and blood. If the only son who is killed at the front has no brother because his parents coldly dreaded to play their part in the Great Adventure of Life, then our sorrow is not for them, but solely for the son who himself dared the Great Adventure of Death. If, however, he is the only son because the Unseen Powers denied others to the love of his father and mother, then we mourn doubly with them because their darling went up to the sword of Azrael, because he drank the dark drink proffered by the Death Angel.

In America today all our people are summoned to service and sacrifice. Pride is the portion only of those who know bitter sorrow or the foreboding of bitter sorrow. But all of us who give service, and stand ready for sacrifice, are the torch-bearers. We run with the torches until we fall, content if we can then pass them to the hands of other runners. The torches whose flame is brightest are borne by the gallant men at the front, and by the gallant women whose husbands and lovers, whose sons and brothers are at the front. These men are high of soul, as they face their fate on the shell-shattered earth, or in the skies above or in the waters beneath; and no less high of soul are the women with torn hearts and shining eyes; the girls whose boy lovers have been struck down in their golden morning, and the mothers and wives to whom word has been brought that henceforth they must walk in the shadow.

These are the torch-bearers; these are they who have dared the Great Adventure.